The Umpire Was Blind!

The Umpire Was Blind!

Controversial Calls by MLB's Men in Blue

Jonathan Weeks

McFarland & Company, Inc., Publishers
Jefferson, North Carolina

LIBRARY OF CONGRESS CATALOGUING-IN-PUBLICATION DATA

Names: Weeks, Jonathan, author.
Title: The umpire was blind! : controversial calls by MLB's men in blue / Jonathan Weeks.
Description: Jefferson, North Carolina : McFarland & Company, Inc., Publishers, 2020. | Includes bibliographical references and index.
Identifiers: LCCN 2020021781 | ISBN 9781476680323 (paperback) | ISBN 9781476639215 (ebook)
Subjects: LCSH: Baseball—Umpiring—United States—Anecdotes. | Baseball umpires—United States—Anecdotes. | Baseball—United States—History—Anecdotes. | Major League Baseball (Organization)—History—Anecdotes.
Classification: LCC GV876.W45 2020 | DDC 796.357/3—dc23
LC record available at https://lccn.loc.gov/2020021781

BRITISH LIBRARY CATALOGUING DATA ARE AVAILABLE

ISBN (print) 978-1-4766-8032-3
ISBN (ebook) 978-1-4766-3921-5

© 2020 Jonathan Weeks. All rights reserved

No part of this book may be reproduced or transmitted in any form or by any means, electronic or mechanical, including photocopying or recording, or by any information storage and retrieval system, without permission in writing from the publisher.

Front cover: National League umpire Hank O'Day (second from left, facing camera) confers with his American League counterpart and members of the Philadelphia Athletics and New York Giants during the 1905 World Series (Boston Public Library)

Printed in the United States of America

McFarland & Company, Inc., Publishers
  Box 611, Jefferson, North Carolina 28640
  www.mcfarlandpub.com

Contents

Preface	1
Introduction. The Devil We Know: A Very Brief History of Umpiring	3

Part One. The Umpire Giveth, the Umpire Taketh Away: Streaks and Records Helped or Hindered by Umpires — 9
- Johnny Vander Meer's Consecutive No-Hitters — 9
- Joe DiMaggio's 56-Game Hitting Streak — 13
- Don Larsen's Perfect World Series Game — 17
- Bob Shaw's Balk-a-Thon — 20
- Don Drysdale's Consecutive Scoreless Innings Streak — 23
- Orel Hershiser's Consecutive Scoreless Innings Streak — 27
- The 1998 Home Run Chase (Featuring Mark McGwire and Sammy Sosa) — 30
- Kerry Wood's 20-Strikeout Performance — 34
- Armando Galarraga's Near-Perfect Game — 37
- Max Scherzer's Near-Perfect Game — 40

Part Two. The Road to October: Critical Calls During the Regular Season — 43
- Bob Ferguson's Campaign Against Gambling — 43
- Tim Hurst and the Beer Glass Incident — 45
- Soggy Games in Pittsburgh: Round 1 — 47
- Soggy Games in Pittsburgh: Round 2 — 50
- Fred Merkle's Infamous Blunder — 52
- Stuffy McInnis's Gift Homer — 59

- Germany Schaefer Steals First Base — 61
- Bill Brennan Imposes His Iron Will — 64
- The Indecision of Charles Johnston — 67
- Red Jones's Fourteen Ejections — 70
- Two Balls in Play at Wrigley Field — 72
- Don Money's Nullified Grand Slam — 74
- The Pine Tar Game — 77
- Wild Card Tiebreaker Game — 81
- Bill Hohn's Fist Bump — 84
- 19-Inning Marathon Ended by Jerry Meals's Blown Call — 86

Part Three. The Victors and the Spoils: Playoff Controversies — 89
- The Jeffrey Maier Game — 89
- Livan Hernandez's 15-Strikeout Performance — 92
- The 1998 ALCS Disaster — 95
- 1999 ALCS: The Phantom Tag and Other Issues — 98
- Pierzynski and the Uncaught Third Strike — 101
- Midges Invade Jacob's Field — 104
- 2009 Playoffs: The Fall Guys — 106
- 2010 Playoffs: Bad Calls in Multiple Rounds — 111
- 2012 NL Wild Card Game: Improperly Invoked Infield Fly Rule — 114
- 2015 ALCS Game 6: A Wet, Wild Finish in Kansas City — 117
- 2016 NLCS Game 4: Angel Hernandez's Blown Call at Home Plate — 120
- 2017 NLDS Game 5: Nationals Lose on Account of Jerry Layne's Mistakes — 123

Part Four: Legends of the Fall: Infamous World Series Debates — 127
- 1885 World's Championship Series: Umpire David Sullivan's Hot Mess — 127
- 1911 World Series Game 5: The Run That Shouldn't Have Counted — 130
- 1925 World Series Game 3: Sam Rice's Mystery Catch — 135

- 1935 World Series Game 3: Moriarty Defies Landis with 3 Ejections — 138
- 1948 World Series Game 1: Bill Stewart's Blown Pickoff Call on Phil Masi — 142
- 1955 World Series Game 1: Jackie Robinson Steals Home — 145
- 1969 World Series Game 5: The Old Shoe Polish Trick — 149
- 1970 World Series Game 1: Ken Burkhart's Miraculous Behind-the-Back Call — 152
- 1975 World Series Game 3: Armbrister Interferes with Fisk — 155
- 1978 World Series Game 4: Reggie Jackson Interferes with Infield Throw — 158
- 1985 World Series Game 6: Don Denkinger's Blown Call at First Base — 161
- 1998 World Series Game 1: Rich Garcia Gives Tino Martinez an Extra Pitch to Work With — 164
- 2006 World Series Game 2: Kenny Rogers and the "Smudgegate" Affair — 166
- 2011 World Series Games 3 and 7: Ron Kulpa and Jerry Layne Make a Mess of Things — 170
- 2013 World Series Game 3: Cardinals Score Game-Winner on Obstruction Call at Third Base — 172
- 2017 World Series Game 5: Bill Miller's Oddly Shaped Strike Zone — 175

Notes — 179
Bibliography — 187
Index — 197

Preface

Let's face it—umpires are only human.

For well over a century, the activities on major league baseball fields have been dramatically affected by the flawed decisions of officials. In late August of 2008, a rule was implemented by commissioner Bud Selig allowing crew chiefs to call for video reviews on questionable home runs. (Video review had been used just once in the majors prior to then—during the 1999 season.) The rule proved beneficial less than a week later when an apparent homer hit by Alex Rodriguez of the Yankees was disputed by Tampa Bay Rays manager Joe Maddon. Crew chief Charlie Reliford examined the footage and allowed the call to stand.

From 2008 through 2010, the use of video replay was invoked more than a hundred times, resulting in several dozen overturned home run calls. After much debate, a new regulation was established in 2014, allowing each manager one official challenge per game with a new one being granted each time a dispute is upheld. In addition to home run calls, managers can now challenge a number of other situations, including fair-foul rulings and fan interference calls.

The use of video replay has served to drastically reduce the number of bitter disputes. John Thorn, the official historian of Major League Baseball, remarked, "Gone are the days when a Bobby Cox, Lou Piniella, Sparky Anderson or Earl Weaver could combine cathartic exercise with theatrical relief in disputing an umpire's judgment call. The modern skipper just signals for the replay booth."[1]

Before the advent of video replay, controversy on the field was common, and the face of baseball history was irrevocably altered by the questionable judgments of umpires on multiple occasions. For instance:

- In 1908, a game-winning hit by Giants infielder Al Bridwell was disallowed, ultimately costing the New Yorkers a pennant.

- In the 1985 World Series, an erroneous decision by umpire Don Denkinger helped the Royals to a championship.
- In 2011, umpire Jim Joyce spoiled what should have been a perfect game for Tigers pitcher Armando Galarraga when he blew a call at first base on the final out of the game.

Legendary Giants pitcher Christy Mathewson once quipped: "Many baseball fans look upon an umpire as a sort of necessary evil to the luxury of baseball, like the odor that follows an automobile."[2] Defending his own limitations as well as those of his peers, Hall of Fame arbiter Billy Evans contended that: "The public wouldn't like the perfect umpire in every game. It would kill off baseball's greatest alibi—'we was robbed.'"[3] At the very least, umpires are an inescapable necessity. And despite their many faults, they have played an integral role in shaping the game's past, as we shall see on the pages that follow.

Introduction

The Devil We Know: A Very Brief History of Umpiring

During Spring Training of 1950, Brooklyn Dodgers President Branch Rickey introduced an electronic umpire to the team's Vero Beach training camp. An inveterate trendsetter, Rickey had no intention of replacing umpires with machines. He saw the innovation as more of a teaching tool. But the implication was clear—that automatons could do an equivalent job to the men in blue, if not better.

Skipping straight to the epilogue, Rickey's machine never caught on. Still, the argument has persisted to the present day. In 2016, an episode of the HBO series *Real Sports with Bryant Gumbel* helped bolster the popular belief that umpires—particularly those behind home plate—are incompetent. After analyzing roughly a million major league pitches over a three and a half year period, Yale professor Toby Moskowitz told *Real Sports* reporter Jon Frankel that more than 30,000 erroneous ball/strike calls are made each season for an overall accuracy rate of eighty-eight percent.

Not an especially impressive number to say the least.

Writing for the *Kansas City Star* in 2017, journalist Lee Judge groused about a blown call made by home plate umpire Marty Foster in a game between the Royals and Twins. In many televised games, networks superimpose computerized graphics on the screen so fans at home can see which pitches land within the strike zone. These graphics are generally considered to be extremely accurate. Analyzing the network data, Judge determined that Foster missed thirteen calls during the game, including a critical one that should have given the Royals their second out of the ninth inning.

Commenting on computerized strike zones, Chicago TV producer Marc Brady said: "Humans have bad days. Computers don't. Maybe the sun angle affects the umpire's view of a pitch … or maybe he's just freezing and wants to go home. A computer has nowhere to go."[1] Thinking along those lines, former major leaguer Eric Byrnes pondered: "Why do millions of people sitting at home get to know whether or not it's a ball or strike, yet the poor dude behind home plate is the one who's left in the dark?"[2]

Why indeed?

Well, the answer is rather complex. Aside from the fact that baseball is a sport steeped in tradition, there are other obvious reasons. Not everyone supports the idea of an automated strike zone. Multimedia sports personality Joe Giglio cautioned that: "As with any technological advancement, it could come with issues. If the strike zone was 'off' or malfunctioned, baseball would either have to empower the umpire to make the correct call or deal with the missed pitches."[3] Former National League umpire Harry Wendelstedt went one step further, proposing humorously: "If they did get a machine to replace [umpires], you know what would happen to it? Why, the players would bust it to pieces every time it ruled against them. They'd clobber it with a bat."[4]

With offense on the decline and strikeouts dramatically on the rise in the majors, MLB commissioner Rob Manfred arranged with the independent Atlantic League to implement various experimental changes. In addition to moving the pitching rubber back from its standard sixty-feet, six-inch placement, Atlantic League president Rick White agreed to begin using "robot umpires" during the 2019 season.

The so-called "robo-umps" don't look anything like Arnold Schwarzenegger's character in the *Terminator* movies. The technology is actually known as TrackMan. It's a 3D Doppler radar system that precisely measures the location, trajectory and spin rate of hit and pitched baseballs. The device can be precisely aligned to the strike zone to determine balls and strikes. Most major league parks already have the devices in place, though they have mostly been used for coaching and scouting purposes.

The Atlantic League experiment is part of a tentative three-year agreement that will run through the 2021 campaign. Data will be submitted to MLB evaluating the effectiveness of the policy changes. Since the eight-team Atlantic League plays a 140-game schedule, there will be plenty of data for MLB to work with before a final decision is made.

No matter how the Atlantic League trial turns out, the fact of the matter is that home plate umpires (in some capacity) are likely here to stay. And it's difficult not to sympathize with them given the demanding nature of their jobs. According to retired American League arbiter Nestor Chylak, officials are expected to "be perfect on the first day of the season and then get better every day."[5] Adhering to an extremely convoluted rulebook, they make hair-trigger decisions knowing that their calls will affect the fortunes of the players and teams involved. They are among the most vilified figures in all of sports. Many of the insults hurled at them have become clichés. A few of the more charitable ones are as follows:

- You drop more calls than AT&T!
- I thought only horses slept standing up!
- Flip over the plate and read the directions!
- Is your rulebook written in Braille?!

Despite their imperfections, umpires have played a vital role in the game's history. Former major league commissioner A. Bartlett Giamatti described the public perception of umpires in figurative terms: "Baseball fits America well because it expresses our longing for the rule of law while licensing our resentment of law givers."[6] That resentment has flourished for a very long time.

On October 6, 1845, attorney William Rufus Wheaton served as an umpire in the first recorded game, which was an intra-squad match played by the Knickerbocker Base Ball Club. Umpires were still presiding over games by the time the National Association of Base Ball Players (the sport's first governing body) was formed in the late 1850s. Though there was no formal dress code in the early days, umpires wore clothing that distinguished them from players, typically consisting of a top hat, cane and Prince Albert coat.

As the sport grew in popularity after the Civil War, it became professionalized. In 1878, The National League instructed home teams to pay umpires five dollars per game. An official staff of twenty umpires was assembled by NL President William A. Hulbert the following year. Founded in 1882, the rival American Association followed suit, offering umpires $140 per month with a daily allowance for travel expenses. Arbiters in both leagues wore uniforms with caps and formal jackets not unlike those of today.

Umpiring could be extremely hazardous during the first century of major league play. In addition to frequent streams of verbal abuse, the men in blue were routinely assaulted by players and fans alike. At the end of his career, umpire Joe Rue asserted: "I've been hit by mud-balls and whiskey bottles and had everything from fruits and vegetables thrown at me. I've probably experienced more violence than any other umpire who ever lived."⁷ Baseball historian John Thorn remarked of the early days: "In the late–1800s, a player who had a pugilistic background might be better equipped to handle a rowdy player than a banker or a doctor or a dentist."⁸ It should come as no surprise then that Billy McLean, the game's first professional umpire, was a skilled boxer.

During the nineteenth century, officials not only worked in hostile environs, but they also worked alone. This allowed players to get away with murder. With the umpire's attention frequently diverted, opponents resorted to unsportsmanlike conduct, tripping and shoving one another on the basepaths. A favorite tactic of baseball's pioneers was to push a runner off the bag after signaling for a pickoff throw from the pitcher. Some base-runners even went so far as to cut directly across the diamond on the way to home instead of rounding second and third.

Player protests often led to assorted unpleasantries. According to Thorn, the familiar cry of "Kill the umpire" was a very tangible threat. "Home team fans typically claimed that the umpire was in the fix. Kicking dirt on an umpire's suit took on a kind of symbolism. The idea is, by kicking dirt, you attack the institution, you attack the partiality of the umpire."⁹

Most umpires were impartial, but a handful were not. In 1882, Detroit Wolverines President William G. Thompson became suspicious of some calls made by arbiter Dick Higham. A private detective hired by Thompson discovered that Higham had been conspiring with a notorious gambler to fix games. Higham was subsequently fired and banned from baseball. He remains the only umpire ever to be permanently exiled from the sport.

In the 1880s, umpires began wearing large chest protectors known as "balloons" or "mattresses." With this cumbersome piece of equipment in place, officials were forced to look directly over the catcher's head. This resulted in more "high" strikes being called. Though the American League continued to use balloon protectors well into the twentieth century, NL umpires, inspired by Hall of Famer Bill Klem, took to wearing smaller guards beneath their coats. This allowed them to look directly over the catcher's shoulder nearest the batter. As a result, NL arbiters gained a reputation for calling "low" strikes.

By the 1930s, umpiring had become a respectable profession. Recognizing the need to properly instruct suitable candidates, NL arbiter George Barr opened the first training school in 1935. Barr's American League counterpart, Bill McGowan, opened a second academy for umpires four years later. The schools dramatically improved the quality of the game. Not only were graduates more cognizant of the rules, but they were also taught to be impartial and professional. Umpires with fiery temperaments were gradually rooted out of baseball.

Though cultural diversity was sorely lacking among umpires in the early days, there was a steady influx of Irish, German, Slavic and Jewish officials beginning in the 1890s. Sadly, it wasn't until 1966 when the color barrier was finally broken in the majors. After logging more than a dozen years of minor league experience, Emmett Ashford was promoted to the American League. This opened the door for Art Williams, who became the first black umpire in the NL during the 1972 campaign. Hispanic umpires would be represented soon afterward with the appearance of Armando Rodriguez (AL-1974) and Rich Garcia (NL-1975).

Recognizing the need to be legally protected in their profession, National League arbiters united to form the NL Umpire's Association in 1963. With the assistance of Chicago attorney John J. Reynolds, salaries were successfully increased. When umpires Bill Valentine and Al Salerno rallied for AL unionization in 1968, they were fired by league President Joe Cronin. The Major League Umpires Association was formed to represent both leagues in the wake of this unfortunate incident.

Today, major league umpires make a fairly comfortable living. Rookie arbiters are paid more than $100,000 per-season while veteran officials receive more than three times that amount. Candidates toiling in the minors, however, are barely scraping by. As of 2017, a full season of Double-A ball netted an umpire around $2,700 per month. The job is anything but glamorous as travel arrangements are not provided for. Arbiters are obligated to transport themselves all over the country, driving through the night sometimes.[10]

Ascension to the big leagues carries inherent pressures. Umpires are expected to make the correct decision on every play and with the advent of instant replay, they are frequently proven wrong in front of legions of fans. They deal with sullen managers and explosive players, often taking the blame for the failures of both. In short, it's a lonely, thankless job. Former National League umpire Lee Ballafant, who presided over games for twenty-two seasons, once quipped sourly: "I can truthfully say that I never did like umpiring. I stayed with it because I had to eat."[11]

Whether we sympathize with them or not, it is an irrefutable fact that the decisions of umpires have dramatically altered the fabric of baseball history. In the heat of the moment, mistakes are often made and the consequences of these mistakes have been monumental at times.

PART ONE

The Umpire Giveth, the Umpire Taketh Away: Streaks and Records Helped or Hindered by Umpires

••••••••••••••••••

Johnny Vander Meer's Consecutive No-Hitters
June 11–June 15, 1938

Though his lifetime statistics appear rather ordinary on the surface, Johnny Vander Meer showed flashes of brilliance throughout his career. From June 11 through June 15, 1938, the hard-throwing left-hander was arguably the best pitcher in the majors. Given the micro-management of today's hurlers, Vander Meer's back-to-back no-hitters are a feat that will likely remain unmatched for a very long time (and perhaps forever). Thanks to a blown strike call, Vander Meer almost lost his bid for immortality.

Born in Prospect, New Jersey, Vander Meer grew up in Midland Park, which is located about fifty miles from New York City. At the age of fourteen, he developed peritonitis (a serious intestinal condition) and nearly died. After two months in the hospital and five weeks confined to his bed at home, he decided to drop out of high school. He worked as an engraver while playing baseball on the side. In 1932, he tossed several no-hitters at the amateur level and got noticed by scouts. The Dodgers assigned him to their farm system, but a shoulder injury delayed his ascent to the majors. He ended up being sold to the Reds. In 1936, he was named Minor League Player of the Year by *The Sporting News*. He made his major league debut the following season.

During spring training of 1938, Cincinnati manager Bill McKechnie helped Vander Meer tame the wildness that had plagued him periodically to that point. The extra work paid great dividends as he got off to a 5–2 start with a 2.77 ERA. He began his June 11 assignment against Boston as a little-known prospect, but within the next few days, he was elevated to superstar status.

The Bees (formerly and subsequently known as the Braves) were a middle of the road team in 1938. Managed by Casey Stengel, they finished in fifth place with a league-worst batting average of .250. They were certainly no match for Vander Meer on June 11 as he faced just twenty-eight batters, walking three and striking out four. The game was played in a brisk one hour and forty-five minutes. When it was over, Vander Meer had secured himself a reputation as one of the most promising young players in baseball. It was the first National League no-hitter since 1934 and the first by a lefty in seven years.

Vander Meer had no idea prior to his June 15 start against Brooklyn that he was on the verge of making history. In fact, the thought of a second no-hitter never even crossed his mind. "If I had known it had never been done before, it would have put more heat on me," he said years later.[1]

The 1938 Dodgers were a seventh-place team managed by Hall of Famer Burleigh Grimes. Despite their lowly position in the standings, there were some legitimate offensive threats in the lineup, including Cooperstown great Kiki Cuyler and prolific RBI-man, Dolph Camilli. Catcher Babe Phelps hit .308 that year while outfielder Ernie Koy flirted with the .300 mark all season.

The umpire that evening was Bill Stewart, a former pitcher who had been signed by the White Sox before an arm injury derailed his path to the majors. When baseball was not in season, he worked as a referee in the National Hockey League. In 1937, he had set his whistle aside to serve as coach of the Chicago Blackhawks. Despite a lackluster 14–25–9 regular season showing, he guided the team to an improbable win over the Toronto Maple Leafs in the Stanley Cup Finals. Stewart was a diminutive figure at 5-foot-6 and his size would inadvertently jeopardize Vander Meer's no-hit bid.

The game started with more fanfare than Vander Meer was accustomed to. It was the first night game in Brooklyn history and, to celebrate it, there were pre-game festivities with fireworks and celebrity appearances. Busloads of supporters from Vander Meer's hometown joined a capacity crowd at Ebbets Field. There were so many people milling about in the grandstand that the public address announcer was obligated to repeatedly warn spectators that the game would not begin until the aisles were clear. Vander Meer warmed up three separate times before he finally took the mound. When he did, he wasn't terribly sharp, walking five batters through eight innings and relying on his defense to bail him out. He muddled through until the ninth, when things began to unravel.

Early in the game, Vander Meer had been throwing very strongly. As his velocity began to wane, he started mixing in curves. By the ninth inning, he had resorted to old habits, becoming characteristically wild. After Buddy Hassett grounded out, Vander Meer walked the bases full, prompting a visit from Bill McKechnie. "Listen—those hitters are more scared than you are," said McKechnie. "Just pour that ball in there."[2]

Bearing down, Vander Meer induced a sharp grounder off the bat of Ernie Koy, resulting in a force out at the plate. This brought up shortstop Leo Durocher with two outs. Durocher was a lifetime .247 hitter, but fared much better during his career with runners in scoring position. With the count even at 1–1, he lifted a deep drive to left field that brought the crowd to its feet. Even Brooklyn fans were cheering for Vander Meer at that point and there was a collective sigh of relief as the ball hooked foul. The next pitch should have ended the game, but Stewart botched the call.

Vander Meer's 1–2 offering caught the outside corner for strike three. Unfortunately, catcher Ernie Lombardi came out of his crouch too early and Stewart misjudged it, calling ball two. The under-sized Stewart was having difficulty seeing around the hulking Lombardi, who stood 6-foot-3 and weighed well over two-hundred pounds. Stewart also admitted later that he was having trouble spotting the ball under the glare of the newly installed lights. Justifiably irritated, Lombardi exchanged words with Stewart, who admitted that he had missed the pitch. Unfortunately, there was no reversing the call at that point. If Vander Meer wanted his name in the record books, he would have to dispose of Durocher—Again! Tension in the stadium was palpable as Durocher lifted a harmless fly ball to Harry Craft in center field.

Disaster averted!

According to Vander Meer, Stewart was the first one to greet him after the game. "Johnny, I guess if you hadn't got him, I would have blown it for you," he said apologetically.[3] It would not be the last time Stewart would come under fire. During the 1948 World Series, he made a controversial decision that resulted in a Game 1 loss for the Indians (details of which can be found in another chapter). Stewart maintained good rapport with players throughout his career. Asked about his strategy for handling disputes, he told a reporter: "Never lie to 'em. If you make a mistake, own up to it. I always try to."[4]

Before Vander Meer's next start against the Bees, there was a lot of talk about a third consecutive no-hitter. It was beginning to weigh heavily upon the young hurler. "All the publicity, the attention, the interviews, the photographs were too much for me," he reminisced years later.[5] Under unimaginable pressure, Vander Meer took the mound at Boston's "Bee Hive" and tossed three more hitless innings before yielding a single to future batting champion Debs Garms. He recalled being immensely relieved. "I think if I'd have had a ten-dollar bill in my baseball pants, I'd have gone over to first base and handed it to Garms," he joked.[6]

Vander Meer finished the 1938 campaign with a 15–10 record and 3.12 ERA. Though he would appear on four All-Star teams during his career, he would continue to be plagued by periodic wildness. He averaged five walks per nine innings and retired with a 119–121 lifetime record. Demoted to the minor leagues in 1952, he threw another no-hitter before his playing days ended. He managed at the minor league level and was inducted into the Cincinnati Reds Hall of Fame.

After leaving umpiring behind in 1955, Stewart worked as a scout for the Indians and Senators. He was later appointed head coach of the United States National Hockey team. His *New York Times* obituary described him as "an affable and articulate man with a fantastic memory and remarkable drive" off the field.[7] He was inducted into the U.S. Hockey Hall of Fame in 1982.

Vander Meer's remarkable feat has been seriously challenged only once—by Nolan Ryan. On July 15, 1973, Ryan tossed a no-hitter (his second of the season), striking out seventeen Detroit batters. At one point during the game, Tigers' jokester Norm Cash came to the plate carrying a table leg in place of a bat. When umpire Ron Luciano prompted him to find a more suitable piece of lumber, Cash argued comically that it didn't matter since he had no chance of getting a hit anyway. Four days later, Ryan held the Orioles hitless for seven innings at Anaheim. In the eighth inning, he hit leadoff batter Brooks Robinson with a pitch then coughed up a bloop-single to light-hitting shortstop Mark Belanger. Ryan admitted that he had entered the game believing he could tie Vander Meer's record and that it became a source of distraction for him.

Joe DiMaggio's 56-Game Hitting Streak
May 15–July 16, 1941

Joe DiMaggio played alongside some of the brightest icons in baseball history. Nearly all of them had wonderful things to say about "The Yankee Clipper." Mickey Mantle once commented: "Heroes are people who are all good with no bad in them. That's the way I always saw Joe DiMaggio. He was beyond question one of the greatest players of the century."[8] Bob Feller echoed that sentiment, remarking: "[Ted] Williams was the greatest hitter I ever saw, but DiMaggio was the greatest all around player."[9] Stan Musial, who surpassed DiMaggio's numbers in nearly every statistical category, offered flatteringly: "There was never a day when I was as good as Joe DiMaggio."[10]

Few athletes have been more revered than "Joltin' Joe." During his lifetime, he was associated with Hollywood starlets and heads of state. Songs were composed in his honor. And he was even referenced in Ernest Hemingway's Pulitzer Prize–winning novel, *The Old Man and the Sea*. There are a number of records in professional sports that are considered impregnable. Of them all, DiMaggio's 56-game hitting streak is generally regarded as the most impossible to surpass.

Born in 1914 to immigrant Italian parents, DiMaggio grew up in San Francisco. The immediate

Joe DiMaggio salutes his bat during the 1941 campaign. He should also have paid homage to umpire Steve Basil, whose blown call at first base kept DiMaggio's fabled 56-game hitting streak alive (Library of Congress).

family, which included eight children, lived in a small four-room house. DiMaggio's father fished for crabs and the boys were expected to help. But young Joe disliked the profession, avoiding all the chores associated with it.

At age seventeen, DiMaggio began his minor league career with the San Francisco Seals of the Pacific Coast League. In 1933, he hit safely in sixty-one consecutive games—a PCL record that still stands. He spent portions of four seasons on the farm before joining the Yankees. By the time he began his assault on the major league record books in 1941, he had played on five All-Star teams and captured an AL MVP award.

DiMaggio began the 1941 season on a tear and then fell into a horrendous mini-slump that dropped his batting average considerably. He and his then wife, Dorothy Arnold, were expecting their first child and various members of the press hypothesized that he was suffering from pre-parental jitters. Whatever the case, very few sportswriters took notice when he began "The Streak" on May 15 with an RBI single in a blowout loss to the White Sox.

There were plenty of things going on to draw attention away from DiMaggio's exploits. Europe was embroiled in war and, as German aggression continued overseas, president Franklin Delano Roosevelt issued his famous "Unlimited National Emergency" speech. Elsewhere in the world of baseball, Red Sox slugger Ted Williams spent the entire season chasing—and ultimately reaching—the elusive .400 batting average mark at the plate. Another major development, Lou Gehrig passed away on June 2 after a heroic battle with Amyotrophic Lateral Sclerosis. Meanwhile, DiMaggio's skein went virtually unnoticed until he extended it to twenty games.

In his acclaimed biography, *Joe DiMaggio: The Hero's Life*, Pulitzer Prize–winning author Richard Ben Cramer pointed out: "It was only after the fact that 'The Streak' shone as a portent of America's brilliant rise to superpower, and made DiMaggio her poster boy for valor, victory and God-given grace."[11] Better late than never, the sporting world eventually caught on.

Like any illustrious sporting achievement, DiMaggio got some very lucky breaks along the way. On May 18, the Yankees faced the Browns at home on "I Am an American Day." To the immense pleasure of the patriotic masses, DiMaggio went 3-for-3. But those numbers were most definitely skewed. His first hit was a squibber to third that was badly mishandled by infielder Harlond Clift. His second hit bounced off the glove of right fielder Chet Laabs. Perhaps inspired by a sense of civic pride, official scorer Dan Daniel awarded DiMaggio a single and a double.

PART ONE. THE UMPIRE GIVETH, THE UMPIRE TAKETH AWAY   15

As "The Streak" began to take up newspaper space and capture the imaginations of fans, immense pressure was put on umpires to make the right decisions. During one record-tying game, DiMaggio was said to have turned his head to question a strike call. The arbiter reportedly swallowed hard before issuing an immediate apology.

"The Streak" was in serious jeopardy on multiple occasions. In fact, DiMaggio extended it during his final plate appearance nearly a dozen times. But never was he more in danger of losing it than on June 10 at Chicago's Comiskey Park. After a pair of groundouts and an infield pop-up, the Yankee icon came to bat in the seventh inning against right-hander Johnny Rigney, who was one of Chicago's top hurlers in those days. DiMaggio smashed a sizzling grounder to third, where the sure-handed Dario Lodigiani was stationed. "Lodi" could only block it with his body, but he recovered in time to nail the Yankee centerfielder at first by a quarter of a step. Fortunately for DiMaggio, first base umpire Steve Basil saw things differently, making a "safe" call on the play.

Basil, who had turned to umpiring after his playing career stalled out at the Class-D level, was in his sixth year of major league service. Though generally even-tempered, he was not afraid to assert his authority when his calls were held in question. Never was this more apparent than in June of 1938, when he tossed three members of the St. Louis Browns out of a game for arguing balls and strikes.

According to AL arbiter Joe Rue, Basil was a bit of a tattletale who was constantly trying to curry favor with MLB officials. In particular, he had established intimate relationships with umpire supervisor Tommy Connolly and AL president William Harridge. "Basil was always playing up to Connolly," Rue asserted bitterly. "And he'd run to Connolly and Harridge with everything."[12]

There was no need to seek the counsel of league officials on the date in question. In fact, the White Sox hardly protested at all as DiMaggio's streak was extended to twenty-five games. Basil's call proved to be of monumental importance when Joe D. grounded into a double play in his final at-bat of the day. Had Basil made the correct decision, "The Streak" would have been divided into two roughly equal halves—impressive, for sure, but not exactly the stuff of which legends are made.

The events of July 17, 1941, have attained an almost mythical quality. DiMaggio had pushed his streak to fifty-six games and was on his way to Cleveland's Municipal Stadium in a cab when the driver, recognizing the iconic outfielder and his teammate Lefty Gomez, said ominously: "I got a feeling if you don't get a hit in your first at-bat today, they're going to stop you." (Several versions of the quote exist) Flabbergasted, Gomez snapped: "Who the hell are you? What're you trying to do—jinx him?"[13]

Gomez might have been on to something.

The jinx appeared in the form of Indians third baseman Ken Keltner, who made a pair of spectacular stops to rob DiMaggio. "The Streak" ended that day and "Joltin' Joe" hit safely in his next sixteen games. Many years after the fact, he claimed to have had an encounter with the mysterious Cleveland cab driver. "Now this is thirty years later," DiMaggio asserted. "He apologized and was serious. I felt awful. He might have been spending his whole life thinking he had jinxed me, but I told him he hadn't. My number was up."[14]

Regarding numbers, DiMaggio's were impressive. During "The Streak," he hit .408 with fifteen homers and 55 RBI. When it began, the Yankees were in fourth place sitting five and a half games out. By the time it was over, the New Yorkers had moved into first and built a six-game lead. Perhaps the most impressive feature of DiMaggio's skein, he struck out only five times in 223 at-bats. He would whiff just thirteen times all season.

Interestingly, Keltner's slick glovework cost DiMaggio a major endorsement. The Yankee slugger had a deal set up with Heinz 57 ketchup, but when "The Streak" ended at fifty-six games, the company retracted its offer. DiMaggio told the press he was glad it was over, but confided to friends later that he was upset.

Though Williams hit .406 in 1941, the MVP award ultimately went to DiMaggio. It was a personal victory for Joe D., who held the Red Sox slugger in great contempt. "He throws like a broad and runs like a ruptured duck," the Yankee outfielder once quipped.[15] Hobbled by ongoing injuries, DiMaggio's career (rendered even more memorable by nine World Series rings) ended in 1951. Even after he died in 1999, he never completely faded from public consciousness. "Some say his calm and quiet style was a result of his shyness," wrote one biographer after his passing. "Some claim he was cold and aloof. It doesn't matter. On the ball field, Joe DiMaggio was Fred Astaire: all class, all the way."[16]

As for Basil, he retired from umpiring after the 1942 slate with more than a thousand games to his credit. A lifelong resident of Texas, his name has faded into the mists of time. Since no one really wanted "Joltin' Joe" to fail, Basil's errant call has gone largely unmentioned over the years. And no one has come terribly close to surpassing "The Streak"—not even DiMaggio himself, who never had another twenty-game string after his brilliant summer of 1941.

Don Larsen's Perfect World Series Game
October 8, 1956

In nearly one hundred and fifty years of major league baseball history, only twenty-three perfect games have been thrown. Of those twenty-three, only one occurred during the World Series. In the wake of Don Larsen's 1956 postseason masterpiece, a writer from *The San Francisco Chronicle* referred to him as "the last person in baseball who might be expected to pitch a perfect game."[17] It may not even have been possible without the help of home plate umpire, Babe Pinelli, whose controversial strike call ended the game.

Born in Michigan City, Indiana, Larsen's family moved to San Diego during World War II. His mother was a housekeeper and his father worked in a department store. At Point Loma High School, Larsen became a multi-sport star and was offered several basketball scholarships. He signed with the St. Louis Browns instead, explaining later that he "didn't have much interest in going to college and studying [his] life away."[18]

After toiling in the minors for four seasons, Larsen was drafted into the U.S. Army during the Korean War. He served in a variety of non-combat assignments and was discharged in 1953. He made his major league debut that same year. Though his numbers weren't terribly impressive, he led the St. Louis staff in innings pitched and complete games. After a disastrous follow-up season, he was traded to the Yankees in a blockbuster deal involving over a dozen players.

Larsen was known for his love of the nightlife, a propensity that allowed him to blend well with notorious Yankee carousers Mickey Mantle, Billy Martin and Whitey Ford. During spring training one year, Larsen ran his car into a mailbox at 5:30 a.m., inspiring manager Casey Stengel to remark: "The man was either out too early or too late."[19]

On the mound, Larsen had good control and employed a variety of pitches, including a curve, change-up and fastball. He was pretty handy with a bat as well—good enough to be used as a pinch-hitter more than sixty times during his career. Yet, despite his vast potential, he was an under-achiever. One teammate described him as such: "He probably had a lot more ability than ninety-five percent of all the pitchers in baseball ... but he was a lazy type."[20]

During the 1950s, the Yankees and Dodgers faced each other in the

World Series four times. There was hardly a weak spot to be found in the Brooklyn lineup. In addition to a quartet of Hall of Famers (Duke Snider, Jackie Robinson, Roy Campanella and Pee Wee Reese), the Dodgers had Gil Hodges, a perennial All-Star and eminent home run threat. Avenging decades of futility, they defeated the Yankees in the 1955 Fall Classic, capturing the first championship in modern franchise history.

On the eve of Larsen's historic performance in 1956, the Series was knotted at two games apiece and Casey Stengel had not yet chosen a starter. Larsen, who was available since he had only lasted 1.2 innings in a disastrous Game 2 outing, told a reporter from *The New York Daily Mirror* that he was up to the task. "I'm just liable to pitch a no-hitter," he added half-jokingly.[21] That statement proved to be prophetic.

Earlier in the year, Larsen had been tipping his pitches. This became problematic during a late-season series at Fenway Park, when Red Sox coach Del Baker was able to accurately read every offering in advance. Taking corrective measures, Larsen got together with Yankee pitching coach Jim Turner to alter his mechanics.

Using a no-windup delivery, Larsen breezed through the Dodger lineup with just a handful of scary moments. In the second inning, Jackie Robinson ripped a ball to third base that bounced off Andy Carey's glove. Shortstop Gil McDougald grabbed it in time to throw Robinson out. In the fifth inning, Gil Hodges launched a drive to the warning track in left-center field, where Mickey Mantle made a nice running catch. The next batter, Sandy Amoros, smashed a pitch toward the right field stands. Hank Bauer tracked it to the wall and breathed a sigh of relief as it hooked foul by a matter of inches. "I was the happiest guy in the park," he told reporters after the game.[22] The afternoon was refreshingly free from drama for Larsen after that.

As Larsen's perfect game continued into the late innings, his teammates adopted the customary practice of avoiding him. Larsen tried desperately to get someone to speak to him, even going so far as to corner Mickey Mantle in the runway. But the Yankee idol refused to engage with him.

With two outs in the ninth inning, Dodger manager Walter Alston pinch-hit for pitcher Sal Maglie, who had held the powerful Yankees to just two runs on five hits. His replacement was Dale Mitchell. An outfielder by trade, Mitchell had appeared on two All-Star teams and led the AL in hits during the 1949 slate. Traded to Brooklyn in late–July of 1956, he compiled a .292 average down the stretch. He was excellent off the bench, banging out 49 pinch-hits during his career with 31 RBIs. Mitchell saw four pitches from Larsen that afternoon and decided that only one of them was good enough to hit. He fouled it off, remarking after the fact: "If you miss your pitch, you're out of business."[23] In the end, it was umpire Babe Pinelli who put him out of business.

A self-proclaimed juvenile delinquent, Pinelli had turned his life around by pursuing a career in baseball. He enjoyed four productive seasons as Cincinnati's starting third baseman. During his playing days, he earned a reputation as a hot-head, engaging in multiple on-field brawls—including an infamous scrape with umpire Bill "Lord" Byron. But Pinelli's temperament changed dramatically when he joined the National League umpiring staff. Between 1951 and 1955, he issued just six ejections, receiving the nickname of "The Soft Thumb."

Before the final pitch of Larsen's perfect game, the hurler admitted to being so nervous that his knees were shaking. Yankee catcher Yogi Berra set a low target on the outside corner. Pinelli was looking over Berra's right shoulder (a standard practice for NL umpires), making it a bit more difficult to accurately call outside strikes. Game footage shows that Larsen's offering was off the plate and that Berra was forced to reach for it slightly. Mitchell checked his swing acceptably by 1950s standards. Pinelli may have been fooled by Larsen's efficiency that afternoon or perhaps he wanted to leave his mark on baseball history. Whatever the case, Mitchell didn't argue with Pinelli's strike call as Berra rushed the mound and joyfully jumped into Larsen's arms. Mitchell later told his friend, Hall of Famer Bob Lemon, that the pitch was so far outside, he couldn't have reached it if he had tried.

Legions of second-guessers have long contended that Pinelli made the wrong decision, but the arbiter didn't lose any sleep over it. "Larsen hit the corner with a beautiful fastball [that was] just high enough. It was easy to call and I called it."[24]

End of story.

Yankee backstop Yogi Berra, who had caught two no-hitters thrown by Allie Reynolds in 1951, raved about the effectiveness of Larsen's pitches during his memorable Game 5 start. "He only shook me off twice," Berra contended, "but each time he finally signaled for the original pitch. He was great. In fact, I've never caught a greater pitcher than Don was."[25]

Larsen lasted fourteen seasons in the majors, retiring with a lackluster 81–91 record and 3.78 ERA. He later worked as a salesman. At the time of this writing, he was living in Idaho and still making periodic appearances at Yankee Stadium. He sold most of his memorabilia over the years, including the uniform he wore during the most brilliant game of his career.

In the wake of Larsen's masterpiece, Pinelli was snubbed by reporters and league officials. He received no commendation for his performance nor was he asked to share his observations. Fellow crew member Tom Gorman considered the oversight to be shameful. Pinelli announced his retirement after the Series was over, ending a career that had spanned twenty-two seasons. "Why go on?" he remarked. "I won't see a better pitched game."[26]

Aside from Larsen's magnum opus, there has been only one other postseason no-hitter. In Game 1 of the 2010 NLDS, Phillies ace Roy Halladay retired the first fourteen Cincinnati batters he faced before issuing a walk to outfielder Jay Bruce. The Hall of Fame right-hander quickly regained his control and disposed of the next thirteen hitters, completing a near-perfect game. Remarkably, Halladay had been perfect against the Florida Marlins earlier in the season.

Bob Shaw's Balk-a-Thon
May 4, 1963

There are certain records in baseball that no player would ever want to be associated with. Despite a successful major league career that included a trip to the World Series, Bob Shaw is largely remembered for one horrific afternoon on the mound. During a luckless outing against the Cubs, the right-handed junk-baller raised the bar for most balks committed in a single game. The stigma might have proved embarrassing to Shaw had more people actually understood precisely what a balk is.

According to *Pro Baseball Insider*, a balk can be defined as a situation in which "the pitcher tries to intentionally deceive the runner. It can be a flinch on the mound after the pitcher gets set, a deceptive pick-off attempt, or even just as simple as dropping the ball once you become set."[27] If a balk is called, all runners are entitled to move up a base. It sounds straightforward, but is not. Every pitcher has a unique set of quirks on the mound and the motions that constitute intentional deceit are somewhat open to interpretation. Outspoken arbiter Ron Luciano once admitted that he never called balks because he didn't understand the rule. Considering that balks are rare (occurring an average of once per every 289 innings pitched during the regular season), Luciano was probably not alone.

PART ONE. THE UMPIRE GIVETH, THE UMPIRE TAKETH AWAY   21

Before the 1963 season, NL umpires were forced to scramble for their rulebooks as President Warren Giles issued an ordinance compelling arbiters to crack down on balks. In the first twenty games of the season, twenty infractions were called. The trend continued to great excess during Shaw's infamous outing on May 4.

Born in the Bronx, Shaw starred in three different sports during high school. He had his sights set on the Ivy League, but his grades wouldn't allow it, so he accepted a football scholarship to St. Lawrence University. Since the scholarship didn't include room and board, Shaw was forced to sleep on the floor of his friend's dorm room. When the Detroit Tigers offered him a $1,000 bonus to enter their farm system, he gladly agreed.

In 1954, Hall of Famer Joe Gordon helped Shaw alter his pitching mechanics during a dismal season with the Durham Bulls. A simple adjustment to his grip prompted a rapid rise up through the minors. He was eventually traded to the White Sox.

In his second full major league season, Shaw led the American League with a .750 winning percentage while compiling a handsome 2.69 ERA. His efforts helped propel Chicago to a long overdue World Series appearance. Shaw made two starts against the L.A. Dodgers, winning one and losing another as the White Sox dropped the Series in six games.

Traded in June of 1961, Shaw ended up with the Kansas City A's and, later, the Milwaukee Braves. Though he averaged less than three runs per nine innings during the 1963 campaign, he was giving runs away for free on May 4. Facing the Cubs at County Stadium in Milwaukee, he entered the game with a 0–1 record. The Cubs had an impressive lineup in those days, featuring Hall of Famers Billy Williams, Ron Santo and Ernie Banks— none of whom needed the generous gifts that Shaw was about to bestow upon them.

With two outs in the top of the first, Williams singled, bringing up the dangerous Santo. Home plate umpire Al Barlick saw something suspect in Shaw's delivery and called a balk, advancing Williams to second. It was just a preview of impending disaster as Santo walked and Banks struck out, ending the inning without any damage.

The game was tied at one apiece in the third when trouble began in earnest. Williams opened the frame with a walk. With Santo at the plate, Barlick called another balk on Shaw, pushing Williams to second. Clearly rattled, Shaw ended up balking Williams to third and then home, giving the Cubs a 2–1 lead.

The Braves tied the score, but Shaw's day of infamy was not yet complete. In the top of the fifth, he was called for his fifth infraction of the game (a record that still stands). He came completely unglued at that point, walking the next two batters to force in a run. After arguing with Barlick about the arbiter's rapidly disappearing strike zone, Shaw ended up getting tossed out (an act of kindness on Barlick's part, some would say).

Incredibly, Milwaukee reliever Denny Lemaster joined the festivities in the eighth, drawing yet another balk call from Barlick. This ran the daily total up to six—more than any team has ever committed in a single game.

Evaluating Shaw's performance many years later, a *Stack Magazine* writer commented humorously: "One balk can be forgiven. Two balks and it's like 'Hey, guy on the mound, please stop balking!' But, five balks—FIVE?! Even if, as a pitcher, you didn't understand what constituted a balk, after you got called for it—I don't know—say, THREE times, maybe you'd start to figure out what you were doing wrong.... Let's hope his manager isn't holed up in some insane asylum, curled up in a ball and rocking back and forth as he mutters 'Bob Shaw' over and over again."[28]

The author of those words needn't have worried. Manager Bobby Bragan remained at the Braves helm for portions of three more seasons before embarking upon a successful career as a minor league executive. The umpire who issued the record-setting balk calls wound up in the Hall of Fame. Al Barlick, known for his thunderous strike calls and dramatic hand signals, was the sixth umpire to be enshrined at Cooperstown in 1989. But the 1963 campaign was one he would surely have liked to forget.

Thanks to Warren Giles's war on balks, National League umpires were constantly under fire. Fed up with the state of affairs, Barlick mouthed off to the press. "We umpires have to shoulder too much of the blame," he griped. "We didn't write the rules, [we] just make certain none is violated. Now everyone is on us about our balks. Our instructions are to call balks when the pitcher fails to pause in his delivery with men on base and we're following orders."[29]

After umpiring a game between the Reds and Mets on June 15, Barlick contacted the league secretary and threatened to quit. At the time, there was no supervisor of umpires in the National League (unlike the American League) and Barlick felt that Giles was not offering enough support to NL crews. His grievance was taken very seriously. Giles issued a public apology of sorts and granted Barlick a brief leave of absence. He then called an emergency meeting of the rules committee to soften his stance against balks.

Controversy resurfaced in 1988, when the rule was rewritten to make balk calls more uniform throughout the majors. A clause was added stipulating that pitchers must "come to a single complete and discernible stop with both feet on the ground."[30] The results were disastrous. Six weeks into the season, a record for balks had already been set. By the time the last regular season pitch had been thrown, the cumulative balk total in both leagues stood at 924—nearly five times the major league average. Sportswriters have often referred to the 1988 campaign as "The Year of the Balk." Four different pitchers came close to tying Bob Shaw's single-game record that season, ultimately falling short. In January of 1989, the rule was changed back to its prior form. Balks have remained relatively uncommon since then.

The most prolific offender in baseball history is Steve Carlton, who was charged with ninety balks during his career. Dave Stewart of the Oakland A's holds the single season record with sixteen. It should come as no surprise that he attained that dubious honor in 1988.

Bob Shaw ended up playing for seven teams in eleven seasons. He finished his major league career with a 108–98 record and 3.52 ERA. When his playing days were over, he served as a pitching coach for the Brewers and managed in the Florida State League. Having learned a thing or two from his mistakes over the years, he wrote an instructional manual on pitching before he passed away in 2010.

On a final note, Shaw, Stewart and Carlton are not the only players whose careers will forever be associated with balks. Another infamous incident occurred during the 1961 All-Star Game at Candlestick Park. Built over a landfill that extended into San Francisco Bay, the stadium was known for its blustery conditions. During the game in question, Giants pitcher Stu Miller was rocked by a sudden gust of wind, forcing him to falter in his delivery enough to draw a balk call. The infraction led to a run that sent the game into extra innings. Fittingly, Miller was charged with a blown save.

Don Drysdale's Consecutive Scoreless Innings Streak
May 14–June 8, 1968

In 1961, baseball experienced an offensive surge marked by the sudden emergence of several flash-in-the pan sluggers. Baltimore's Jim Gentile led the league with 141 RBIs. Detroit's Norm Cash captured a batting title with a lofty .361 mark. And Roger Maris of the Yankees pushed the single-season home run record to sixty-one. Those players would never come close to matching those numbers in any other season. Feeling that the tides had turned unfairly in favor of hitters, Commissioner Ford Frick endorsed the expansion of the strike zone. Offense began to slowly dwindle as a result, reaching a low-point in 1968, which has often been referred to as "The Year of the Pitcher."

Remarkable pitching feats were relatively common during the 1968 campaign. A total of 339 shutouts were thrown that year as batting averages plummeted to an all-time low of .230 in the AL and .243 in the NL (second lowest). Additional highlights included Catfish Hunter's perfect game (the first regular season AL perfecto since 1922), Bob Gibson's 1.12 ERA (lowest of the post–Deadball Era), and Denny McLain's thirty-one victories (highest total since Dizzy Dean in 1934). Most impressive of all, perhaps, was Don Drysdale's streak of 58.2 consecutive scoreless innings.

Born in Van Nuys, Los Angeles, Drysdale attended the same high school as actor Robert Redford. Following the advice of his father, he waited until he was sixteen to start pitching. Within a couple of years, he had worked his way up to the Triple-A level. He earned himself a permanent roster spot with the Dodgers in 1956.

Tall and sturdily built at 6-foot-5, 200-plus pounds, Drysdale was often referred to as "Big D." He had plenty of natural ability, but used intimidation to gain an edge. From 1958 through 1961, he led the National League in hit batsmen every year, prompting Hall of Famer Orlando Cepeda to remark: "The trick against Drysdale is to hit him before he hits you."[31]

Drysdale borrowed his strategy from one of the most aggressive pitchers of all time, Sal Maglie, who was nicknamed "The Barber" because of his tendency to throw at hitters. After playing alongside Maglie for portions of two seasons, Drysdale developed a two-for one-rule. If one of his teammates got knocked down, he knocked down two on the other team. Instructed by manager Walter Alston to walk a batter one day, Drysdale plunked him instead. "Why waste four pitches when one will do?" he explained. "Sooner or later you have to say 'it's my ball and half the plate is mine.' Only I never let on which half of the plate I wanted."[32]

Strong-arm tactics worked to his advantage as Drysdale won at least fifteen games during seven seasons. He led the NL with twenty-five victories in 1962, capturing a Cy Young Award. Highly durable, he reached the 300-inning threshold in four straight campaigns while leading the league in strikeouts three times. His crowning achievement came during the offensive implosion of 1968, when he strung together six consecutive shutouts.

Before Drysdale, the American League record for consecutive scoreless innings belonged to Walter Johnson of the old Senators, who went 55.2 frames without allowing a run during the 1913 slate. In the National League, the standard had been set by "King Carl" Hubbell of the Giants, who assembled a string of 45.1 scoreless innings in 1933. During Drysdale's six shutouts, he faced twelve Hall of Famers (including pitchers) and ran up a total of forty-two strikeouts. But he came close to blowing it before he surpassed Hubbell's mark. With a little help from umpire Harry Wendelstedt, he was able to keep the streak alive.

On May 31, Drysdale faced the San Francisco Giants at home. He got through eight innings unscathed before courting disaster. First baseman Willie McCovey walked to open the ninth. Left fielder Jim Ray Hart followed with a single, bringing up right fielder Dave Marshall, who walked to load the bases. With the streak in serious jeopardy, Drysdale ran up a 2–2 count on catcher Dick Dietz before hitting him in the elbow with a pitch. Just when all seemed lost, Wendelstedt intervened, resorting to a seldom invoked rule which states that a hit batsman is not entitled to first base if he makes no effort to avoid the pitch. In Wendelstedt's opinion, Dietz had allowed himself to be hit. "I saw it immediately," the arbiter asserted. "That's not the type of thing that you can miss. He started to back away and then stuck his elbow into the ball. I immediately said 'No, no, no, you tried to get hit with it.' This was just so evident that I acted instinctively."[33]

Wendelstedt was not alone in his belief. Dietz's teammate, Ron Hunt,

Wendelstedt's controversial interference call on Giants catcher Dick Dietz allowed Dodger hurler Don Drysdale to extend a scoreless streak that ultimately reached 58.2 consecutive innings (National Baseball Hall of Fame Library, Cooperstown, N.Y.).

who at one time held the painful record for most career beanings, said: "[Dietz] stood there like a post. It was a high slider and he didn't make an attempt. We'd seen a lot of those things where it was or wasn't called, when it wasn't such a big deal."[34]

Though Drysdale's streak was certainly of great significance, Wendelstedt insisted he had acted impartially. "I couldn't care less about the man's record," he contended. "You do what you think is right. It's part of my job."[35]

Perhaps trying to save a little face, Dietz argued the call and later refused to admit to any indiscretion. "I was protecting the plate," he insisted. "Don threw one of those slippery pitches—he threw a spitball—so I was hanging over the plate protecting myself."[36]

Despite Wendelstedt's timely gift, Drysdale was still in a no out, bases loaded jam. Composing himself, he got Dietz on a shallow fly. Ty Cline followed with a grounder that resulted in a force-out at home. Jack Hiatt then popped out to end the game, extending Drysdale's streak.

Describing the reaction of visiting players on that fateful evening in Los Angeles, columnist Jim Murray wrote: "The Giants, to a man, behaved as if Wendelstedt had just dropped a match into a baby carriage."[37] After the game, San Francisco manager Herman Franks expressed his bitterness with the decision. "It was the worst call I've ever seen," he grumbled. "If Drysdale breaks the record now, he and Wendelstedt should share it. Hell, put Wendelstedt's name on the trophy first."[38]

Against the Pirates at home on June 4, Drysdale recorded his sixth consecutive shutout, breaking a record held by Doc White of the 1904 White Sox and moving within striking distance of Johnson's all-time mark. Still bitter about the Dick Dietz incident, Herman Franks accused Drysdale of doctoring baseballs. Responding to Franks' charge, Phillies skipper Gene Mauch approached umpire Augie Donatelli during Drysdale's June 8 start and requested a shakedown. Donatelli performed a rudimentary inspection and instructed Drysdale not to rub the back of his neck or touch his cap for the remainder of the game.

Drysdale tossed four and two-thirds scoreless innings before the Phillies put an end to his historic streak. With runners on first and third, pinch-hitter Howie Bedell lifted a sacrifice fly to left field, scoring teammate Tony Taylor. Interestingly, it was Bedell's only RBI of the year and one of only three he collected during his entire career.

Surrounded by reporters after the game, Drysdale said; "I think all good things have to come to an end. I knew it would happen sooner or later."[39] Asked how long he thought the record would stand, he answered, "There's always somebody around who can break a record. This gives everybody a target to shoot at. I wish all the luck and will be the first to congratulate him if I'm still around to do it."[40]

For Drysdale, the 1968 campaign was his last great effort. Hampered by chronic shoulder issues, he was forced into retirement at the age of thirty-three. He went on to a long career in broadcasting. His record of consecutive scoreless innings lasted until 1988, when it was broken by Orel Hershiser.

Harry Wendelstedt's career was not defined by the controversial call that saved Drysdale's streak. The arbiter had a long, industrious career that spanned thirty-three major league seasons. Known for the dramatic chainsaw motion he used to signal strikeouts, the Baltimore native called five no-hitters during his big league tenure—a record shared with Hall of Famer Bill Klem. Wendelstedt owned and operated his own umpiring school from 1975 until his death in 2012, sending more arbiters to the big leagues than all the other schools combined.

Addressing the offensive collapse of 1968, officials in both leagues agreed to lower the height of the mound from fifteen to ten inches. The concept of three-ball walks was also discussed, but in the end it was decided that a return to a smaller strike zone would be a more practical solution. Results were seen immediately with collective batting averages rising in both leagues during the 1969 slate.

Orel Hershiser's Consecutive Scoreless Innings Streak
August 30–September 28, 1988

It is a well-established fact that history often repeats itself—especially in baseball. Any well-informed fan would have felt an intense feeling of déjà vu on September 23, 1988, at Candlestick Park in San Francisco. On that night, Orel Hershiser surpassed an old National League record set by Carl Hubbell for consecutive scoreless innings pitched. That record had previously been broken by Don Drysdale, who had also played for the Dodgers. An even more striking parallel—both men relied on controversial calls from umpires to exceed Hubbell's mark.

Born in Buffalo, New York, Hershiser lived in Detroit and Toronto before spending his high school days in New Jersey. He didn't make the varsity baseball squad at Cherry Hill East until eleventh grade. Even after setting a school record for most strikeouts in a single game, he remained undrafted after his graduation. He attended Bowling Green University in Ohio and made the Mid-American Conference All-Star team during his junior year. In 1979, he pitched a no-hitter against Kent State. The Dodgers claimed him in the seventeenth round of the amateur draft not long afterward.

Initial scouting reports on Hershiser alleged that he had a weak fastball and a flawed curve in addition to being easily rattled. But Dodger manager Tom Lasorda had faith in the young hurler, describing him as "a hard worker" who was "aggressive, even daring, on the mound."[41] Looking to instill confidence in Hershiser, Lasorda gave him the rugged nickname of "Bulldog," which the right-hander believed was more for his manager's benefit. "I think it makes him think I'm tough and can work myself out of jams," Hershiser told a reporter.[42]

A September call-up in 1983, Hershiser posted a 3.38 ERA in eight appearances. He served in a variety of roles the following year, winning eleven games as a starter and reliever while finishing third in Rookie of the Year voting. During the 1985 slate, he established himself as ace of the Dodger staff with a 19–3 record. His winning percentage was tops in the NL that year.

In his prime, Hershiser had a variety of effective pitches, including a sinking fastball, a sharp curve and a four-seamer. He had all of them working for him in September of 1988, when he made his mark on baseball history. On August 30, he finished a 4–2 win over the Expos with four shutout innings. It was the beginning of a remarkable run.

From September 5 through September 28, Hershiser held opponents scoreless in six consecutive starts. He was on the verge of surpassing Hubbell's mark of 45.1 consecutive shutout innings, set in 1933, when things nearly fell apart. Facing the Giants in San Francisco, Hershiser yielded a single to Jose Uribe to open the third inning. Giants pitcher Atlee Hammaker then beat out a bunt to second base. After centerfielder Brett Butler reached on a fielder's choice, advancing Uribe to third, Ernie Riles hit a grounder to Steve Sax. Sax, who would later develop serious problems making infield relays, threw accurately to shortstop Alfredo Griffin. Griffin got the force at second, but as he was pivoting to complete the double play, Butler plowed into him, causing his throw to sail over the head of first baseman Tracy Woodson. Uribe crossed the plate and the run appeared on the scoreboard. Before the dust had settled, however, third base umpire Paul Runge came to Hershiser's rescue.

Runge, who was in his sixteenth year of major league service, contended that Butler had veered to the right of second base and interfered with Griffin's throw, resulting in an automatic out at first. Runge had developed a reputation for allowing players and managers to speak their minds. But despite the protestations of San Francisco skipper Roger Craig, the arbiter was not inclined to reverse his call. The inning was over and the run erased. More importantly, Hershiser's streak was still going.

Tremendously relieved, Griffin told a reporter after the game: "Butler slid at the base and hit me and made me make a bad throw. But the umpire made the right call. It made me feel better because it would have crushed me." No one was more thankful than Hershiser, himself, who ran off the field shouting: "Dick Dietz revisited!" (On a humorous side note, he remarked that no one in the dugout knew what he was talking about.)[43]

On September 28, Hershiser engaged in a pitching duel with right-hander Andy Hawkins of the Padres, who was having one of the finest seasons of his career. Both men worked their way through nine innings without yielding a run. There was far more at stake for Hershiser. Having completed fifty-eight consecutive scoreless frames, he was on the verge of claiming the all-time record for himself.

"I really didn't want to break it," said Hershiser. "I wanted me and Don to be at the top, but the higher sources said they weren't taking me out of the game." Drysdale, who was on the broadcasting crew that night, chuckled when informed of the comment. "I'd have kicked him right in the rear if I'd have known that," he said. "I'd have told him to get his buns out there and get them."[44]

Hershiser did exactly that, though the inning wasn't pretty. A wild pitch and two ground outs advanced San Diego's Marvell Wynne to third base. After an intentional walk to Garry Templeton and a stolen base (which was discounted due to defensive indifference), Hershiser retired Keith Moreland on a fly ball to right field. The all-time record was now solely in Hershiser's possession. During a post-game press conference, Drysdale was asked about the streak. Fittingly, he pointed to Hershiser and said: "You listen to him now."[45]

Though the postseason didn't officially figure into Hershiser's totals, he tossed eight more scoreless innings against the Mets on October 4 before yielding an RBI double to Darryl Strawberry. He was named MVP of the NLCS and World Series as the Dodgers knocked off the A's in five games. A lock for the Cy Young Award at season's end, Hershiser enjoyed several more productive campaigns afterward. He won twelve or more games six times and helped three different clubs to postseason appearances.

Since then, he has worked as a broadcaster, pitching coach, motivational speaker and professional poker player. He has also co-authored several books along the way.

Runge remained a member of the National League staff through the 1997 campaign. Over the course of his career, he worked in nine National League Championship Series, four World Series and three All-Star Games. He shared the record for most NLCS appearances with several others until Bruce Froemming claimed it for himself in the year 2000. After retiring from his on-field duties, Runge served as director of NL umpires for two years. Interestingly, the Runges were the first three-generation family of umpires. Paul's father, Ed, served as an AL arbiter for seventeen seasons and his son, Brian, worked on the unified major league staff for fourteen years.

Hershiser's record has not been seriously challenged over the past several decades. In 2014, Brandon Webb of the Diamondbacks and Clayton Kershaw of the Dodgers both tossed more than forty consecutive innings of shutout ball, but neither surpassed Hubbell's mark. Zack Greinke of the Dodgers moved ahead of "King Carl" in 2015, though his streak ended at 45.2. "I've never thrown a ball in my whole career as good as Greinke and Kershaw are throwing," Hershiser said respectfully. "I'm not even in that realm. These guys are on a different level."[46]

The 1998 Home Run Chase
(Featuring Mark McGwire and Sammy Sosa)

In 1994, an ongoing players strike resulted in the cancellation of the World Series. It was the first season without a Fall Classic in ninety years. Several important milestones were left in limbo as big league ballparks closed their gates on August 12. Tony Gwynn, who had been chasing the .400 mark all year, settled for a career-high .394 batting average. On pace to break Roger Maris's single-season home run record, Matt Williams of the Giants ended up with 43 long balls. And the Expos, the winningest team in the majors at 74–40, were forced to wait another year for a World Series bid—a prize that would ultimately escape their grasp.

Referred to by various sources as baseball's "most embarrassing moment," the strike lasted a total of 232 days while costing players and executives more than $1 billion. "It was tough," Commissioner Bud Selig recalled. "There was a lot of anger everywhere, particularly amongst our fans."[47] Many fans expressed their disapproval by staying away from ballparks in 1995 as attendance dropped significantly.

In the wake of the strike, enthusiasm within the sport waned considerably among players as well. Pitcher Dave Stewart admitted to a reporter: "I never felt the same way about baseball again after that … the passion I have for the game has never been the same."[48] Reflecting on the strike a decade after the fact, veteran pitcher Mike Mussina remarked: "I think the experience of ten years ago showed both sides that the game is too important to too many people, and we need to find better ways to accomplish things."[49]

Major league attendance remained somewhat stagnant until 1998, when baseball got a desperately needed shot in the arm. It came in the form of a dramatic home run duel waged by Mark McGwire and Sammy Sosa. Writing for *Sports Illustrated*, Emmy Award–winning analyst Tom Verducci eloquently stated: "The chase by McGwire and Sosa of [Roger] Maris's record 61 home runs—and then of each other—spread the religion of baseball. Cardinals and Cubs games had the feel of revival meetings…. And baseball, a setup line to cruel jokes during and after the 1994–95 strike, regained its honor. Hardly anyone complained about the length of games or nitpicked about Nielsen ratings. Hallelujah!"[50]

McGwire, the eventual victor of "The Chase," had been a star for the University of Southern California. He played for Team USA in the 1983 Pan American Games and 1984 Olympics before being drafted by the Oakland A's. In 1987, he set a home run record for freshmen (later broken by Aaron Judge of the Yankees) on his way to claiming Rookie of the Year honors.

Early photos of McGwire depict him as tall and somewhat lean, but as the years wore on, he became a hulking giant at 6-foot-5, 250 pounds. "Any time a guy that big steps to the plate—they're few and far between, thank God—it's kind of hard not to notice him standing there," pitcher Kevin Brown said of McGwire during his peak. "The sun just disappears for awhile."[51]

Unfortunately, McGwire's chances of being elected to Cooperstown took a nosedive when he admitted to using performance enhancing drugs (PED's) after his retirement. Though he spent roughly half of his sixteen seasons nursing various injuries, he averaged one homer per every 10.6 at-bats—the best ratio of any slugger in history, including the legendary Babe Ruth. In Oakland, McGwire formed a potent tandem with teammate

Jose Canseco. The aptly named "Bash Brothers" guided the A's to three consecutive World Series berths beginning in 1988. Canseco left the club in 1992, leaving McGwire to carry the bulk of the heavy hitting until 1997, when he was traded to the Cardinals.

Co-star of the 1998 home run duel, Sammy Sosa came from humble beginnings. Born into a poor Dominican family in San Pedro de Macoris, he and his siblings lived in an abandoned hospital for awhile after his father passed away. Sosa helped support his kin by selling oranges and shining shoes. Originally a product of the Rangers farm system, he was traded to the White Sox in 1989 and the Cubs three years later.

Like McGwire, Sosa's early baseball cards portray him as being of slender build. But in contrast to "Big Mac," he never admitted to using PED's and was never officially fingered for it—even after a 2009 *New York Times* article implicated him (citing anonymous sources). Known for his energy and enthusiasm, Sosa had a habit of sprinting onto the field to assume his right field position and then blowing kisses to fans—a personal trademark. His power remained long after the storied 1998 campaign as he averaged fifty homers per year from 1999 to 2004. He still holds Cubs team records for home runs and slugging percentage.

"The Chase" did not begin in earnest until summer. There was little competition between the two players in April, when McGwire collected eleven home runs to Sosa's six. Heading into June, McGwire had more than doubled Sosa's output, but as the weather grew warmer, "Slammin' Sammy" began to live up to his nickname. He would pass McGwire briefly in mid–August then again in late–September though he would ultimately fall short. Sosa remained supportive throughout, especially on September 8, when McGwire drilled his 62nd homer off Steve Trachsel in Chicago, breaking Roger Maris's record. Sosa greeted McGwire after he had touched all the bases and wrapped him in a bear hug. There was never any bad blood between the two rivals as Sosa felt compelled to point out in his postgame comments. "Remember that we play against each other, but we're not enemies," he affirmed. "…We're in this together."[52] They certainly were as Sosa eclipsed Maris's mark less than a week later.

On September 20, McGwire was busy putting distance between himself and Maris when controversy reared its ugly head. In an 11–6 win against the Brewers at County Stadium, he belted his 65th clout of the season. He would have finished the game with sixty-six had umpire Bob Davidson not rendered a questionable decision in the fifth inning. "Big Mac" smashed a scorching liner toward the left-center field bleachers, located roughly 392 feet from home plate. "The Chase" had literally captivated millions at that point and fans were flocking to ballparks from far and wide to get their hands on a piece of history. A pair of spectators—one from Wisconsin and another from Iowa—grabbed McGwire's blast near the yellow home run line above the outfield wall. The ball landed in the glove of a physical education teacher named Michael Chapes and ended up in a t-shirt that Allen Riesbeck had draped over Chapes's mitt.

Davidson sprinted toward the fence and ruled that the two fans had reached over the yellow line, thereby downgrading McGwire's homer to a ground rule double. "The ball got there in about half a second," Davidson recalled. "I got out there as fast as I could and I saw it ... the fan was leaning over and the ball hit below the yellow line.... I saw the ball good."[53] Though he never argued with the decision, McGwire begged to differ, telling a reporter: "The man who caught the ball never came over the yellow line. The replay shows he didn't. But then again, it's a judgment call."[54] Had the home run duel been staged in 2008 or later, Cardinals manager Tony LaRussa could have challenged the call. But in 1998, that luxury didn't exist. St. Louis owner William DeWitt Jr., petitioned Commissioner Bud Selig to review the game footage for a possible reversal, bur nothing ever came of it.

Interestingly, the ball was knocked from Riesbeck's possession when other fans in proximity rushed to get in on the action. It was snapped up by Johnny Luna—an 18-year-old from Queens, New York. Chapes—the fan who had brought his glove to the game—was escorted out of the park by security and fined over $500. Talking to reporters after the game, he disputed Davidson's fan interference call. "I'm only 5'7"," he said. "My arms aren't that long. It was a home run."[55] Though the call would not prevent McGwire from winning "The Chase," history was altered irrevocably (albeit without serious consequences) that night.

In 2001, Barry Bonds of the Giants left McGwire and Sosa both in the dust, cracking seventy-three home runs. The record is considered tainted, however, due to Bonds's involvement with the infamous BALCO steroids scandal. McGwire issued a tearful apology to sportscaster Bob Costas in 2010, admitting that he had also used steroids. Sosa, who officially announced his retirement in 2009, has maintained his innocence to the present day.

With his playing days now behind him, McGwire has remained in the game as a coach for the Cardinals, Dodgers and Padres. Having failed to garner the necessary support, his name no longer appears on the primary ballot for Cooperstown induction. As for Sosa, he was still eligible at the time of this writing, though he received an insignificant portion of the 2019 vote.

Davidson would come under fire on multiple occasions during his career. A series of disputed calls earned him the nickname of "Balkin' Bob," a moniker that followed him for the remainder of his big league tenure. In 2012, he was suspended briefly in the wake of a heated argument with Phillies manager Charlie Manuel. MLB officials explained that Davidson was being punished for "repeated violations of the Office of the Commissioner's standards for situation handling."[56] Davidson's intolerance for verbal abuse was well-known. His 156 lifetime ejections place him among the top five of all-time in that category. Spectators were not exempt from Davidson's wrath as he twice had fans removed from ballparks for misbehavior. He was once cited as the fourth worst umpire in a *Sports Illustrated* players poll. Despite his intemperance, he kept his job for thirty major league seasons.

In the wake of Bonds' tarnished home run record, baseball toughened its stance against performance-enhancing drugs. From 2002 through 2018, the fifty-home run plateau was reached eleven times by ten different players. Entering the 2020 campaign, nobody had surpassed Babe Ruth's old mark of sixty (set in 1927). Marlins slugger Giancarlo Stanton came up just short in 2017, ending the season with a total of fifty-nine.

On a final note, Michael Chapes, the fan who had McGwire's discounted 66th home run ball torn from his grasp, sued Johnny Luna for possession of the souvenir in a Milwaukee County court. By then, Luna had turned the ball over to a 40-year-old bridge painter named Gerald Diglio, who promised him a big payday. Chapes pledged to offer the ball to McGwire if it was returned to him, but he never got it back. His lawyer commented bitterly: "Having the ball stolen from you after you've caught an historic home run, being kicked out of the park after being held for an hour with drunks in a holding cell and slapped with a $518 fine? The only thing that's missing is [baseball commissioner] Bud Selig letting out the air in his tires when he goes out to the parking lot."[57]

Kerry Wood's 20-Strikeout Performance
May 6, 1998

Since strike calls are highly subjective, it logically follows that pitchers are aided by the decisions of umpires in every high-strikeout performance.

This principle was carried to great extremes on the above date, when Kerry Wood of the Cubs tied a major league record for most punch-outs in a game.

Born in Texas, Wood put on a baseball glove for the first time at the age of four. He grew up idolizing Nolan Ryan and began working on a curveball in Little League. Originally a shortstop, he took to the mound when his junior varsity coach issued an open call for pitchers. While playing for Grand Prairie High School, Wood struck out 152 batters and posted a 14–0 record. He was the fourth overall pick in the 1995 entry draft.

Ascending rapidly through the Cubs farm system, Wood was called to the majors in April of 1998. He struck out seven in his debut but made an early exit after giving up four runs to the Expos. His ERA stood at 5.89 on the eve of his fifth big league start, which has been referred to by multiple sources as one of the greatest games ever pitched. It's unfortunate that less than sixteen thousand fans were on hand at Wrigley Field to witness it.

Wood's opponents that day were the Astros—a team that would capture the NL Central Division easily with 102 wins. In addition to Hall of Famers Jeff Bagwell and Craig Biggio, Houston had corner outfielders Derek Bell and Moises Alou, who combined for sixty homers and 232 RBIs that year. Using a nasty assortment of fastballs, curves and sliders, Wood held the aforementioned players to a combined 0-for-13 at the plate with nine whiffs.

The game got off to an ominous start when catcher Sandy Martinez and second baseman Craig Biggio both ducked out of the way of Wood's first offering, which split the heart of the plate. The ball struck umpire Jerry Meals in the mask, leaving him briefly stunned but (thankfully) uninjured. Wood and Martinez seemed to be in sync after that.

Assessing Wood's performance that day, infielder Jeff Blauser said: "I've seen Greg Maddux throw complete game shutouts in under two hours. But as far as a pitcher being overpowering, Kerry's game has to rank right up there. He throws heat, but his curveball is so good that you see guys' knees buckling on balls that break over the outside corner."[58]

There were plenty of calls being made *off* the outside corner as well. In fact, game footage indicates that Meals was allowing Wood roughly three to six inches of leeway around the plate. In the fifth inning, all three batters were retired on called strikes, two of which were borderline at best. Even Wood openly admitted: "The thing that sticks out is I got some pretty generous calls."[59] Meals, who was in his first year as a full-time umpire, gained a reputation for having an inconsistent strike zone. One sportswriter groused that his shortcomings behind the plate were "infuriatingly, blatantly evident."[60]

Another feature of the game that drew a great deal of attention was a questionable decision by the official scorer, which deprived Wood of a no-hitter. In the third inning, Astros infielder Ricky Gutierrez grounded a ball between third and short. Chicago's third baseman, Kevin Orie, moved a few steps to his left, but didn't reach low enough. The ball nicked his glove and bounced into shallow left field. In the late innings of a typical no-hitter, it would almost definitely have been ruled an error. But the official scorer had no idea that Gutierrez would be the only Houston player to reach base safely that afternoon. Wood tried to squelch the ongoing controversy years later by declaring it was a hit, but many Cubs fans continue to debate the play today.

In the late innings of the ballgame, which was played in less than two and a half hours (short by modern standards), it began to rain. This probably helped Wood's cause to an extent. A scout who was in attendance commented: "The conditions were perfect because it was overcast and tough to pick up the ball."[61] By the seventh inning, the relatively sparse crowd was on its feet every time Wood got two strikes on an Astros hitter. The right-handed flame-thrower didn't realize he had set a record until former pitcher Steve Stone told him during a post-game television interview. Wood gave credit to the Chicago faithful who stuck around in spite of the wet conditions. "The fans are great here and the adrenaline I had was because of [them]," he said.[62] Only one player before Wood had ever struck out twenty opponents in a game—Roger Clemens, who actually turned the trick twice during his career. In 2016, Max Scherzer of the Washington Nationals joined Wood and Clemens in the elite 20-strikeout club.

Wood finished the 1998 campaign with a 13–6 record and 3.40 ERA—numbers good enough to capture Rookie of the Year honors. After his promising debut, Wood's career was rather star-crossed. During spring training of 1999, he tore a ligament in his arm, undergoing Tommy John surgery. It was a long road back to health and he would reach the 200-inning threshold just twice in his fourteen seasons. In 2007, he was converted to a reliever, saving a total of 63 games over a six-year span. When his ERA skyrocketed to 8.31 in 2012, he disappeared from the majors. He averaged more than ten strikeouts per nine innings during his big league tenure.

Still active through 2019, umpire Jerry Meals is one of the shortest arbiters in the game at 5-foot-8. As is the case with almost any official, some of his decisions have invited controversy—most notably in 2011 when he was cited by MLB for blowing a call at home plate in the nineteenth inning of a game between the Braves and Pirates (details of which can be found in a later chapter). Regarding his strike calls in Kerry Wood's gem, Meals contended years later that the zone was much different in the late–'90s. Perhaps, but a careful examination of the video footage reveals that even those parameters were stretched to an extent.

Over the course of three decades, Meals has solidified his pitcher-friendly reputation. In particular, he has a propensity for calling strikes on the outside corners. He was exceptionally liberal during Wood's 20-strikeout performance as illustrated by the ten K's credited to opposing pitcher Shane Reynolds. Eleven of the thirty punch-outs recorded that afternoon were on called third strikes.

Armando Galarraga's Near-Perfect Game
June 2, 2010

Armando Galarraga's major league career was rather unremarkable. He played for four teams in six seasons, never recording an ERA below 3.73 and never finishing with double-digit win totals after his rookie year. But in the world of baseball, remarkable pitching feats often spring from improbable sources. On June 2, 2010, Galarraga attained perfection only to have his accomplishment nullified by one of the most flagrant mistakes in the history of umpiring.

Born in Cumana, Venezuela, Galarraga attended Los Riscos High School and was the only alumnus to have reached the majors at the time of this writing. He originally signed with the Expos, but was dealt to the Rangers by the Washington Nationals in 2005. In February of 2008, he was traded to Detroit, where he enjoyed the most successful season of his big league career.

A right-hander, Galarraga was tall and well-proportioned at 6-foot-3, 230 pounds. Employing a combination of sinkers, sliders and change-ups, he had a tendency to lose the plate at times. In his 2007 debut, he averaged more than seven walks per nine innings but he had no trouble locating the strike zone during his near-perfect game a few seasons later.

Four days prior to Galarraga's magnum opus, Roy Halladay of the Phillies pitched the twentieth perfect game in major league history. And three weeks before then, Dallas Braden of the A's was perfect against the Tampa Bay Rays. Had first base umpire Jim Joyce not grievously erred on what should have been the last out of Galarraga's gem, the game would have set several extraordinary precedents, including most perfectos in a season and shortest span between them. Instead, Galarraga settled for a masterfully pitched shutout.

The game took place at Comerica Park in Detroit, which has long carried a reputation for being friendly to pitchers. Galarraga faced a fifth-place Indians' squad that was without a single .300 hitter in the lineup. There were few power threats either with Shin-Soo Choo being the only player to exceed the 20-homer mark that season.

Galarraga was not especially overpowering, getting most of his outs on grounders. Only three of his opponents went down on strikes. The game moved at a brisk pace, taking less than two hours from start to finish. In the ninth inning, more than 17,000 attendees witnessed a glaring example of diamond injustice.

Second baseman Mark Grudzielanek led off with a deep fly ball to left-center field. Austin Jackson had to cover a lot of ground before making a spectacular grab on the run. Catcher Mike Redmond followed with a ground ball out to second base. On the verge of making history, Galarraga induced another harmless grounder off the bat of Jason Donald. It bounced between second and first, where Miguel Cabrera fielded it and threw to Galarraga in plenty of time. Unfortunately, Joyce flat out missed the call. Cabrera stood there flabbergasted with his hands on his head as Galarraga smiled and ambled slowly back to the mound.

"Something just instinctually told me he was safe," Joyce later said. A veteran of twenty-four major league seasons, he thought he had made the right call until he heard Detroit players shouting from the dugout. Tigers skipper, Jim Leyland, came out to inform Joyce that he had made a glaring mistake. "You blew it, Jim," were his exact words.[63]

After Galarraga had retired Trevor Crowe for the game's final out, Leyland confronted Joyce again, telling him to review the game footage. Joyce headed to the umpire's locker room and did exactly that. Upon encountering the incontrovertible evidence, he began shouting and cursing his blunder. "He was beside himself," crew chief Marvin Hudson said. "I felt tremendously bad for him."[64]

Before the following day's game, Galarraga compassionately told reporters: "I feel sad because everyone knows I pitched a perfect game, but

[Joyce] is just a human being. He came over and apologized. I forgave him."⁶⁵ Joyce was scheduled to work behind the plate that day and, in a gesture of good will, Galarraga presented the lineup card to him. Joyce reportedly could not even read the names through tears.

In the wake of his erroneous call, Joyce received numerous death threats. A security team was assigned to him for every road trip—an arrangement he did not relish. "I wish I was still invisible, I really do," he remarked in 2011. "I wish that I could go back to being the old Jim Joyce, that this didn't happen and that everything was normal."⁶⁶ In spite of a handful of regrettable decisions, Joyce was ranked by *ESPN* and *Sports Illustrated* as the top umpire in the majors on multiple occasions. And his reputation was enhanced even further in 2012, when he saved the life of an Arizona Diamondbacks food service worker by administering CPR.

Joyce's career continued through 2016. Questioned about the Galarraga incident several months after his retirement, Joyce described it as the most difficult situation he ever faced on the diamond. But there was an upside to it as well. "In the same vein, it was my best time," he told an *MLB News* correspondent, "—the way that players, fans and everybody in-between gave me a lot of support."⁶⁷

Interestingly, Joyce had been stationed at second base for Dallas Braden's perfect game. Joyce and Galarraga teamed with author Daniel Paisner in 2011 to write a book about the hurler's ill-fated brush with glory. As a condition of the book's release, Joyce was prohibited from umpiring during any of Galarraga's assignments from that point forward.

Galarraga made his last major league appearance in 2012. He finished his professional career in the Mexican League three years later. In 2016, he joined the Yankee organization as a minor league instructor.

Like the 1968 campaign, 2010 has often been referred to as the "Year of the Pitcher." Had Galarraga received due credit for his accomplishment, it would have been one of seven no-hitters thrown that season. And Galarraga's pitch count would have been the lowest of any perfect game. Across the majors, 329 shutouts were thrown in 2010—the most since 1972. Additionally, fifteen pitchers collected at least 200 strikeouts, tying an all-time record.

An appeal was made to the commissioner's office to amend the outcome of Galarraga's near-perfect game, but Bud Selig ultimately denied it. Feeling bad for the young hurler, General Motors North American President Mark Reuss compensated him with a brand-new Chevy Corvette. The hurler was taken completely off guard by the gift. "I still don't believe it," he told members of the press. "I'm in shock."⁶⁸

Max Scherzer's Near-Perfect Game
June 20, 2015

Like Armando Galarraga in 2010, Max Scherzer came within a hair's breadth of tossing a perfect game, ultimately losing it on account of a questionable umpiring decision. But in contrast to Galarraga, who settled for a one-hit shutout, Scherzer at least walked away with a no-hitter to his credit.

One of the most striking physical features of Max Scherzer is his eyes. He was born with a genetic anomaly known as heterochromia iridum, which affects approximately one in two-hundred people. It sounds much worse than it actually is. Scherzer has one blue and one brown eye, a trait that has not hindered his rise to stardom in any perceptible way.

Hailing from Chesterfield, Missouri, Scherzer was a standout at Parkway Central High School. He was drafted by the Cardinals in 2003 but opted to attend the University of Missouri at Columbia instead. In 2006, he was drafted again—this time by the Diamondbacks. He would bounce up and down from the majors to the minors for portions of three seasons before landing a full-time roster spot with the Tigers in 2010. He was later traded to the Washington Nationals.

Over the last several seasons, Scherzer has emerged as one of the top pitchers in the game, capturing three Cy Young Awards. He uses a low three-quarter delivery that is almost sidearm. In addition to his four-seam fastball, which tops out at around ninety-nine miles per hour, he keeps hitters off balance with sliders and change-ups that travel in the low-to-mid-eighties. Occasionally, he mixes in an even slower curve.

On June 20, 2015, Scherzer pitched the finest single-game effort of his career, remaining perfect until his one hundred and third pitch of the afternoon. His opponents, the Pirates, were among the hottest team in the majors at the time, having won twenty-one of their previous twenty-seven games. With two outs in the ninth, Scherzer was facing Jose Tabata, a native Venezuelan with a lifetime .275 average. Tabata put together a fine at-bat, working the count even at 2–2 before fouling off three of Scherzer's deceptive offerings. The next pitch was a hanging slider that hovered near Tabata then broke downward. The part-time outfielder made no effort to avoid the pitch. In fact, he dropped the pad on his left elbow directly into it, spoiling Scherzer's perfect game. Though his actions were illegal, umpire Mike Muchlinski chose not to employ a rule which states that a batter is not entitled to first base if he makes no effort to avoid being hit. Infamously applied by Harry Wendelstedt in 1968, the same rule allowed Don Drysdale to assemble a streak of 58.2 scoreless innings. Scherzer kept his cool and retired Josh Harrison on a deep fly to left-center field, salvaging a no-hitter.

Tabata waited until a lot of negative feedback had percolated on the internet before offering his side of the story. "I thought the slider was going to break, but it kind of stayed floating," he explained. "People don't understand that these are the instincts people have. I wasn't looking to get hit. I wanted to get a hit."[69] Scherzer, who blamed himself for hitting Tabata in the first place, held no grudges—even if Tabata had done it on purpose. "I don't blame him for doing it," he said. "Heck, I'd probably do the same thing."[70]

Scherzer's remarks failed to effectively squelch the controversy. Writing for *Sports Illustrated*, Cliff Corcoran contended that Scherzer had been short-changed and blamed the other umpires on Muchlinski's crew for not speaking up. In Corcoran's opinion, Muchlinski was less culpable since his view was likely obscured by catcher Wilson Ramos's glove. *NBC Sports* analyst, Bill Baer, raised another interesting point, arguing that even if Tabata had intentionally leaned into Scherzer's pitch, his actions were no different than a catcher framing a ball off the plate to draw a strike call. "Both players are attempting to exploit a grey area in order to maximize their team's odds of winning," he wrote.[71]

There are several factors working against Baer's absolution of Tabata. For starters, the Pirates were trailing the Nationals, 6–0, at the time of the infraction and had very little chance of beating Scherzer, who was masterful all afternoon. Second, Tabata was wearing an enormous elbow pad that was likely on the cusp of being illegal. And last but certainly not least, Tabata did more than stand idly by as he was hit. Video footage irrefutably confirms the fact that he actively moved toward the pitch in violation of the rules. So, if a grey area exists, it is extremely grey indeed. Perhaps Grant Brisbee of *SB Nation* stated it most poignantly when he opined: "Sticking the elbow out just to break up the [perfect game] is like calling the IRS on your neighbor because you're jealous of his new boat."[72]

Though Scherzer certainly had reason to feel cheated, he moved on with his career unhindered. In May of 2016, he struck out twenty Detroit opponents, tying a record shared by Roger Clemens and Kerry Wood. At seasons' end, he became only the sixth player to capture the Cy Young Award in both leagues. The following year, he recorded an immaculate inning (three outs/nine strikes) against the Philadelphia Phillies and took the Cy Young Award again, joining an elite group of pitchers to be honored on three occasions.

As of 2019, Muchlinski was in his fourteenth season of big league service. A lifelong resident of Washington, he worked in six different minor leagues before becoming a full-time member of the MLB umpiring staff. Aside from the unfortunate Scherzer game, his career has been relatively drama-free to date. Statistics show him to be rather pitcher-friendly and his ejection record indicates that he has little tolerance for players who challenge his calls behind home plate.

Aside from Armando Galarraga, there are several pitchers who have shared Scherzer's misfortune over the past two decades. Hall of Famer Mike Mussina carried two perfect games into the ninth inning during his career. In 2001, he came within one strike of attaining perfection against the Red Sox, yielding a two-out single to pinch-hitter Carl Everett with a 1–2 count. Pitching for the Rangers in 2013, Yu Darvish was perfect for 8.2 innings before coughing up a single to Marwin Gonzalez of the Astros. In 2017, Dodger southpaw Rich Hill suffered an even worse fate, losing his perfecto on a ninth inning error by third baseman Logan Forsythe. In the tenth, Hill lost a no-hitter, shutout and win on a single pitch when he surrendered a lead-off homer to Pittsburgh's Josh Harrison.

PART TWO

The Road to October: Critical Calls During the Regular Season

••••••••••••••••••

Bob Ferguson's Campaign Against Gambling
Mutuals vs. Canaries, July 24, 1873

More than a century after his death, Bob Ferguson is largely remembered for his colorful nickname—"Death to Flying Things." But there are other aspects of his career that set him apart. In addition to being the game's first switch-hitter, he remains the only man to serve as a player, manager, umpire and league president at the same time.

In 1871, baseball officially became professionalized with the formation of the National Association. Ferguson, who had begun his amateur career in 1863, was appointed player-manager of the New York Mutuals. While additionally serving as a substitute umpire, he led the Mutuals to a sluggish fourth-place finish. When rumors of game fixing surfaced at season's end, he left the club and joined the Brooklyn Atlantics.

With a reputation for integrity, Ferguson was elevated to the position of league president. He took a firm stance against gambling—specifically bookmaking, side betting and pool selling, which sometimes led to the throwing of games. On July 4, 1873, suspicion arose that several Atlantics players had conspired to intentionally drop a game against the Mutuals. Less than three weeks later, the Atlantics lost to the Baltimore Canaries under questionable circumstances. Ferguson stormed the gambling area and confronted odds makers, challenging them to a fight and vowing to drive them out of baseball. In the wake of the incident, a writer from *The*

Brooklyn Eagle declared: "This is the first instance on record that either a player, a captain of a club nine, or the manager of any professional club has had the courage to boldly and publicly denounce the gambling frauds which have brought such odium upon professional playing."[1]

Ferguson carried his good intentions too far on July 24. While umpiring a game between the Mutuals and Canaries at Brooklyn's Union Grounds, he was involved in one of the ugliest incidents in baseball history. Entering the game, the Canaries were sitting in second place with a 23–13 record. In stark contrast, the Mutuals were several games below .500 and floundering near the bottom of the standings.

Throughout the game, Ferguson was subjected to verbal abuse from Mutuals catcher Nat Hicks. A notorious umpire baiter, Hicks was a fine defensive player who was among the first to stand directly behind the batter (a courageous move considering that catchers wore no protective equipment in those days). Despite his prickly nature, Ferguson tolerated Hicks's barbs until the final inning, when he completely lost his composure.

New York led, 8–5, before a glaring series of defensive lapses (one of them by Hicks) led to a five-run Baltimore outburst in the ninth. Between innings, Hicks got into a heated dispute with teammate John Hatfield. Accusations of foul play were exchanged. Coming off his recent showdown with gamblers, Ferguson jumped into the argument, accusing Hicks of deliberately trying to sink the Mutuals. When Hicks called Ferguson a "damn liar," the arbiter went berserk, grabbing a bat and breaking Hicks's arm in two places.

After order was restored, the Mutuals overcame a 10–8 deficit on timely hits by Bobby Mathews, Count Gedney and Dave Eggler. Eggler was on second when Hatfield hit a line drive that was mishandled by Davy Force in left field. Eggler crossed the plate with the winning run. Though fans were elated with the victory, they hadn't forgotten about Ferguson's assault on Hicks. As they flooded onto the field, police surrounded the arbiter and escorted him safely out of the stadium.

Hicks was out of action for two months. In the absence of a suitable replacement, the Mutuals were forced to cancel several games. Between July 25 and August 6, they played just once. Standing in proximity to batters without protection led to multiple injuries for Hicks over the course of his career. He nearly lost an eye at one point and ended up retiring with less than three hundred games to his credit.

Ferguson issued a formal apology to Hicks and resigned as an umpire. Since he served as league president, no punitive action was taken against him. From 1876 to 1884, he managed and played for five different clubs. He returned to umpiring when his playing days ended. Explaining his game strategy to a *New York World* reporter one day, he said: "Never change a decision, never stop to talk to a player. Make 'em play ball and keep their mouths shut...."[2] Despite Ferguson's efforts to free the sport from the influence of gamblers, the fixing of games continued with regularity for several more decades.

On a humorous final note, Ferguson's famous nickname (which he curiously shared with teammate Jack Chapman) was not the only memorable one of the era. Had an Old-Timer's game been staged at the dawn of the twentieth century, Ferguson could have shared the field with Buttercup Dickerson, Peek-A-Boo Veach and Ice Box Chamberlain, among others.

Tim Hurst and the Beer Glass Incident
Reds vs. Pirates, August 4, 1897

At 5-foot-5, the diminutive umpire Tim Hurst was known to some as "Tiny Tim." But true to the words of an iconic *Star Wars* character, he proved that "size matters not." The pugnacious Hurst was known to keep players under control with both words and fists. Hailed by a writer from *Sporting Life* for "having the finest brand of keen-cutting, kill-at-a-thousand-yards sarcasm of any umpire in captivity,"[3] his fiery disposition eventually drove him out of baseball.

With a reputation for making highly accurate decisions, Hurst had an interesting way of maintaining order behind the plate. "Never put a catcher out of a game," he told a *New York Herald* reporter. "If the man in back of the bat is sassy and objects to your calling of balls and strikes, keep close behind him while doing your work and kick him every time he reaches out to catch a ball. After about the third kick, he'll shut up."[4]

Sometimes Hurst's feisty temperament led to amusing results. In a possibly apocryphal anecdote provided by historian Fred Lieb, Hurst allegedly made a call that went against Cincinnati's third baseman, Arlie Latham. Latham tore off his glove and kicked it in protest. It landed at the feet of Hurst, who promptly kicked it right back to Latham. The festivities didn't end there. According to Lieb, the two men booted the glove all the way to the outfield fence.

On a number of occasions, Hurst's outbursts were less than entertaining. Such was the case on the date in question, when the Pirates met the Reds at League Park in Cincinnati for a doubleheader. The Reds breezed to a 14–3 win in the opener then exploded for four runs in the first inning of the finale. Things took an ugly turn in the second inning when Hurst called Cincinnati's leftfielder Bug Holliday out at second. Holliday raised a protest, insisting that he had been unfairly tripped by infielder Dick Padden. Hurst stood firm on his ruling and the crowd roared its disapproval. Having traded blows with Reds catcher Heinie Peitz a few days earlier, Hurst was immensely unpopular among fans in Cincinnati.

One ornery spectator threw a heavy beer glass in Hurst's direction, striking the arbiter in the back or the foot (accounts vary slightly). Another glass landed a few feet away from Hurst, provoking his wrath. He offered the following statement to a *Sporting Life* correspondent: "I thought in a second I ought not to stand and be slugged without defending myself. I picked up the glass that had just dropped near me and, as I hurled it underhanded, the spectators in that part of the stands were all in a bunch. I did not throw the missile at a particular person, but I saw it hit someone in the head. The man it struck I do not know. I was sorry after I had done it because I knew I had lost my temper."[5]

Hurst's inadvertent target was a local fireman named James Cartuyvelles. The glass struck him over the right eye, opening a deep gash that bled copiously. A few members of the crowd rushed the field in an attempt to get at Hurst, but police were able to ward them off. Cartuyvelles was transported to the hospital. Assuming he had sustained a serious injury, Hurst was arrested and ushered out the back of the stadium into a paddy wagon. He was charged with assault and battery at the Oliver Street station house.

In the wake of Hurst's unexpected departure, umpire Red Bittman was forced to finish the game alone. It was one of only ten big league assignments he drew in his career. The Pirates chipped away at Reds starter Frank Dwyer, tying the game and chasing him from the mound. But the game ended up being called on account of darkness in the sixth inning with the score knotted at four.

Hurst was bailed out later that evening by Cincinnati team treasurer Ashley Lloyd. When additional charges surfaced against him, National League president Nicholas Young terminated his contract. Hurst managed the Browns to a dismal 39–111 record in 1898 then worked as a boxing promoter/referee before reappearing as an umpire in the American League.

In 1909, Hurst's volcanic temper got the best of him again during a doubleheader between the A's and White Sox. After dropping the opener, 2–1, the ChiSox built a four-run lead in the finale. They failed to hang on as the A's battered pitcher Doc White for five runs in the seventh. The Philly onslaught continued in the eighth, when one of the most infamous confrontations between a player and umpire took place.

With runners on base, Hall of Famer Eddie Collins singled and moved to second, where he appeared to be safe on a dropped relay. Hurst blew the call, believing there was some sort of interference on the play. This drew the ire of Collins, who stated his opinion on the matter somewhat indelicately. Describing Hurst's reaction, *Philadelphia North American* sportswriter Jimmy Isaminger used the following lines: "...the umpire distributed a mouthful of moistened union-made tobacco in the direction of youthful Eddie, who immediately called Tim's attention to the Board of Health ordinance which prohibits expectorating in public places."[6]

Fans went out of their minds, throwing cushions and bottles in Hurst's direction after the game. It took police nearly half an hour to get him safely out of the stadium. After a full investigation of the spitting incident, Hurst was fired by AL president Ban Johnson. Cast out of baseball, he resumed his career as a sports promoter. He later made a living selling real estate.

Soggy Games in Pittsburgh: Round 1
Pirates vs. Superbas, July 4, 1902

There are many factors an umpire can't control. One of them is the weather. In 1902, arbiters Bob Emslie and Hank O'Day had their hands full as heavy rains in Pittsburgh led to some highly irregular events on the field.

The summer of 1902 was a wet one for the Pirates, resulting in the postponement of more than a dozen games, a majority of which occurred between April and June. By the time July rolled around, the Bucs were ready to play under almost any circumstances. The doubleheader that took place on July 4 was among the most bizarre in history.

With a capacity of 16,000, Exposition Park in Pittsburgh was located near the banks of the Allegheny River. When heavy rains swept through the region before the scheduled Fourth of July festivities, water began seeping under the outfield fence. This was not an unusual occurrence. In fact, sportswriters and fans sometimes referred to the park's deep recesses as "Lake Dreyfuss"—an allusion to the team's popular owner.

Barney Dreyfuss had immigrated to America from Germany with little money and a limited grasp of the English language. Within a few years, he had become part-owner of the Louisville Colonels. When the National League down-sized before the 1900 campaign, Dreyfuss purchased half the Pirates shares and arranged to have his best players, among them the great Honus Wagner, transferred to Pittsburgh. The team was instantly catapulted into contention, capturing four pennants in the first decade of the twentieth century. Fans grew to love Dreyfuss's dedication to the Pirates and to the sport itself.

Regardless of his good intentions, Dreyfuss wasn't about to allow the profits from an Independence Day doubleheader slip through his fingers on account of a river that didn't recognize its boundaries. By the time the gates opened for the morning game, floodwater had closed to within a hundred feet of second base and was knee deep in some spots. Grounds crews had spread sawdust on the infield to get it in shape, but umpire Bob Emslie was forced to bend the rules in order to accommodate play.

A former pitcher, Emslie won thirty-two games in 1884 before a sore arm ended his playing career. Asked to officiate an International League game when the arbiter unexpectedly fell ill, he performed well enough to land a minor league contract. He became a National League umpire in 1891 and held onto the position for thirty-three seasons.

Emslie was prematurely bald and wore a hairpiece, earning him the nickname of "Wig." Cantankerous Giants' manager John McGraw strapped him with the additional handle of "Blind Bob," but that one was seldom used. Though he earned a reputation for being quick with a smile, it seems doubtful Emslie was smiling much when he saw the condition of the ballpark in Pittsburgh that day. Since much of the outfield was under water, he consulted with team captains to determine a course of action. It was agreed that balls hit into "Lake Dreyfuss" would count as singles.

More than 12,000 fans braved the damp conditions that morning to see the Pirates take on the Brooklyn Superbas. Led by Hall of Fame manager Ned Hanlon, the Superbas finished a distant second to the Bucs in 1902. Even with Willie Keeler, a two-time batting champion, in the lineup, they lost fourteen of twenty head-to-head meetings against Pittsburgh, getting outscored by a cumulative total of fifty-four runs.

The sodden field created some unforgettable moments. Stationed in right field, Keeler went into ankle deep water to catch a drive off the bat of player/manager Fred Clarke in the sixth inning. In the next frame, Cozy Dolan waded up to his knees in center field to grab a hard smash by Pittsburgh's Honus Wagner. Dolan became completely drenched later that inning when he fell tracking a fly ball hit by third baseman Tommy Leach.

Emslie maintained order throughout and the Pirates won the first meeting, 3–0. Between games, heavy showers passed through the region again and water crept even closer to second base. Emslie found himself in an unenviable position—he could risk upsetting Dreyfuss by calling the game off or continue the doubleheader in marginally unplayable conditions. In the end, he decided that the show must go on.

Dolan, who committed twenty outfield errors for the Superbas that season, stole the spotlight again in the afternoon game when he plodded into the lagoon to make a one-handed grab on a liner hit by Clarke. He received an appreciative round of applause from the crowd of 9,000-plus, who likely had no idea they were witnessing one of the strangest games ever played. The Pirates took the second match, 4–0, polishing off an eight-game winning streak—their second longest of the year.

The use of special ground rules was not an uncommon practice in the early part of the twentieth century. Stadiums were much smaller and teams were hesitant to turn away paying customers. At times, overflow crowds were so large that adjustments had to be made to accommodate them. It was not unusual to see fans camped out along the foul lines or, on rare occasions, in front of outfield wall, creating situations similar to the flood game in Pittsburgh.

Before Game 3 of the 1903 World Series, thousands of trespassers broke through a cordoned off area at the Huntington Avenue Grounds in Boston. The game was already oversold and evacuating the park would have been impossible at that point. Police were able to secure a fifty-foot stretch beyond the infield and a thirty-foot expanse behind home plate. Umpires Hank O'Day and Tommy Connolly decided that balls hit into the outfield crowd would count as ground rule doubles. A total of seven were hit that day as the Pirates won the game, grabbing a 2–1 Series advantage.

Soggy Games in Pittsburgh: Round 2

Pirates vs. Reds, October 4, 1902

By October 4, the Pirates had built a twenty-seven-game lead over their closest rivals and stood just one win away from claiming the all-time single-season record. No one wanted this more than Barney Dreyfuss, who wasn't about to let another round of storms spoil his club's chances. Though the Allegheny River stayed within its natural confines that afternoon, the weather was drizzly and the field was spongy. Dreyfuss had to pressure umpire Hank O'Day into allowing the game to be played.

Mired in fourth place more than thirty games out of the running, the Cincinnati Reds had little motivation to show up at Exposition Park on a brisk, soggy afternoon. Hall of Fame player/manager Joe Kelley spitefully announced before the game that he intended to blemish the Pirates' record. He delayed the team's arrival until the very last minute, hoping fans would stay away if they didn't see the Reds onsite. Players showed up just prior to game time and, following Kelley's lead, they sat on the bench smoking instead of warming up.

When O'Day promptly ordered Kelley to present a lineup, the latter made a mockery of the proceedings by placing everyone out of position. Pittsburgh manager Fred Clarke protested, insisting that Kelley should behave in a more sportsmanlike manner, but under the rules, O'Day had no authority to tell Kelley where to put his players.

The game began with a battery of Jake Beckley and Rube Vickers. Beckley, a Hall of Fame first baseman, had never pitched before. Vickers, a rookie hurler, had no experience as a catcher. The results were predictable as Beckley allowed eight runs in four innings and Vickers was charged with six passed balls—a new single-game record. To Kelley's great delight, Vickers really hammed it up, repeatedly pulling a handkerchief out of his pocket and loudly blowing his nose.

With the Pirates leading, 8–1, Kelley inserted a more capable pitching tandem, sending Cy Seymour to the mound and transferring catching responsibilities to Heinie Peitz. Seymour had appeared in over a hundred games on the mound before moving to the outfield full-time. Peitz was a catcher by trade and a pretty good one at that. But the Reds' rebellious behavior continued with players smoking cigars on the field throughout and blowing smoke in the faces of opponents. Some even wandered into the stands to procure refreshments.

The ever-stoic O'Day rarely lost his composure on the diamond. A quiet recluse with few interests aside from baseball, it has been said that he never cracked a smile during his entire career. Another source described him as a "strange character who lived in a shell, emerging only when he visited the field to render his decisions."[7] He had little tolerance for blatant insubordination as evidenced by his high ejection rate. When Kelley came to the plate with a cigar in his mouth, O'Day decided that a line had been crossed and demanded he put it out. Kelley, who was clearly enjoying himself at that point, complied.

The Pirates breezed to an 11–2 win, prompting a writer from the *Pittsburgh Press* to remark: "While the Reds were acting more like monkeys than men, the champions were doing the best they knew how."[8] A correspondent from the *Cincinnati Enquirer* was even more derisive, referring to the game as "disgraceful" and commenting that "taken as a game of ball, the story isn't worth ten lines."[9] Dreyfuss felt guilty about charging money for the farcical game and, in the late innings, he instructed stadium employees to wander the stands notifying fans that refunds would be available at the box office. "We're not going to take money from our friends under false pretenses," he told a reporter.[10]

Kelley defended his actions after the game. "We put a team on the field and there is no rule compelling us to allow them to name the positions they'll play," he said. "As it was, anybody who opened the gates ought to be arrested."[11] Dreyfuss threatened to have Kelley charged with unbecoming conduct on the field, but nothing ever came of it.

An interesting side note: In addition to Beckley and Seymour, Deadball superstar "Turkey Mike" Donlin shared pitching responsibilities that day. Primarily an outfielder, Donlin had appeared in three games as a pitcher for the St. Louis Perfectos three years earlier. Cincinnati fans saw very little of him in 1902 since he was serving a six-month jail sentence for disorderly behavior. During a drunken binge, Donlin had urinated in public and assaulted a pair of chorus girls, prompting the Orioles to release him. He didn't make his first appearance for the Reds until August.

Any comments made by O'Day concerning the Reds' behavior on that wet October afternoon appear to be lost to time. The Pirates record for wins in a season was short-lived, lasting until 1904, when the Giants gathered 106 victories. Two years later, the Cubs annihilated both of those marks with 116 wins—the most ever in a 154-game schedule.

There have been other farcical games in baseball history. In 1912,

Senators owner/manager Clark Griffith started an annual tradition of staging a novelty game at seasons' end providing it didn't affect the standings and opponents agreed to it. Umpires were made aware of the arrangement beforehand. On October 4, 1913, the Senators faced the Red Sox with legendary pitcher Walter Johnson stationed in center field. Johnson, winner of 417 games during his Hall of Fame career, stole two bases and made an appearance as an infielder. He had no idea that his performance that day would have lasting repercussions.

The Senators held a seven-run lead in the ninth, when Johnson was called to the mound. He lobbed fat pitches to two Red Sox batters, both of whom hit safely. He was then replaced with back-up catcher Eddie Ainsmith, who had no prior pitching experience. Ainsmith promptly surrendered a bases-clearing triple. The Senators hung on for a 10–9 win and Johnson ended up claiming a Triple Crown. Because the game was played for fun, no runs were charged to Johnson and his ERA stood at 1.09—the lowest mark in history by a pitcher with at least 300 innings of work. Many years later, a researcher discovered the oversight and correctly charged the runs Johnson, raising his ERA to 1.14. Though the mark was still good enough to retain the 1913 Triple Crown, it was no longer a record. That honor now belongs to Bob Gibson, who tossed over 300 innings and posted a 1.12 mark in 1968.

Fred Merkle's Infamous Blunder
Cubs vs. Giants, September 23, 1908

In her critically acclaimed book, *Crazy '08*, author Cait Murphy elegantly states that "every baseball season is like a Dickens novel—a tale told in installments, until in the last chapter, known as the World Series, all the loose ends are tied up and the heroes go home. In 1908, there are simply more chapters, more incidents, more characters, more surprises and more drama than in any other."[12] There is little doubt that the 1908 campaign was among the most enthralling in baseball history. And no recollection of it would be complete without mention of poor Fred Merkle.

Merkle, just nineteen years old and playing in his first full season, committed a minor mistake with major consequences during the heart of the 1908 pennant race. Though he would prove himself to be an excellent hitter, a swift base runner and a competent fielder in subsequent years, the mistake would hover over him like a black cloud. In a famous photo taken near the end of Merkle's career, he appears morose and much older than his years. Even in death, he couldn't shake his association with one regrettable on-field incident. The headline of his *New York Times* obituary read: "Giants 1st Baseman's 'Boner' in Failing to Touch 2nd Led to Loss of '08 Pennant."[13] Stated more accurately, that headline could have read: "Giants First Baseman's Reputation Was Destroyed by Controversial Umpiring Decision."

The inscrutable O'Day looks somewhat miserable in this photograph. His infamous call on Fred Merkle in 1908 indirectly cost the Giants the pennant (Library of Congress).

Managed by a hot-headed autocrat with a gangster-esque nickname, the 1908 Giants were among the most powerful teams of the Deadball Era. Manager "Mugsy" McGraw had no tolerance for mediocrity. Describing McGraw's temperament, third baseman Arlie Latham once joked: "He eats gunpowder for breakfast and washes it down with warm blood."[14] Though his culinary tastes contradicted Latham's remark, McGraw fussed, cussed, and brawled his way to ten pennants and three World Series titles during a managerial career that spanned more than thirty seasons.

The contentious McGraw had a plentiful crop of gifted players to work with in 1908. Generally considered the greatest pitcher of the era, Christy Mathewson won thirty-seven games for the Giants that year while working an exhausting total of 390.2 innings. Roger Bresnahan, an innovative defensive catcher with enough foot-speed and patience to appear as a leadoff batter, could be counted on every third or fourth day to reliably handle "Matty's" signature pitch—the "fadeaway." Mike Donlin, a lifetime .333 hitter who moonlighted as a Hollywood actor, carried the offense with a team-high 106 RBIs. Any runners left behind were proficiently driven across the plate by centerfielder Cy Seymour, whose 92 ribbies were third-best in the NL.

On Chicago's West Side, the Cubs were building a dynasty. In 1906, they set a record for wins in a season that has stood the test of time. They followed with 107 more victories in 1907, capturing the first World Series title in franchise history. The 1908 incarnation of the club was well equipped to give McGraw's mighty Giants a run for their money.

The Cubs' success was built on pitching, defense and timely hitting. A childhood mishap had left Chicago's ace hurler, Mordecai Brown, with deformed fingers. It was an unexpected blessing as he learned how to make the ball curve or sink dramatically when he gripped it a certain way. A twenty-game winner every year from 1906 to 1911, Brown had a strong supporting cast behind him. Right-hander Ed Reulbach gathered no fewer than seventeen victories in five consecutive seasons. And Orval Overall, a towering figure for the era at 6-foot-2, 214 pounds, led the NL in shutouts twice in that same span.

The Chicago infield was anchored by a marvelously efficient double-play trio that would be immortalized in a poem written by columnist Franklin Pierce Adams. But many opponents had less eloquent things to say about Joe Tinker, Johnny Evers and Frank Chance. Chance, who also served as manager, was a fine first baseman and a scrapper at the plate. His on-base percentage exceeded the .400 mark during eight seasons. Tinker, a wide-ranging shortstop with sure hands and a strong arm, was known for his uncanny ability to deliver clutch hits in key situations. The loquacious Evers, a nuisance to opponents and umpires alike, was a self-proclaimed student of the sport. His vast knowledge of the rulebook proved highly useful on September 23, when he stole a game from the Giants and a tranquil future from the ill-fated Fred Merkle.

Prior to the "Merkle Game," the Cubs and Giants had battled for supremacy all season. There was no love lost between the two clubs. In fact, players treated one another with contemptuous disregard. "Friendly competition would have been unimaginable," remarked a writer from the *Associated Press*. "No diplomacy was necessary then, these teams hated each other, cursing and fighting right on the field."[15]

The Giants led Chicago by three and a half games on September 20. But a doubleheader sweep by the Cubs in a head-to-head meeting on September 22 locked the two teams in a first-place tie. Fate intervened the following morning, when New York's regular first baseman, Fred Tenney, woke up with a severe case of lower back pain. McGraw penciled Merkle, whose only other start that year had come on June 26, into the lineup.

The pitching matchup featured the illustrious Mathewson against Jack Pfiester, whose remarkable success facing New York earned him the nickname of "Jack the Giant Killer." According to his SABR biography, the side-winding southpaw compiled a 15–5 record against the Giants with seven shutouts during a career that spanned eight seasons. The infamous showdown took place at the Polo Grounds in New York. Six thousand seats had been added to accommodate the devoted fans who frequently streamed through the turnstiles and stood elbow-to-elbow in every available corner.

The umpires that afternoon, Hank O'Day and Bob Emslie, were both seasoned veterans. Referred to by fellow arbiter, Bill Klem, as a "misanthropic Irishman," the perpetually stoic O'Day had little tolerance for misbehavior.[16] Only two umpires in major league history exceeded his lofty total of 185 lifetime ejections. Emslie was a bit on the cheerier side, though he was extremely unyielding when his decisions were challenged.

The game began, as always, with bad blood between the two clubs. Giants infielder Buck Herzog had been spiked the day before by Chicago's Frank Chance. Adding insult to injury, Pfiester hit New York's Moose McCormick with a fastball in the second inning. As McCormick lay in a heap inside the batting circle, Giants physician Joseph Creamer provided state-of-the-art medical attention by dousing McCormick's head with a bucket of cold water. There was a moment of comic relief when Emslie's hairpiece was knocked askew in a collision with Mike Donlin. For the most part, however, the game had all the levity of a medieval joust.

Through eight innings, both pitchers fared well. Joe Tinker's inside-the-park homer in the fifth represented the only run off Mathewson. Tinker enjoyed remarkable success against "Matty" throughout his career, prompting the latter to remark that the Cubs Hall of Famer was the toughest NL opponent he had ever faced. Mike Donlin's RBI single in the sixth accounted for New York's only score off "The Giant Killer." Things settled down after that until the ninth.

Mathewson had no difficulty disposing of the Cubs in the top of the frame. In the home half of the ninth, Pfiester got Cy Seymour on a grounder to Evers. Art Devlin followed with a solid hit to center field. He was erased at second base on a fielder's choice. With McCormick on first, Merkle—soon to be forever disgraced—singled to right field. Pfiester was now in a two out jam with runners on first and third. He had injured a tendon at some point during the game and his pitching arm was bulging. But in the spirit of the early twentieth century, he stayed on the mound to face the game's final batter. His first pitch to Al Bridwell was a waist-high fastball. The light-hitting Giants shortstop was ready for it, drilling it past Evers into right-center field. This set off a chain of unfortunate events.

Umpire Bob Emslie scrambled to avoid being hit and fell down. McCormick crossed the plate with what should have been the winning run, but Merkle, instead of touching second base, veered off toward the clubhouse in right-center field. Though the move would invite a host of derogatory epithets, among them "Bonehead" and "Leatherskull," it was a fairly common practice for the era. The rule requiring a runner on first or second to advance to the next base on a walk-off hit was little known and seldom enforced. But the studious Johnny Evers had been doing his homework.

During a game between the Pirates and Cubs on September 4, Evers had drawn umpire Hank O'Day's attention to an identical situation. After Pittsburgh's rookie first baseman Warren Gill failed to touch second on a game-winning hit in the bottom of the tenth, Evers retrieved the ball, stepped on the bag and appealed to O'Day. The arbiter ruled against Evers since he was working alone that afternoon and had not been paying attention to Gill's activities. A precedent had been set and Evers knew it.

As euphoric fans swarmed onto the field at the Polo Grounds to celebrate what they assumed was a glorious victory for the home team, Evers shouted at outfielder Solly Hofman to toss him the ball. Hofman scooped it up and attempted a relay, but it ended up in the hands of Giants pitcher Joe McGinnity. When Cubs players tried to wrestle it from McGinnity's grasp, he reportedly heaved it deep into the stands. Refusing to be deterred, Evers somehow produced a ball—likely not the game ball, but a ball nevertheless. He stepped on second and stated his case to O'Day.

The field had become a rather dangerous place to be with random fights breaking out between rowdy fans. Resuming the game would have been virtually impossible at that point. O'Day and Emslie were escorted by police to a safe place under the stands. Reviewing the play, Emslie admitted he had been on his backside during the immediate aftermath and could not reliably determine if Merkle had touched second base. O'Day ruminated over this for a few moments and made the most controversial ruling of the Deadball Era. As the arbiters were ushered out of the stadium under police protection, O'Day shouted to a throng of reporters: "Merkle didn't run to second. The last run don't count. It's a tie game."[17]

After Emslie and O'Day had submitted their reports to National League President Harry Pulliam, a meeting was called to evaluate the details. Pulliam ruled in favor of the umpires, officially declaring the game a tie on account of darkness. This didn't sit well with executives from either team and the NL Board of Directors was assembled to hear both sides of the story. It was decided that the game would be replayed on October 8. Umpires Bill Klem and Jimmy Johnstone drew the assignment.

Interestingly, the replay was almost unnecessary. While the Cubs and Giants were scrambling to gain an edge in the standings, the Pirates were in the thick of the race all season. Led by Hall of Fame player/manager Fred Clarke, the Bucs spent a total of sixty-three days in first place. They held a two and a half game lead on July 27. But even a 13–2 run from September 19 through October 4 wasn't enough. At the close of play on October 7, the Giants and Cubs were deadlocked in first place with Pittsburgh sitting a half game out. At the root of this scenario was another controversial umpiring decision.

Facing the Cubs in Chicago on October 4, the Pirates had a chance to clinch the pennant. Ensuring his team the best chance of success, Clarke sent staff ace Vic Willis to the mound against Chicago's top hurler, Mordecai Brown. More than 30,000 fans crammed themselves into the West Side Grounds, which had been built to accommodate a crowd roughly half that size. The Cubs led, 2–0, through five innings, but the Pirates quieted the hometown faithful with a two-run rally in the top of the sixth. Rising to the challenge, Chicago regained the lead and carried a 5–2 advantage into the ninth. With Honus Wagner on first, Pirates second baseman Ed Abbaticchio hit a long fly ball into the overflow crowd in right field. It could have counted as a double or homer, but umpire Hank O'Day wasn't quite finished making an indelible mark on the 1908 season. He called the ball foul and was promptly mobbed by a throng of hysterical Pittsburgh players. Caving to the pressure, O'Day appealed to his crewmate Cy Rigler. Rigler upheld O'Day's decision and Abbaticchio failed to reach base. The rally died and the Pirates were eliminated. In a classy gesture, Pittsburgh owner Barney Dreyfuss visited the Chicago clubhouse accompanied by Clarke to offer congratulations.

An urban legend has persisted for years that a woman sitting in the right field stands was injured by Abbaticchio's drive and later filed a claim against the Cubs. Making the story even more provocative, the woman's ticket stub allegedly proved that she had been sitting in fair territory. Investigating the legend, *Baseball Digest* founder Herbert Simons sorted through records of every Chicago court case in a two-year span and found no evidence of a lawsuit. It simply didn't exist.

On October 7, Giants team doctor Joseph Creamer offered Klem a $2,500 bribe to steer his calls in favor of New York. Though the offer amounted to roughly a year's salary for Klem, he staunchly refused. The following morning, he reported Creamer's actions to Pulliam and asked to be excused from his assignment. Unfortunately, there were no substitutes available on such short notice. Incredibly, the officious Creamer approached Klem again shortly before game time, but the arbiter stood his ground. Creamer would later be run out of baseball for his actions.

Describing the scene at the Polo Grounds that afternoon, Cubs hurler Mordecai Brown remarked: "It was as near a lunatic asylum as I ever saw."[18] Hundreds of fans tried to sneak into the park under cover of darkness but were thwarted by night watchmen. By dawn, a large crowd had already lined up outside the ticket office. Thousands of fans sought vantage points on Coogan's Bluff—a steep precipice overlooking the stadium. They settled on rooftops and billboards. Some even clung to telegraph poles. At least two fans were killed in falls from perilous heights.

Several Chicago players received death threats. When the team's train arrived at Grand Central Station, players were verbally abused by an assembly of hostile fans. By 10:30 am, there were more than five-thousand people outside the Polo Grounds. Tickets sold out in roughly an hour, prompting multiple fights.

Prior to the first pitch, restless fans tried to set fire to a fence separating them from the field. When that didn't work, they tore it down. Police used fire hoses to repel them. On the other side of the stadium, several enterprising individuals tried to gain admission by digging a tunnel. Their efforts were fruitless.

Attendance was officially recorded at 40,000, but there were undoubtedly more people on hand to see Christy Mathewson square off against Jack Pfiester. Chicago's "Giant Killer" ended up being pulled in the first inning after coughing up an RBI double to Mike Donlin. The New Yorkers carried a 1–0 lead into the third inning, when the Cubs exploded for four runs off the ailing Mathewson, who had woken up with a sore arm. It was all the offense Chicago would need that day as Mordecai Brown slammed the door on the Giants, scattering four hits over eight innings while collecting his 29th win of the season.

Several Cubs players were accosted while leaving the field. Pfiester had his arm slashed with a knife and Frank Chance was attacked from behind. He fell hard, hurting his neck. Shortly afterward, an unruly mob tried to batter down the door to the visitors' clubhouse. Police drew their guns, prompting the crowd to disperse. When Chicago players finally arrived at the team's hotel, an anonymous fan threatened to blow up their train. Each of these regrettable events could be traced to O'Day's controversial call on September 23.

O'Day's decision has been referred to by multiple sources as the most courageous ever made by an umpire on the field. If this is an accurate statement, then the single most courageous act by a ballplayer can be attributed to Fred Merkle for continuing his career with the Giants. He played in portions of eight more seasons for New York after his infamous blunder. At one point during his disastrous 1909 follow-up, in which he hit .191 without a single homer, he said to McGraw: "Listen to them hoot. You're making a mistake keeping me here." McGraw turned to Merkle and said reassuringly: "I wish I had more players like you. Don't listen to those weathercocks. They'll be cheering you the next time you make a great play."[19] McGraw never blamed Merkle for his mistake. In fact, he cited several games the Giants should have won in 1908 that would have given them the pennant.

Merkle's ill-timed baserunning maneuver introduced a new slang term to the American vernacular. From that point forward, "to Merkle" meant not to show up. For years, Merkle dodged reporters and fans who invariably wanted him to recount the incident. While this proved to be a source of great anguish for him, it was Cubs fans who felt the most sorrow. After disposing of the Tigers in the 1908 World Series, the club waited more than a hundred years to bring a championship to Chicago.

As for O'Day, the stress of umpiring eventually led to serious stomach problems that kept him out of action for an extended length of time. Referring to the many traumas experienced by O'Day over the years, AL arbiter Silk O'Loughlin commented: "Look at O'Day. He's one of the best umpires, maybe the best today, but he's sour. Umpiring does something to you. The abuse you get from the players, the insults from the crowds, and the awful things they write about you in the newspapers take their toll."[20] By the time he called his last game in 1927, O'Day had presided over no-hitters in four decades. After leaving umpiring behind, he worked as a scout and served in an advisory capacity to the NL.

Stuffy McInnis's Gift Homer
Red Sox vs. A's, June 27, 1911

AL president Ban Johnson would have cringed had he attended a ballgame in the current era. While most games last more than three hours nowadays, most early–twentieth century contests were completed in two hours or less. Even so, Johnson felt that play should move at a brisker pace. Attempting to speed things up, he imposed restrictions on warm-up pitches in 1911. Stated quite plainly, it was a terrible idea.

During a July 27 meeting between the A's and Red Sox, Johnson's new rule was put to the test. Entering the game, the A's were sitting in second place with a 40–20 record. Among the strongest teams in the majors, they were on their way to a second consecutive World Series title. The Red Sox were nearing the end of a rebuilding phase, having been absent from post-season play for nearly a decade. The pitching matchup featured two of the era's most dominant hurlers: Smoky Joe Wood for Boston against Charles Bender of the A's.

The umpiring crew that afternoon consisted of Jack "Rip" Egan behind home plate and Jack Sheridan at first base. Egan, a former pitcher, had spent most of his playing career in the minors before getting roughed up in his only big league start for the Senators. Sheridan, whose umpiring career had begun in 1885, was among the most influential arbiters of the era. He had instituted the practice of crouching (as opposed to standing up straight) behind the plate to call balls and strikes. Universally admired by peers, Hall of Famers Bill Klem and Billy Evans were both said to have modeled their on-field habits after Sheridan.

The A's pecked away at Wood, chasing him from the game early. Reliever Ed Karger wasn't much better, staking Philly to a 6–3 lead through seven innings. As the teams were switching sides before the top of the eighth, Karger and catcher Les Nunamaker hustled onto the field to exchange a few quick tosses (in defiance of Johnson's rule). Two A's players hadn't even left the field yet and Boston's centerfielder Tris Speaker was engaged in friendly banter with second baseman Eddie Collins. Several of Collins's teammates were still looking for their gloves, which were routinely left on the field between innings in those days. While all this was taking place, Philly first baseman Stuffy McInnis improvised a devious strategy. As Karger continued to throw to Nunamaker, the sly infielder crept slowly toward the batter's box, taking practice swings to maintain his innocence. And then—timing it perfectly—he swatted one of Karger's warm-up tosses into unoccupied outfield territory.

The ball rolled all the way to the wall as McInnis began rounding the bases. Boston players, assuming the inning hadn't started yet, made no effort to chase after it. Neither Egan nor Sheridan were in position when the pitch was struck, but both were following the play closely as McInnis came steaming around third. After McInnis crossed the plate, Egan counted the run, setting off a storm of controversy.

Boston skipper Patsy Donovan argued that, since the umpires and fielders were not ready, the inning had not formally begun. Philly manager Connie Mack claimed that Karger had violated the warm-up pitch rule and any ball that crossed the plate should be counted as a live pitch. After hearing both sides of the debate, Egan stuck to his original call.

Regardless of Johnson's rule, a careful review of the play indicates that Egan made the wrong decision. At the beginning of any inning, action cannot officially begin until an umpire is set and a "time in" is indicated. Therefore, in the case of Stuffy McInnis, the ball should have been declared dead. The Red Sox lodged a protest to the league office, but it was overturned by Johnson. One contemporary remarked that the domineering AL executive "lived and died believing that baseball was perfected in order to serve him as a gigantic chess board on which to move his living pieces."[21] In a rare display of flexibility, Johnson rescinded the ban on warm-up pitches shortly afterward.

Germany Schaefer Steals First Base
Senators vs. White Sox, August 4, 1911

With more than ten years of experience to his credit entering the 1911 season, umpire Tommy Connolly probably thought he had seen just about everything on the diamond. He didn't count on the antics of Germany Schaefer—one of the most eccentric and unpredictable ballplayers in history. Schaefer challenged Connolly's knowledge of the rules when he successfully executed a steal of first base—a stunt that had presumably never been attempted before.

Schaefer grew up in the Levee District of South Chicago, which was notorious for crime and prostitution. He had a pleasant childhood nevertheless and matured into an easygoing young man. He was already twenty-nine years old by the time he became an everyday player in the majors. Though he rarely hit for average or power, he was known for his boundless energy and daring exploits on the basepaths.

Ever the showman, Schaefer received the nickname of "Prince" for his dramatic flair. In a game against the White Sox, he was called upon to pinch-hit for the Tigers with two outs, a runner on and his team trailing by a run. As he stepped to the plate, he addressed the crowd, referring to himself as "Herman the Great—acknowledged by one and all to be the greatest pinch-hitter in the world."²² He then plainly stated his intentions of hitting a home run into the left field bleachers. On the first pitch from Chicago's Doc White, he did exactly that. As he rounded the bases, he slid into each one. Upon crossing the plate, he bowed to the crowd and thanked them for their attention.

Schaefer resorted to various other stunts over the years. After going deep against Hall of Famer Rube Waddell one afternoon, he carried his bat with him and pointed it like a rifle, taking imaginary shots at the hurler as he rounded the bases. Frequently used as a first or third base coach, Schaefer was known to eat popcorn in the coach's box or sit on the ground using bats as oars to "row" across the grass. He was also seen on many occasions walking the baselines like a tightrope. Numerous photos of Schaefer depict him clowning around. In one picture, he is wearing mitts on both hands and smiling mischievously. "Is humorous coaching of value to a team?" He proposed to a reporter one day. "I think so. It is valuable for two reasons. It keeps our fellows in good spirits and it sometimes distracts our players."²³ Schaefer provided the ultimate distraction during a 1911 game against the White Sox.

Traded to Washington in the middle of the 1909 campaign, Schaefer reached his prime, hitting .294 from the point of the transaction to the end of the 1914 slate. He had an excellent year in 1911, compiling a career-high .334 batting average. On August 4 of that season, Schaefer's Senators were locked in a scoreless tie with Chicago. In the bottom of the ninth, Schaefer was on first base with teammate Clyde Milan representing the winning run at third. Looking to draw a throw from White Sox catcher Fred Payne, Schaefer bolted for second, arriving there safely.

Germany Schaefer was known for his unorthodox behavior on the ball field. In 1911, he created a sticky situation for umpire Tommy Connolly when he "stole" first base during a game against the White Sox (Library of Congress).

His efforts were wasted as Payne held onto the ball. Before the next pitch, Schaefer took his lead on the first base side of the bag—a tactic that appeared counterintuitive on the surface. But there was method to Schaefer's madness. As pitcher Doc White made an offering to Senators hitter Kid Elberfeld, Schaefer ran back to first, completing the first known documented "steal" of that station. Again, Payne alertly held onto the ball, not wanting to risk throwing it away and allowing Milan to score.

White Sox manager Hugh Duffy, who had compiled the highest single-season batting average of the Deadball Era at .440, was confused about what he had just seen and came out to argue with Connolly. As Duffy began to state his case, Schaefer took advantage of the situation and headed toward second base again. His actions achieved the desired effect as he got caught in a rundown, prompting Milan to bolt toward home. Unfortunately for the Senators, Milan was tagged out, inviting a fresh round of controversy.

Schaefer contended that the out shouldn't count since the White Sox had ten men on the field at the time (counting Duffy). Connolly rejected the appeal, pointing out that Duffy had not been an active player since 1906. There were at least two other pending issues, however: Schaefer's "steal" of first base and the question of whether or not a "time out" had been assumed when Duffy stepped onto the field to argue the play. In the end, both points were moot as Connolly upheld the "steal" and the out at home.

The game was not decided until the bottom of the eleventh, when the Senators loaded the bases and scored their only run on a ground ball hit to shortstop Lee Tannehill. A writer from the *Washington Times* recognized Schaefer's unprecedented achievement, remarking that "such a play will not be duplicated in a cycle of baseball."[24] Explaining himself to reporters after the game, Connolly stated bluntly that, under existing rules, Schaefer "had a perfect right to go from second back to first."[25]

Remarkably, Connolly had never even seen a baseball game until his family emigrated to the U.S. from Manchester, England. By then, he was in his mid-teens. Captivated by the sport, he spent long hours studying the rulebook. He got noticed by major league umpire Tim Hurst while calling games for the YMCA. He joined the National League staff in 1898 but defected to the fledging American League in 1901 to escape the unruliness that plagued the senior circuit at the dawn of the twentieth century.

Umpiring crews were small in Connolly's day and, over the course of his career, he employed the practice of staying behind home plate when first base was open and moving behind the pitcher's mound with a runner on. If a runner made it to second, he would move back behind home plate. Though not a common practice for the Deadball Era, Connolly felt it gave him a better view of third base and kept him close to home if there was a play. "An umpire just couldn't cover every base," he said in later years. "But we did the best we could. I have no regrets."[26]

Germany Schaefer continued his clowning throughout his career as a player and coach, attracting legions of fans. Historian Fred Lieb once observed: "Everybody loves the jovial, droll, pock-marked Dutchman."[27] Sportswriter Malcolm Bingay commented that Schaefer was "the soul of baseball itself with all its sorrows and joys, the born troubadour of the game."[28] Interestingly, Schaefer bombed in his Vaudeville debut. Dressed as a leprechaun and dancing a jig, he was literally dragged off the stage along with double-play partner Charley O'Leary when the comedy routine failed to amuse a Chicago crowd.

Shortly after Schaefer's passing in 1919, a new regulation was instated forbidding runners to mirror the tactics he had used in the memorable 1911 game. The rule, which still stands today, states that a runner is out if "after he has acquired legal possession of a base, he runs the bases in reverse order for the purpose of confusing the defense or making a travesty of the game."[29] Connolly, who was still in service as an umpire when the new rule went into effect, never got a chance to invoke it during his career. Appointed chief of the AL staff in 1931, he later became the first umpire (along with Bill Klem) to be elected to the National Baseball Hall of Fame. His thirty-one years of AL service were a record that stood until 1999.

Bill Brennan
Imposes His Iron Will
Giants vs. Phillies, August 30, 1913

In the heat of the moment, umpires are often forced to make unpopular calls knowing full well there will be consequences. During a 1913 game between the Giants and Phillies, arbiter Bill Brennan rendered a decision that may have been more personal than practical. His actions inadvertently led to the replacement of NL president Thomas Lynch.

A robust man standing 6-foot-2 and weighing close to 250 pounds, Brennan had a booming voice that commanded attention. He was no stranger to controversy. In 1912, Phillies owner Horace Fogel alleged that the pennant race was fixed and that Brennan was at the center of an umpires' conspiracy. Brennan threatened to file a libel suit against the outspoken proprietor then changed his mind when Fogel was permanently banished from baseball. The arbiter could never have guessed he would be embroiled in another intense debate less than a year later.

The Phillies got off to a hot start in 1913, occupying first place from May 9 until June 30, when the Giants passed them in the standings. Despite major contributions from NL home run king Gavvy Cravath and Hall of Fame pitcher Pete Alexander, the Phillies never regained the lead. But things were still very much up in the air when the teams met on August 30.

The ill-fated game took place at Philadelphia's Baker Bowl, which was known as a hitter's paradise. The park's most striking feature was the right-field wall, which stood a mere 280 feet from home plate and made life extremely difficult for pitchers. Though the August 30 matchup should have been an outstanding one—Christy Mathewson for the Giants versus Alexander for the Phillies—neither hurler was especially brilliant that afternoon. Mathewson had his share of difficulty at the Baker Bowl over the years, staking opponents to a .288 batting average and .308 on-base percentage—the worst numbers of any ballpark in which he made at least ten starts. Alexander, winner of 373 games and four Triple Crowns, was not always effective against the Giants, getting tagged for 132 extra-base hits and a .320 OBP in ninety-nine appearances.

Brennan was behind the plate that day with crewmate Mal Eason stationed at first base. Eason had pitched at the major league level for six seasons before his dreadful 36–73 won/loss record drove him to umpiring. His career as an official was somewhat brief as well, lasting less than a thousand games. He was never selected to work in a World Series.

The Giants looked as if they would breeze to a win, battering Alexander for six runs through three innings. But right-hander George Chalmers took over and completely shut down the Giants' attack. New York led, 6–0, until the sixth, when Philly rallied for five runs off Mathewson. John McGraw believed his ace would settle down but he was wrong. "Matty" yielded a two-run homer to third baseman Bobby Byrne in the seventh then coughed up an insurance run an inning later.

Trailing, 8–6, in the ninth, McGraw called upon Moose McCormick to pinch-hit for first baseman Fred Merkle. Chalmers retired McCormick, but on his way back to the dugout, McCormick motioned angrily to the centerfield bleachers and complained that fans had distracted him by waving their straw hats. Responding to the grievance, Brennan walked out to centerfield and barked at bleacherites to move from their seats. He was promptly greeted with jeers and catcalls. Unable to control the crowd, the arbiter approached Philly team captain Mike Doolan and instructed him to order the fans to move. Doolan laughed aloud and said it would not be possible.

Refusing to take "no" for an answer, Brennan then held a conference with McGraw. When he had finished, he spoke to acting Phillies manager Hans Lobert (who had taken over after Red Dooin was ejected earlier in the game). Again, Brennan insisted the crowd be moved and, again, he was told by members of the Philly squad that the request was impractical. Instead of abandoning his mission, the arbiter stalked out to centerfield and ordered an on-duty policeman to disperse the crowd. This didn't sit well with the officer, who informed Brennan he was under no obligation to take orders from umpires. Fans were clamoring for the game to resume at that point and Brennan, who had encountered enough resistance for one day, declared the game a forfeit in favor of the Giants.

Angry mobs gathered outside the stadium, throwing bricks and other projectiles. Giants infielder Tillie Shafer was hit in the back of the head. Police were forced to draw their guns in order to get players and officials to their trains safely. Brennan ended up being knocked to the ground and pummeled by fans—twice—but he managed to get back to his feet and escape. In their haste to flee the scene, Giants players boarded the wrong train.

The events that followed were almost as dramatic as the post-game riot. Responding to a Philly appeal, NL president Thomas Lynch reversed Brennan's decision, contending that the arbiter's actions were not supported by the standard playing rules or special ground rules. When the Giants launched a counter-appeal, the NL board of directors overruled Lynch and demanded that the game be resumed on October 2 at the precise point where it had been preempted.

Brennan spent most of September in the hot seat. A fan named Henry Russell claimed that the arbiter had trampled him on the way out of the stadium and a warrant was reportedly issued for Brennan's arrest in Philadelphia. This prompted rumors that Brennan would be fired, but he hung onto his job until season's end.

Any parallels to the infamous Merkle game were nullified when the Giants clinched the pennant prior to October 2. The August 30 debacle came to a quiet conclusion when Red Murray grounded out and Chief Meyers singled to right. McGraw tried to make things interesting by inserting

Eddie Grant as a pinch-runner and sending Larry McLean up to pinch-hit for Fred Snodgrass, but Grant was forced at second for the final out of the game.

Brennan was later featured in a syndicated cartoon drawn by Giants pitcher/illustrator Al Demaree. In the single-panel comic, Brennan was described as "a man who has the courage of his convictions."[30] Standing by those convictions, he quit his job around the same time that Lynch was ousted as NL president. Brennan worked in the short-lived Federal League during both seasons of operation. When the circuit folded after the 1915 slate, he was out of the majors. He returned for one more NL campaign in 1921. He later served as a college football coach for multiple schools.

The Indecision of Charles Johnston
Yankees vs. Indians, August 6, 1937

In any game, there are pivotal junctures in which the judgments of umpires directly affect the final score. An arbiter must be prepared to render those judgments with accuracy and stand by them. In a showdown between the Yankees and Indians, umpire Charles Johnston failed to meet those requirements not once, but twice.

The 1930s were a golden era for Yankee baseball as the club won four consecutive World Series titles. The roster was packed with Hall of Famers, among them immortals Lou Gehrig and Joe DiMaggio. In 1937, the Bombers annihilated the competition, finishing thirteen games ahead of the second place Tigers. By the time they hosted the Indians at home on the August 6, they had built a comfortable lead in the standings.

In his second season of big league service, umpire Charles Johnston drew the home plate assignment that day. His crewmates were George Moriarty and Brick Owens, who had over six thousand games of major league experience between them.

Though the Indians managed a distant fourth place finish in 1937, they had some very capable players in their lineup. First baseman Hal Trosky averaged thirty homers and 127 RBIs per year between 1934 and

1939. A six-time All-Star and eventual Hall of Famer, centerfielder Earl Averill combined strong defense with timely hitting. Flame-thrower Bob Feller, who reached the majors at the age of seventeen, gradually developed into one of the most dominant hurlers of the era.

Playing against the Yankees could be extremely frustrating for opponents. The Indians finished behind New York in the standings every year from 1926 through 1939. Even Feller—one of the all-time greats—compiled a losing record against the Bombers with an ERA three-quarters of a run above his lifetime average. "I would rather beat the Yankees regularly than pitch a no-hit game," he once declared.[31]

The pitching matchup on August 6 featured the teenaged Feller versus right-hander Bump Hadley, a fast-baller who had a tendency to lose the plate. The Yankees tagged Feller for two runs in the second, but the Indians answered with a run in the fourth and three in the sixth on a homer by Trosky. The Tribe led, 5–2, before the Yankees rallied to tie the score in the ninth inning. In the top of the tenth, Trosky hit his second home run of the game off Johnny "Fireman" Murphy. Another dramatic Yankee comeback was sullied by the incompetence of Johnston in the bottom of the frame.

The Yankees had runners on second and third with one out when Red Rolfe appeared to check his swing on a pitch in the dirt. Johnston called strike three after catcher Frankie Pytlak tagged Rolfe. Yankee skipper Joe McCarthy came out to argue. In the ensuing debate, Johnston—perhaps a bit flustered—complicated matters by stating that Rolfe had foul-tipped the ball. When McCarthy pointed out that this would entitle Rolfe to another chance at the plate, Johnston changed his mind, claiming that Rolfe had checked his swing and the pitch should be counted as ball three. This irritated Indians manager Steve O'Neill, who demanded to know why Johnston had reversed his original call. Completely overwhelmed at that point, Johnston appealed to Moriarty for help. The veteran arbiter overruled Johnston, declaring Rolfe out on the play. The situation became even more befuddling shortly afterward.

Joe DiMaggio stepped up and hammered a pitch inside the third baseline. Cleveland third-sacker Odell Hale lunged for the ball and knocked it into foul territory with his glove. Hale, never known for his sparkling defense, once inadvertently started a triple play by deflecting a line drive into the glove of a teammate with his head. Johnston raised his hands to signal a foul as Cleveland defenders gave up on the ball. When Johnston waved both Yankee runners back to second and third, McCarthy sauntered angrily onto the field, reminding the arbiter that DiMaggio's liner had been in fair territory when Hale touched it. Either thoroughly confused or looking to avoid culpability, Johnston again turned to Moriarty for assistance. The latter sided with McCarthy, ruling that the runs should count.

The 7–6 Yankee victory did not sit well with O'Neill, who lodged a formal protest, contending that the winning run had scored only because Cleveland's leftfielder, Moose Solters, stopped pursuing the ball when he heard the "foul" ruling. AL President William Harridge took all month to process the appeal. Finally, on August 31, he ordered the game to be replayed. The Yankees squawked about this, but in the end it hardly mattered as they eventually moved on to a World Series victory over the Giants.

This was not the first time that Johnston's questionable decision-making skills had invited trouble. During a game at Comiskey Park in 1936, the Yankees had the bases loaded with one out. When veteran catcher Luke Sewell objected to one of Johnston's calls, White Sox player/manager Jimmy Dykes—among the most combative men of the era—joined the debate. Asserting his authority, Johnston tossed both men out along with back-up catcher Merv Shea, who was spouting off from the bench. Yankee outfielder George Selkirk then drew a walk (one of eleven called by Johnston that afternoon), forcing in a run as the Yankees went on to win, 5–3.

Johnston's performance invited harsh criticism from the Chicago media. When he took the field the following day for a doubleheader, the Comiskey crowd greeted him with a hearty round of boos. In the eighth inning of the second game, Johnston blew a critical call at first base, ruling Chicago outfielder Rip Radcliffe out after Yankee pitcher Pat Malone dropped the ball applying the tag. When third base umpire Bill Summers upheld Johnston's errant call, fans went ballistic, throwing garbage onto the field. In the ninth inning, Summers was forced out of the game after being hit by a thrown projectile.

The American League opted not to renew Johnston's contract in 1938 and he returned to the American Association, where he had gained a majority of his professional experience. He later moved on to the Eastern League. To supplement his income, he worked as an insurance salesman in the offseason. He also officiated football and basketball games. One can only hope he was more effective in that capacity.

Red Jones's Fourteen Ejections
White Sox vs. Red Sox, July 19, 1946

Every umpire has a different tolerance level. Bob Ferguson broke catcher Nat Hicks's arm with a bat for calling him a "damn liar." Tim Hurst spit on Hall of Famer Eddie Collins when the latter disputed a call at second base. Red Jones cleared the entire White Sox bench while trying to determine which player was making crude noises.

In evaluating Jones's unprecedented actions, a writer from the *New York Times* remarked: "What started as an ordinary game on July 19, 1946 has evolved into a sometimes extraordinary tall tale. With every telling, from the initial game-day report to a perennial 'Today in Baseball' blurb, the '14 Men Out' story demonstrates how easily a yarn can be turned into a myth."[32]

Sorting out the facts in the matter is a difficult task indeed. A basic *Google* search of the incident invariably yields at least half a dozen narratives, all of which differ slightly. By some accounts, Jones's ejections occurred in two separate incidents. Other sources claim he thumbed the fourteen players out all at once. Even Red Sox slugger Ted Williams, who was in the thick of things, seems to have gotten a couple of details wrong. Regardless of how the story is told, one irrefutable fact remains: no other umpire has ever victimized a team to that extent.

Interest in baseball reached unprecedented levels in 1946 as players returned triumphantly from World War II. Umpires were told to crack down on beanball wars, which had been a common occurrence during the early part of the decade. By late–July, the Red Sox were running away with the pennant while the White Sox were mired near the bottom of the pack almost twenty games below .500. The ChiSox had just dropped three in a row to Boston and may have been feeling a bit frustrated before game time on July 19.

Williams, one of the greatest natural hitters the sport has ever produced, delivered a two-run double for the BoSox in the first. He came to bat again in the third inning with Dominic DiMaggio on base. Joe Haynes, who served as both a starter and reliever for Chicago, was on the mound. According to Williams: "You had to be alert with Haynes. He was always trying to hit you in the elbow."[33] True to form, Haynes issued a knockdown pitch and Williams hit the dirt. Jones, who was working behind home plate that day, issued a stern warning to the hurler. This is where the details get a little fuzzy.

Sticking only to well-established facts, Jones's warning invited a chorus of catcalls from the White Sox bench. In most published versions of the tale, someone called the arbiter a "meathead." In his autobiography, *My Turn at Bat*, Ted Williams remembered it differently, stating that the language used was more profane. Whatever the case, Jones evicted a handful of players from the bench. One of them was outfielder Ralph Hodgin, who later proclaimed his innocence. "Jones wasn't calling 'em too good and they got to hollering at him," Hodgin recalled. "I was at the end of the bench and he saw me open my mouth, so he threw me out."[34]

In those days, the clubhouses at Fenway were adjacent to one another on the first base side of the field. Opposing players entered via the same tunnel (an arrangement that led to more than one epic fistfight). This compelled the banished White Sox players to parade past home plate on their way out. Among the original crop of ejected individuals, coach Bing Miller (a former star for the Philadelphia A's) sarcastically offered Jones a pair of glasses before exiting the field.

The first round of ejections failed to dampen the spirits of White Sox players, who continued to lay it on thick. Sixty years after the fact, utility infielder Dario Lodigiani finally revealed what provoked Jones's wrath. Apparently, coach Mule Haas (another former A's standout) had a talent for using his mouth to reproduce the sounds of flatulence. When the source of the noises could not be traced and another round of warnings from Jones went unheeded, the arbiter decided to purge the bench of all non-essential personnel. In addition to the starting nine, only a manager, a trainer, a batboy and (comically) coach Mule Haas remained.

As the exiled players strolled past Jones, Wally Moses took a moment to plead his case. "Red, I've been in the big leagues eleven years," said the soft-spoken outfielder. "I've never been thrown out of a game in my life. Honest to Pete, I never said a word to you on the bench." Jones replied less than apologetically: "Wally, I want to tell you. It's like this. It's just like a raid on a whorehouse. The good go with the bad."[35] An inconsequential fact, the Red Sox went on to win that day, 9–2.

As details of the game were recounted, the story took a sharp left turn. On July 31, 1946, *The Sporting News* published a headline that read: "Heckling Ventriloquist Throws Voice, Baffled Red Jones Throws Out 14 Hose."[36] A few weeks later, renowned sportswriter Arthur Daley furthered the misinformation. In 1986, the ventriloquist myth reappeared in Bruce Nash and Allan Zullo's light-hearted sequel to *The Baseball Hall of Shame*. The fable has persisted to the present day.

Over the course of six big league seasons, Red Jones earned a reputation for intolerance, leading the league in ejections twice. He thumbed out twenty-three players in 1946 with fourteen of those expulsions occurring during the infamous game at Fenway Park. Jones's ejections tended to come in bunches as he tossed out multiple players from individual games on nine occasions.

Following his retirement from umpiring, Jones worked in public relations for a beer company and had a brief stint as a TV commentator for the Cleveland Indians. In September of 1969, he recorded some of his stories on a Motown album entitled, *Red Jones Steeerikes Back!*

Though Jones's record of fourteen ejections in a game has yet to be duplicated, it has been challenged on at least two occasions. On August 12, 1984, umpire Steve Ripley and his crew tossed a total of thirteen men (combined from both teams) out of a Braves/Padres game that was marred by multiple beanings and three nasty brawls. The trouble began when Braves hurler Pascual Perez hit Alan Wiggins with the first pitch of the game. The Padres staff threw at Perez every time he came to bat, finally plunking him in the eighth inning. Five fans were arrested for participating in the ugliness.

On April 22, 2000, umpire Mike Everett and his staff had their hands full in a game between the Tigers and White Sox at Comiskey Park as two vicious fights broke out, stemming from a series of beanings. Sox reliever, Keith Foulke, ended up with five stitches. Eleven players were thrown out of the game and, in the aftermath, sixteen members of both teams were suspended. Additionally, twenty-four players, coaches and managers were fined.

Two Balls in Play at Wrigley Field
Cardinals vs. Cubs, June 30, 1959

The prerequisite for being an umpire is the ability to remain alert at all times. Caught up in a dispute behind home plate, arbiter Vic Delmore committed the ultimate act of inattention, introducing a second ball into play during a game between St. Louis and Chicago. The unforgettable blunder would ultimately cost Delmore his job.

In 1959, the Cubs hovered around .500 and were out of contention for most of the season. Aside from Ernie Banks' second consecutive MVP performance, there wasn't much of interest happening at Wrigley Field that year. Delmore helped spice things up a bit on June 30.

(*WARNING:* Readers may need a scorecard to keep up with the events that transpired.)

Bob Anderson, a big right-hander with a lively fastball, was on the mound for the Cubs facing Stan Musial in the fourth inning. With one out and a 3–1 count, Musial appeared to check his swing on a pitch that got a piece of catcher Sammy Taylor before bouncing to the backstop.

Chaos ensued.

Believing that Musial had foul tipped the ball, Taylor didn't even bother to chase after it. He stood there arguing with Delmore for a strike call instead. The ball ended up in the hands of field announcer Pat Pieper, who (according to Anderson) stashed it in the dead ball bag behind home plate. Meanwhile, the opportunistic Musial—playing in his eighteenth major league season—rounded first and headed toward second.

Third baseman Al Dark—a versatile defensive player who appeared at every infield station except for catcher during his career—alertly sprung into action. Musial was on his way to second base when Dark instructed Pieper to hand him any ball from the bag and keep quiet about it. If this version of the story (offered by Anderson to a reporter many years after the fact) is valid, then there were likely three balls in play at Wrigley Field that afternoon since the odds of Pieper producing the actual live ball from a bag full of dead ones are slim.

While Dark was busy taking matters into his own hands, Delmore was still engaged in a dispute with Taylor regarding the walk to Musial. Anderson had wandered over from the mound at that point to share his own thoughts on the topic. Obviously distracted, Delmore handed Anderson a new ball from his pouch.

The results were almost comical.

Anderson rifled the new ball to second. Dark fired the one from the deadball bag to the same destination. The throws arrived at roughly the same time. Anderson's peg sailed into center field, where Bobby Thomson reportedly scooped it up and tossed it into the Cubs dugout to get rid of the evidence. Dark's relay, which many believed was the actual game ball but probably wasn't, ended up being caught by shortstop Ernie Banks. Musial, who had his back to the play and saw Anderson's throw float into the outfield, must have been thoroughly confused when Banks tagged him.

Recounting the incident, Anderson remarked: "To me, the funniest thing was watching Musial, a very [smart] baseball guy wandering around there and wondering 'what the hell is going on, here?'"[37] Musial was smart, indeed, and extremely gifted. During his twenty-two seasons in the majors, he won seven batting crowns and captured three MVP Awards. He became a folk hero in St Louis, where he was known affectionately to fans as "Stan the Man."

Delmore, whose stock went into rapid decline after the regrettable incident, held a conference with his colleagues. Second base umpire Bill Jackowski was among those included. "I felt sorry for Vic," said Jackowski, who worked three World Series and three All-Star games during a distinguished seventeen-year career. "It was a helluva mess."[38] After a ten-minute delay, Musial was ruled out on the play. Cardinals manager Solly Hemus was less than thrilled with the result, threatening to file an official protest, but he withdrew his complaint when St. Louis won, 4–1.

Delmore's infamous blunder at Wrigley field marked the beginning of a downward spiral. When his contract was not renewed at seasons' end, fans from his hometown bombarded NL President Warren Giles with telegrams. Despite the outpouring of support, Giles stood firm on his decision. "Umpires, like ballplayers, have bad days too," Delmore told a reporter dejectedly. "Sometimes when you make a wrong decision, you feel badly about it—worse than anybody else."[39] Sadly, Delmore died from a heart ailment less than a year after the incident. He was only forty-four years old.

At the very least, there was no incriminating video footage left to posterity. Though the game was broadcast by WGN-TV in Chicago, the tape was recorded over and used for other programming. No other footage is known to exist.

Don Money's Nullified Grand Slam
Yankees vs. Brewers, April 10, 1976

Infielder Don Money hit four grand slams during his career. Unfortunately, one of them didn't count. Had New York Yankees manager Billy Martin not successfully convinced the umpiring crew to abide by a call that was made prior to Money's nullified blast, the Brewers would have been celebrating an epic 10–9 comeback victory on the above date.

Entering the 1976 campaign, the Yankees had been excluded from the postseason for more than a decade. A rebuilding project had begun in 1973, when entrepreneur George Steinbrenner assembled a group of investors to purchase the club from the CBS Corporation. The pieces of a championship puzzle were gradually put together as Steinbrenner added new stars to the lineup every year. One of the most important transactions was the installment of Billy Martin as manager during the second half of the 1975 slate.

Known for his volcanic temper, Martin clashed with players, umpires and bosses wherever he went. He was fired and re-hired by Steinbrenner multiple times during his tenure in New York. But he had a knack for turning the clubs he managed into contenders. Before arriving in the Bronx, Martin had led the Tigers and Twins to playoff appearances. He would guide the Yankees to two consecutive pennants before being forced to resign with 69 games remaining in the 1978 campaign.

During his twenty-eight seasons as a major league umpire, Jim McKean made some memorable calls. In 1976, he was pressured by Yankee manager Billy Martin to nullify a grand slam that would have given the Milwaukee Brewers a dramatic walk-off win (National Baseball Hall of Fame Library, Cooperstown, N.Y.).

Martin's competitiveness bordered on being unsportsmanlike at times and he periodically resorted to under-handed tactics. The tone of the 1976 season was set on Opening Day, when Martin claimed the mound at County Stadium in Milwaukee was too low. "It's like pitchers are pitching uphill," he griped before the game, "and if they don't change it, I'm going to ask that my pitchers be allowed to warm up on the mound before the game to get used to it."[40] Whether Martin's complaint was valid or not, Hall of Famer Catfish Hunter faltered for the Yankees, allowing five runs in his first two innings of work.

Following the 5–0 Yankee loss, Martin lodged an official protest. AL president Lee MacPhail ordered umpires to inspect the mound, but by the time they got around to it, necessary corrections (if any were in order) had been made by the County Stadium grounds crew. This didn't please the pugnacious Martin, who made an even bigger stink on April 10, when the teams met again.

The Brewers lineup featured a very young Robin Yount and an aging Hank Aaron, who was playing in his final season. Both players made significant contributions as Milwaukee roughed up starter Ed Figueroa. Trailing 6–0, the Yankees staged a seventh-inning rally, capped off by a two-run Thurman Munson homer. They added five runs in the ninth on timely hits by Chris Chambliss and Lou Piniella.

Looking to overcome a 9–6 deficit, Yount opened the bottom of the ninth for Milwaukee with a single off reliever Sparky Lyle. Pedro Garcia followed with a walk, prompting Martin to replace his bullpen ace with right-hander Dave Pagan. Aside from the events that were about to transpire, Pagan had a largely forgettable career. Pinch-hitter Bobby Darwin reached on Graig Nettles' second error of the game, loading the bases and providing Don Money with a golden opportunity.

Playing in his ninth full season, Money was an excellent defensive third baseman. He had moderate power, peaking at twenty-five homers in 1977. With a 1–0 count, he lifted a pitch deep into the left field seats. He told a reporter after the game: "I had that feeling. It felt right."[41] But as Milwaukee fans began to celebrate an apparent walk-off victory, something felt very wrong for Billy Martin.

Stationed at first base that day, umpire Jim McKean was in his third year of major league service. In 1976, AL umpire supervisor Dick Butler rated McKean as the best on his staff. "He has the perfect temperament," Butler said. "He can listen, he can dish it out. He can be serious and he can be humorous."[42] In spite of Butler's glowing praise, McKean made a costly mistake during the game in question—a mistake he felt compelled to rectify.

As Pagan was set to deliver the 1–0 pitch to Money, the ever-vigilant Martin noticed that Chambliss had called for time at first base. McKean began to raise his arms to honor the request but lowered them when Money connected with Pagan's offering. As Money was rounding the bases, Martin came out of the Yankee dugout to confront McKean. The arbiter initially denied he had granted time, but when second base umpire Nick Bremigan admitted he had seen McKean's arms start to go up, the latter acknowledged his actions. After several minutes of deliberation, players from both teams were ordered back onto the field. Milwaukee's first base coach, Harvey Kuenn, had to be physically restrained as fans booed and littered the field with debris.

Recounting the play years later, Money raised an interesting point. "Billy Martin came running out while waving to his first baseman. Martin claimed [Chambliss] called a time out. The question was: did he have time to call a time out? [Chambliss] said he started to call a time out. I thought: *starting to* and *having enough time* is different."[43]

The game ended anti-climactically. Robbed of a career-defining grand slam, Money flied out. George Scott delivered an RBI sac-fly before Darrell Porter grounded to second, wrapping up a disheartening Milwaukee loss. After the game, Money called McKean "gutless."[44] McKean insisted he had not been intimidated at all by Martin and confirmed to reporters that he had approved the time out.

The Brewers lost 95 games in 1976. The Yankees finished first in the AL East and eliminated Kansas City in the ALCS. They met their match in the World Series, getting swept by Cincinnati's "Big Red Machine." Martin's temper got the best of him during Game 4, when he was ejected by first base umpire Bruce Froemming for a series of snide remarks he made from the dugout.

Jim McKean lasted twenty-eight seasons as a major league arbiter, working his way up to the position of umpire supervisor. He served in that capacity for nearly a decade before being released from his duties along with Rich Garcia and Marty Springstead. Though MLB gave no official reason for the termination, various other sources confirmed it was related to a series of blown calls in the 2009 postseason (a topic discussed at length in a later chapter).

A four-time All-Star, Money moved on to a successful minor league managerial career, serving at the single, double and triple-A levels. In 2007, he was named Southern League Manager of the Year. He later took a job as special director of player development for the Milwaukee Brewers.

The Pine Tar Game
Yankees vs. Royals, July 24, 1983

Many words have been used to describe Billy Martin over the years. More often than not, those words tend to focus on the negative. Despite his many flaws, which were evident to anyone who followed his career as a player and manager, Martin was one of the most brilliant strategists the game has ever seen. Never was this more apparent than on the above date, when he nearly stole a game from the Kansas City Royals.

The Yankees and Royals had a somewhat less than friendly relationship. Having lost three consecutive playoff series to the New Yorkers beginning in 1976, there was lingering resentment among Kansas City players. Though both teams had undergone many changes by the time the 1983 campaign rolled around, the rivalry was still alive and well.

The 1983 pennant race was tight in both divisions. The Yankees tumbled to third place at the All-Star break but were only two games out when they hosted the Royals at home on July 24. In the West, the Royals were trailing the first place White Sox by two games despite having fallen below .500.

Neither starter was terribly effective that afternoon. Shane Rawley was replaced with one out in the sixth after yielding three runs on ten hits to Kansas City. The Yankees answered with three runs of their own in the bottom of the frame, chasing southpaw Bud Black from the mound. By the time the Royals came to bat in the top of the ninth, they were trailing, 4–3.

When reliever Dale Murray yielded a two-out single to U.L. Washington, Martin wasn't taking any chances. He called upon bullpen ace Goose Gossage to face the dangerous George Brett. A Hall of Famer, Brett absolutely killed the Yankees during his career, collecting 79 extra-base hits and 117 RBIs against them. He entered this particular game with a .352 batting average. Earlier in the season, Yankee third baseman Graig Nettles had noticed that Brett's bat was slathered with pine tar from handle to barrel. He pointed this out to Martin, who filed the information away as potentially useful.

It certainly was.

As he had so many times before, Brett rose to the occasion, depositing a Gossage fastball into the right field stands. As Brett was circling the bases, Martin decided it was time to play his trump card. The Yankee skipper marched onto the field and asked home plate umpire Tim McClelland to inspect Brett's bat.

Though only in his first year of full-time major league service, McClelland had already developed a reputation for handling difficult situations with diplomacy. Taking Martin's complaint very seriously, the arbiter laid Brett's bat on the ground against home plate (which is seventeen inches across) to estimate how far the pine tar extended up the handle. At the time, the rulebook stated plainly that the bat handle could not be "covered or treated with any material or substance to improve the grip"⁴⁵ for more than eighteen inches from the end. Any hit attained with an illegal bat was considered void with the batter being automatically declared out.

Upon measuring Brett's bat, it was discovered that the pine tar significantly exceeded the legal limit. Honoring the rules, McClelland signaled for the out. This served to enrage Brett, who bolted out of the dugout like a wild-eyed whirling dervish. He had to be physically restrained by members of the umpiring crew to prevent him from assaulting McClelland. Though manager Dick Howser's argument fell on deaf ears, the Yankees' 4–3 win would not stand for long.

In response to an official protest, AL President Lee MacPhail ruled that the "spirit of the [pine tar] restriction" was to prevent the ball from being discolored and rendered unsuitable for play. In his opinion, Brett had not violated "the spirit of the rules" nor intentionally altered his bat to propel the ball further.⁴⁶ There was a precedent for this decision. On September 7, 1975, a John Mayberry home run had come into question for excessive pine tar. The umpires in that game had allowed the home run to stand and MacPhail had overturned a subsequent protest, citing the same reasons given in Brett's case.

To afford the Yankees a fighting chance, MacPhail ordered the game to be resumed with two outs in the ninth and the Royals leading, 5–4. Brett was retroactively expelled for his tirade along with Howser and coach Rocky Colavito. Hall of Famer Gaylord Perry, who had spear-headed a failed plot to hide Brett's sticky bat in the clubhouse, was also ejected.

Though the Yankees sought to delay the suspended game as long as possible, they were compelled to host the Royals at Yankee Stadium on August 18. Only 1,200 fans attended. In protest, Martin put pitcher Ron Guidry in center field and first baseman Don Mattingly at second. Before the first pitch, Yankee hurler George Frazier threw to first to challenge Brett's home run on the grounds that he had missed the bag on his way around the bases. Word had leaked that Martin might attempt this stunt and, adequately prepared for it, umpire Tim Welke spread his arms, indicating a "safe" call. When Frazier threw to second, arbiter Dave Phillips followed suit. Martin then sauntered onto the field to offer his closing arguments. Anticipating this move, Phillips produced an affidavit signed by all four members of the original umpiring crew declaring that Brett had touched every base. Thwarted at every turn, Martin retreated to the clubhouse. Hal McRae struck out and the Yankees went down in order, bringing the game to an official close.

Disgusted with the outcome, Yankee owner George Steinbrenner commented acerbically: "If the Yankees lose the American League pennant by one game, I wouldn't want to be Lee MacPhail living in New York. Maybe he should go house hunting in Kansas City."[47] The inappropriate remark earned the Yankee executive a hefty fine.

During the offseason winter meetings, the Pine Tar Rule was re-written. As of 1984, a player could not be called out or ejected for having pine tar on his bat, though the bat itself could be removed from the game. Questioned about this development, Billy Martin offered the following statement: "There's no question the rule should have been re-written.... As it was written it was a bad rule and an ambiguous one. But that wasn't my fault. I didn't write the rules. The way this rule was written, I was right, and there was no question of that."[48]

Not long after the infamous pine tar fiasco, George Brett came to bat in a game at Tiger Stadium in which McClelland was stationed behind home plate. The arbiter asked Brett if he wanted to clown around a little and suggested he pretend to inspect Brett's bat. The latter declined, but both men were finally able to share a laugh.

Controversy found McClelland at several other points during his career—especially in the 2007 Wild Card tie-breaker (details in the next section). Despite his occasional lapses, he was once ranked by players as the number one umpire in a *Sports Illustrated* poll. He announced his retirement prior to the 2015 campaign, ending a thirty-three-year career—one of the longest stints by any big league official.

Though the Pine Tar Incident has endured as one of the most celebrated baseball controversies, the game mattered very little in the final analysis as the Yankees finished in third place and the Royals ended up twenty games out of the running. The Royals would bring a World Series title to Kansas City in 1985, but the Yankees would wait much longer, finally ending a dry spell in 1996.

Well over a hundred home runs were lost to rainouts or human error in the years prior to video replay, but very few were of the game-winning variety. Sammy Sosa suffered a fate similar to Brett during a game against the Reds in 1997. The score was tied at one in the ninth, when "Slammin' Sammy" cracked an apparent homer to left field. Third base umpire Frank Pulli ruled the ball fair, but as Sosa was rounding the bases with what would have held up as the deciding run, home plate umpire Greg Bonin overruled the initial call, declaring a foul ball. The game went into extra innings and the Cubs ended up losing, 4–1. Pulli later claimed he had lost Sosa's drive in the lights.

Wild Card Tiebreaker Game
Rockies vs. Padres, October 1, 2007

When you hang around the majors long enough, trouble is bound to find you. Despite his sterling reputation, umpire Tim McClelland landed himself in hot water during the 2007 NL Wild Card tie-breaker game. Lingering doubts remain about McClelland's call on a close play at home plate, which gave the Colorado Rockies a 9–8 win.

On May 22, the Rockies were eight games below .500 and sitting in last place. Few fans or insiders could have predicted then that the club would go 14–1 down the stretch and advance to the NLDS. With two games remaining in the season, the San Diego Padres needed just one win to clinch a Wild Card berth. When they failed to get the job done, a one-game showdown against Colorado became necessary.

Since the Rockies had won ten of eighteen head-to-head meetings, they were given home-field advantage. It was a definite advantage to hitters. At 5,280 feet above sea level, Coors Field has the highest elevation of any major league ballpark. The thin, dry air allows balls to travel farther and wreaks havoc on pitchers. Dramatically illustrating this point, the Rockies led the NL in runs scored at home while ranking last in runs on the road every year from 2012 through 2015.

Neither the Padres nor the Rockies had difficulty generating offense in 2007. The Colorado attack was led by leftfielder Matt Holliday, who captured a batting title that year with a .340 mark. Additionally, he paced the NL in doubles and RBIs. Right fielder Brad Hawpe added 116 ribbies of his own and first baseman Todd Helton chipped in with 61 extra-base hits while batting .320. The San Diego offense was driven by shortstop Khalil Greene and first baseman Adrian Gonzalez, who combined for 57 homers and 197 runs batted in. The Padres had the edge in the pitching department with Cy Young Award–winner Jake Peavy anchoring their staff along with closer Trevor Hoffman, who was baseball's all-time saves leader at the time.

When Rockies manager Clint Hurdle announced to the team that the Padres were sending Peavy to the mound for the tie-breaker game, rookie infielder Troy Tulowitzki joked: "We've got no f---ing chance!"[49] This cracked everyone in the clubhouse up. The Rockies actually weren't worried at all. They had overcome so much to get where they were, players felt destined to win. Hurdle assigned pitching duties to right-hander Josh

Fogg. Though he had the highest ERA among Colorado starters, Fogg had earned the nickname "The Dragon Slayer" for his ability to outduel opposing aces all season long.

As it turned out, neither starting pitcher was up to the task. The Rockies jumped out to an early 3–0 lead, which evaporated in the top of the third when Adrian Gonzalez belted a grand slam off Josh Fogg. Both teams gradually picked away at each other after that. In the eighth, San Diego capitalized on a rare miscue by Matt Holliday, who misjudged a catchable two-out fly, allowing it to sail over his head for a game-tying double. At the end of the ninth inning, the game was knotted at six.

Things remained relatively quiet until the thirteenth inning, when Padres leftfielder Scott Hairston blasted a two-run homer off Colorado reliever Jorge Julio. Julio was replaced by Ramon Ortiz, who was the tenth Rockies pitcher to take the mound. He retired all three of the batters he faced.

Looking to ensure a postseason berth for his club, Padres skipper Bud Black inserted Hoffman into the game. Hoffman knew a little bit about adversity. As an infant, he suffered an arterial blockage, which resulted in the removal of a kidney. During his formative years, he chose baseball because he wasn't allowed to play football or wrestle. A shortstop in the minors, he was converted to pitching when he demonstrated his ability to throw in the 95 mile per hour range. Unfortunately, a rotator cuff injury in 1995 robbed him of his speed. He learned how to throw a nasty changeup instead, which became his signature pitch. A seven-time All-Star, Hoffman received serious Cy Young consideration on four occasions. He was inducted into the Hall of Fame in 2018, but that decision was not based on his performance against the Rockies in the 2007 regular season finale.

Todd Helton told a reporter: "The feeling I had when Hairston hit that home run was painful. Yet we [went] back to the dugout and everybody was saying, 'guys, we never said it was going to be easy.'"[50] It wasn't. In fact, the Rockies needed a little help from home plate umpire Tim McClelland.

Kazuo Matsui greeted Hoffman with a leadoff double. Troy Tulowitzki followed with another double, scoring Matsui. For Hoffman, the nightmare was just beginning as Matt Holliday tripled, tying the game. With nobody out, Helton was intentionally walked. Plenty of managers would have pulled Hoffman at that point, but Black was willing to stake the Padres' entire season on his bullpen ace.

Jamey Carroll, a utility infielder who had originally been inserted as a pinch-runner, stepped in to face Hoffman with the winning run on third.

He had entered the game with a .222 average and later admitted he was shocked to be standing at the plate in such a critical situation. "I knew that Hoffman usually tried to get ahead and get away with his fastball on a first pitch," Carroll said later. "So if there was ever a time to swing at a first pitch, that was it."[51]

Adhering to that strategy, Carroll sent a solid line drive to right field. Though the ball was barely deep enough to get a run in, Holliday took it upon himself to tag and try for home. He was off and running before third base coach Mike Gallego gave him the green light. Brian Giles caught Carroll's liner and made a strong throw that bounced in front of catcher Michael Barrett. Holliday executed a headfirst slide and scraped his chin on the ground. As he slid past the plate, he tried to touch it with his hand, but was impeded by Barrett's left foot. Whether or not he tagged the plate remains up in the air. Holliday himself wasn't even sure, remarking after the game: "The umpire called me safe. That's all I know."[52]

Before the play, McClelland was standing on the third base side of the plate, where he kicked Carroll's bat aside. He scrambled out of the way as Holliday came barreling home and was still in motion as Giles's throw arrived. The arbiter was standing a fair distance away from the action and did not appear to have a direct view. Noting that Barrett had failed to hang onto Giles's relay, McClelland hesitated briefly before rendering a "safe" call. Barrett applied the tag shortly after the signal was made.

The decision continued to haunt Black, who groused to a writer ten years after the fact: "Barrett got his foot out there, Holliday's hand was pushed away and he just kept on going and he never hit home plate."[53] His opinion was a popular one. Jeffrey Marcus of the *New York Times* contended that the Rockies won "with a sleight of hand."[54] Mark Kiszla of *The Denver Post* remarked: "when folks retell this story a hundred years from now, [Holliday] still will not have touched home plate."[55] Numerous other sources agreed.

McClelland himself admitted to having lingering doubts but said that he would make the same call again given another opportunity. "There was no position I could have been in to see it any better," he insisted. "I might have gotten a different look at it, but I don't think I would have gotten a better look at it."[56]

The Rockies made the most of the opportunity, sweeping the Phillies in the NLDS and the Diamondbacks in the NLCS. They finally met their match in the World Series as the Red Sox outgunned them by a cumulative score of 29–10 in four games. As of this writing, the Rockies had yet to return to the Fall Classic. It's interesting to note that, whenever the Rockies magical 2007 season is recounted, the focus invariably shifts back to a questionable call made by one of the game's most respected umpires.

The 2007 Wild Card tie-breaker is not the only one on record. In 2013, a tie-breaker round was necessary in the American League when the Texas Rangers and Tampa Bay Rays finished with identical 91–71 records. The Rangers were awarded home field advantage since they had won the regular series. It didn't help as the Rays jumped out to a 3–0 lead on a third inning homer by Evan Longoria then held on for a 5–2 win. The game was refreshingly free from controversy. Tampa Bay advanced to the Division Series with a Wild Card victory over the Indians but lost to the Red Sox in the ALDS.

Bill Hohn's Fist Bump
Braves vs. Marlins, July 29, 2009

Former MLB Umpire Development Director Mike Fitzpatrick once said that good judgment and character are among the most important qualities an arbiter can have since "the whole integrity of the game rests with the umpire out on the field."[57] To maintain that integrity, an official must be impartial at all times. On the above date, veteran arbiter Bill Hohn dramatically failed to keep up appearances.

In a 2013 interview, Hohn described himself as an aggressive umpire who "took care of things" on the field.[58] At times, he was accused of going to extremes. In 1992, he attempted to have a fan removed from Fulton County Stadium for making a rude gesture at him. In 2010, he ejected Houston pitcher Roy Oswalt for talking to himself. And in 2009, Hohn tossed five members of the Braves in a span of two games, causing many to believe he held a personal grudge against the team.

Hohn's alleged vendetta surfaced on June 21 at Fenway Park. Red Sox right fielder J.D. Drew was facing Braves reliever Eric O'Flaherty in the seventh inning. With the count at 0–2, Hohn called a ball on a pitch that was well within the strike zone. O'Flaherty was visibly upset but held his tongue. On the next offering, Drew lined a ball off the Green Monster in left field, giving the Red Sox a 5–4 lead. O'Flaherty, along with manager Bobby Cox, ended up being ejected for arguing balls and strikes. When

Chipper Jones voiced his disapproval from his third base post, he was tossed out as well.

Hohn's next assignment with the Braves came on July 29 at Land Shark Stadium in Miami. The Marlins were leading, 6–3, in the eighth inning when Atlanta's catcher, Brian McCann, took a 1–0 fastball from reliever Dan Meyer. Replays showed that the pitch was way outside, but Hohn called it a strike. McCann didn't like the decision and blurted in disgust: "Oh, my God!"[59] Hohn glared at him disapprovingly from behind the plate as play resumed. On the next pitch, McCann grounded into a double play, complaining bitterly on his way back to the dugout.

Things escalated when Hohn heard shouting coming from the Atlanta bench. The hot-headed official called time and sauntered over to confront manager Bobby Cox. In the ensuing debate, he pulled the lineup card from his pocket and told Cox that he intended to remove someone from the game. When the Atlanta skipper offered to take the fall, Hohn gladly obliged him. A bit later, McCann got into it again with Hohn as he resumed his catching duties. He was promptly ejected. It was the eighth expulsion issued by Hohn that season.

With his temper already in doubt, Hohn raised serious concerns about his objectivity at the game's conclusion. After centerfielder Nate McClouth struck out, completing a 6–3 Florida win, Hohn engaged in a fist-bump with Marlins catcher John Baker. The gesture created quite a stir around the league.

Chipper Jones called the fist-bump "shocking" and contended that Hohn had a personal bias against the Braves. "I've never seen it before in my sixteen years," he said. "[Players and umpires] exchange banter all the time, but never a handshake or a fist bump."[60]

No formal reprimand was ever issued, but bloggers continued to buzz about the incident for several weeks. Writing for the popular Atlanta Braves fansite, *Tomahawk Take*, Ray Kelsey flamboyantly stated: "Umpires, like judges in a courtroom, are official arbiters, who, when garbed in black, must be absolutely devoid of humanity. They aren't meant to be colorful or mysterious or affable. They are meant to be as impersonal as the chalk lines that determine fair and foul balls—the integrity of the game demands it. For an umpire to display even the slightest lodge type conviviality is wrong."[61]

Hohn, who became a full-time National League arbiter in 1989, grew increasingly intolerant as the years wore on. He issued twenty-one expulsions in his final three seasons—well above the major league average. In addition to his tempestuous relationship with Bobby Cox (whom he banished six times), Hohn had an ongoing feud with manager Jim Fregosi. Asked about his relationship with players over the years, Hohn denied that he had ever crossed any lines. "I never got close to a player or manager and I never spoke much to any of them," he insisted.[62] In the end, it was medical issues—not poor judgment—that chased him into retirement. He called it quits before the 2012 season due to recurrent back and neck problems.

19-Inning Marathon Ended by Jerry Meals's Blown Call
Braves vs. Pirates, July 26, 2011

There's an old Bible verse that says: "The truth will set you free." In more than two decades as a major league umpire, Jerry Meals has faced many inconvenient truths, and he has maintained his integrity by publicly acknowledging his mistakes on more than one occasion. His most glaring error ended an epic duel that involved over forty players and took 609 pitches to complete. He handled the resulting controversy with dignity and professionalism.

Among the most respected umpires of the current era, Meals was promoted to permanent crew chief in 2015. Despite his great success, there are certain games he would probably like to forget—particularly the nineteen-inning marathon at Turner Field.

Entering the 2011 campaign, the Pirates were looking to end a streak of eighteen consecutive losing seasons. They got off to a pretty good start, beginning the last week of July in a first-place tie with the Cardinals, but Meals' conspicuous faux pas in Atlanta somehow triggered an epic Pittsburgh collapse.

At six hours and thirty-nine minutes, the July 26 showdown between the Braves and Pirates was the longest ever played at Turner Field. Fifteen pitchers were used and 391 strikes were recorded. A total of thirty-nine runners were left on base as fifteen consecutive innings elapsed without a run. The temperature was a sizzling ninety-one degrees when play began but had cooled considerably by the time the last pitch was thrown shortly before 2 am.

Most of the scoring took place early on. In the top of the first, Pirates leftfielder Xavier Paul singled off starter Tommy Hanson. Paul stole second and advanced to third on a ground-out by Garrett Jones. Neil Walker drove Jones home with a triple and Pedro Alvarez delivered a run-scoring single. In the second inning, catcher Michael McKenry extended Pittsburgh's lead with a solo homer.

The Pirates' advantage was erased in the third when starter Jeff Karstens allowed five consecutive hitters to reach base. Dan Uggla drove in a run and Jason Heyward collected two RBIs of his own as the Braves rallied to tie the game. The score remained knotted at three until the following morning.

Many among the crowd of 22,000-plus had departed by the time a glimmer of offense suddenly materialized in the bottom of the nineteenth inning. Infielder Julio Lugo drew a one-out walk off reliever Daniel McCutchen. He moved to third on a Jordan Schafer single. Schafer advanced to second due to defensive indifference, bringing right-hander Scott Proctor to the plate. Proctor was Atlanta's eighth pitcher of the night. He had limited experience as a hitter, having logged just four prior plate appearances. With the game on the line, Proctor rapped a routine grounder to third. Alvarez fielded it cleanly as Lugo bolted for home. The throw arrived in plenty of time, allowing McKenry to tag the runner more than a foot in front of the plate. The result appeared obvious to everyone involved—except for Meals, who flagrantly blew the call, handing Atlanta a 4–3 walk-off win.

"The game deserved better," said Pirates manager Clint Hurdle. "You'd like to see the game finished by the players, win or lose, and for it to end that way is as disappointing as it gets."[63]

Meals was ambivalent about his decision initially, commenting to reporters: "I looked at the replays and it appeared he might have got him on the shin area. I'm guessing he might have got him, but when I was out there when it happened I didn't see a tag. I just saw the glove sweep up. I didn't see it hit his leg."[64]

The Pirates lodged a complaint to Commissioner Bud Selig, prompting executive vice president of baseball operations, Joe Torre, to acknowledge Meals' error. "Obviously what he saw initially was different from what you and I saw," Torre said. "I think after reviewing it, Jerry realized he could have made a different call."[65]

In subsequent interviews, Meals took full responsibility for what happened, stating definitively: "On one particular replay, I was able to see that Lugo's pant leg moved ever so slightly.... That's telling me I was incorrect in my decision and that he should have been ruled out and not safe."[66]

Meals' confession did nothing to prevent the Pirates from going into a tailspin. After the disheartening 19-inning defeat, the club embarked on a dismal 3–15 run. This included ten consecutive losses from July 29 through August 7. The Bucs ended the season at 70–92—adding to their long string of sub-.500 finishes. The curse was finally lifted in 2013, when National League MVP Andrew McCutchen guided the club to a Wild Card berth.

PART THREE

The Victors and the Spoils: Playoff Controversies

....

The Jeffrey Maier Game
Yankees vs. Orioles, October 9, 1996

In Game 7 of the 2003 ALCS, Aaron Boone hit a memorable walk-off homer, giving the Yankees their fifth pennant in a six-year span. Before the historic moment, Derek Jeter promised Boone that he would be helped by ghosts. Jeter firmly believed that the spirits of great players and great teams kept watch over Yankee Stadium, causing inexplicable things to happen on the field. The Yankee shortstop had good reason to harbor this belief since he had experienced many strange and wonderful happenings during his tenure in the Bronx. One such incident occurred during Game 1 of the 1996 ALCS.

By the mid–'90s, the Yankees had been excluded from postseason play for more than a decade. Their fortunes changed dramatically with the arrival of the "Core Four"—a quartet of rising superstars that included Jeter, Mariano Rivera, Andy Pettitte, and Jorge Posada. After earning a Wild Card berth in 1995, the Bombers finished on top of the AL East the following year. They made quick work of the Rangers in the ALDS, moving one step closer to their first pennant since 1981.

The 1996 Orioles were a team geared toward offense. While the pitching staff compiled an unwieldy 5.14 ERA, Baltimore hitters ranked first among AL clubs in home runs and third in runs scored. Sporting a quartet of future Cooperstown inductees—Cal Ripken, Eddie Murray, Roberto Alomar and Mike Mussina—the O's placed first in a tight Wild Card race. They bowled over the Indians in the ALDS, earning the right to battle the Yankees for the AL crown.

Game 1 of the ALCS was an epic duel that was decided in extra innings. The Orioles hacked away at starter Andy Pettitte, building a 4–2 lead. A generous bases-loaded walk by Baltimore reliever Armando Benitez in the seventh brought the Yankees one run closer. In the bottom of the eighth, Jeter's "ghosts" finally showed up.

With one out and Benitez still on the mound, Jeter launched a deep fly to right field. Tony Tarasco settled under it and appeared poised to make the catch when a 12-year-old fan named Jeffrey Maier reached over the wall and deflected the ball into the stands. Fans are allowed to keep balls hit into the bleachers but are not permitted to tamper with live ones on the field. Spectator interference is called on such occasions with the play being ruled dead and the batter being called out or awarded a discretionary number of bases. In this case, right field umpire Rich Garcia may not have had a clear view of Jeter's drive as he declared it a game-tying home run.

There were a few moments of umpire Rich Garcia's career he would probably have liked to forget. In Game 1 of the 1996 ALCS, he failed to call fan interference on a game-tying home run by Derek Jeter. The meddling fan, a twelve-year-old boy named Jeffrey Maier, became a minor celebrity in New York (National Baseball Hall of Fame Library, Cooperstown, N.Y.).

Garcia had played on the U.S. Marine Corps baseball team before joining the American League staff in 1975. He was the first Hispanic umpire in the AL. Establishing a reputation as a consistent performer, he was promoted to crew chief in 1985. His blown call on the "Jeffrey Maier Homer" was not one of his finest moments. In fact, it proved to be disastrous for the Orioles as outfielder Bernie Williams blasted a walk-off shot in the bottom of the eleventh, giving the Yankees a 5–4 win. The Orioles lodged a protest to American League president Gene Budig, but the appeal was denied since judgment calls could not be overturned at the time.

Garcia later admitted that Maier had interfered with the play but insisted that the ball was not catchable. Before Game 2, he could be seen on national television laughing with New York fans and signing autographs. Behind this convincing façade, however, the arbiter was deeply troubled. "It was awful," he admitted years later. "I didn't sleep that night. I agonized the whole winter over it. It [ate me] up inside."[1]

The epilogue was favorable for nearly everyone involved. The Yankees ended up being crowned champions of baseball in 1996. The Orioles won the AL East the following year. Jeter went on to collect 200 post-season hits—more than any player in history. After experiencing his fifteen minutes of fame, Jeffrey Maier enjoyed a successful college baseball career with a Division III school, eventually earning a tryout with the Yankees.

Interestingly, Garcia was visited by the "ghosts" of Yankee Stadium again during Game 1 of the 1998 World Series. (Full details of the incident can be found in the next chapter.) In 1999, Garcia participated in a mass resignation spear-headed by union supervisor Richie Phillips. Negotiations backfired and Garcia's resignation was among the many that were unexpectedly accepted. He ended up working as a consultant to the Commissioner's office, landing an eventual promotion to a supervisory position. In 2002, he was placed on probation when it was discovered that he had associated with Florida-based gamblers during the late–'80s.

On a final note, it should be mentioned that Jeter was not alone in his belief that the old Yankee Stadium was "haunted." One of the earliest comments on record can be traced to a 1947 radio broadcast in which Red Barber mentioned the names of several deceased Yankee greats and alleged that they would be present at the World Series that year. In 1962, a *New York Times* writer claimed that the spirits of Babe Ruth and Lou Gehrig still inhabited the stadium. Multiple others have expressed the same belief, including former Yankee manager Buck Showalter, who claimed to have regularly heard eerie noises inside the stadium during the early morning hours. "Everybody believes it," said retired slugger Jason Giambi. "Everybody laughs about it and jokes about it, but I've seen some weird things happen [there]."[2]

Livan Hernandez's 15-Strikeout Performance
Marlins vs. Braves, October 12, 1997

According to detailed statistical analysis, only nine percent of professional ballplayers get called to the majors. Among that elite group, less than fifty percent remain for more than three seasons. Pitcher Livan Hernandez defied the odds in spectacular fashion. His rise to stardom was one of the feel-good stories of 1997.

Born to a poor family in the Villa Clara Province of Cuba, Hernandez carried the Cuban National Team to Junior World Championships in 1992 and 1993. Following a masterful performance in the 1994 World Cup, he fled the country with the help of recruiter Joe Cubas. Signed by the Marlins in 1996, Hernandez joined their starting rotation in June of the following year. He became an overnight sensation, winning his first nine decisions while posting an ERA of 3.18.

The 1997 Marlins were known for their youth and spirit. Most of the players on their roster were below the age of thirty. Of the eight pitchers who made starting appearances during the 1997 slate, Hernandez was the youngest at twenty-two years of age. Prior to that season, the Marlins had never posted a winning record, but with Hernandez leading the way, the club surprised virtually everyone by capturing a Wild Card berth and sweeping the Giants in the NLDS.

Beginning in 1991, the Atlanta Braves made fourteen consecutive postseason appearances (discounting the strike-shortened 1994 season). Numerous members of those squads now have plaques hanging in Cooperstown, including "The Big Three"—a dominant pitching trio featuring Greg Maddux, Tom Glavine and John Smoltz. The 1997 incarnation of the club was comprised of the aforementioned players along with fellow Hall of Famer Chipper Jones. After disposing of the Astros in the Division Series by a combined score of 16–8, the Braves were heavily favored to eliminate the upstart Marlins in the NLCS.

Showing no fear, the Marlins came out swinging, roughing up Maddux in the opener and Smoltz in the third meeting. The series was tied at two games apiece when Hernandez made the first postseason start of his career at Pro Player Stadium in Miami. He was helped tremendously that evening by the generous calls of home plate umpire Eric Gregg.

Gregg was among the most colorful umpires of the modern era. A classic rags-to-riches story, he grew up in an impoverished West Philadelphia neighborhood known as "The Bottom." His father was an alcoholic and his sister died from drug abuse. Gregg had hopes of making it as a player, but weight issues prevented him from progressing beyond the high school level. He got his earliest umpiring experience with a local Little League, entering the minor league system at the age of twenty. When he arrived in the majors, he was among the youngest officials in history.

An enormous man believed by some to be pushing four-hundred pounds, Gregg received the nickname of "The Plump Ump." Renowned for his cheerful temperament, he could occasionally be seen belly-dancing with the Philly Phanatic between innings. He tended bar in the offseason and served as "commissioner" of The Wing Bowl, an annual eating contest held in Philadelphia. Despite his cartoon-like persona, Gregg was a highly respected official, earning six postseason assignments. He was just the third black umpire in history after Emmett Ashford and Art Williams.

The good-natured Gregg was nicknamed "The Plump Ump" for his expansive waistline. In Game 5 of the 1997 NLCS, his strike zone proved to be equally expansive as Marlins rookie Livan Hernandez set a postseason record with fifteen strikeouts. Many of those strikeouts were aided by overly generous calls (National Baseball Hall of Fame Library, Cooperstown, N.Y.).

During his twenty-plus seasons in the majors, Gregg established a notoriously liberal strike zone. Never was this more apparent than in Hernandez's Game 5 start. Using an assortment of fastballs, sliders and slow curves, the rookie right-hander set an NLCS record with fifteen strikeouts. Game footage revealed, however, that Gregg was consistently calling strikes on pitches that were well off the plate. Grilled about his performance in a postgame conference, the arbiter felt compelled to defend himself. "I'm surprised I'm getting these questions about my strike zone," he said. "Did you see anybody throwing helmets? Did you see me eject anybody? Everybody got along well. It was the same for both sides."[3]

While it's true that there were no major squabbles during the game, there was plenty of squawking afterward. Philadelphia journalist Jim Salisbury wrote: "The big umpire from West Philadelphia had a strike zone so wide, he could have slept in it."[4] Braves first baseman Fred McGriff remarked: "You couldn't even have hit some of those pitches."[5] Chipper Jones added: "I know I swung at a couple of pitches that were a foot outside. I asked Eric if they were strikes and he said 'yes.' I couldn't help but chuckle."[6]

Whether Gregg's expansive strike zone benefited both clubs equally remains in question. Though Braves starter Greg Maddux collected nine strikeouts in seven innings of work, only twenty-nine percent of his strikes were called. In contrast, forty-two percent of the strikes recorded by Hernandez were called by Gregg. A compelling fact: Hernandez never came terribly close to duplicating his record-setting performance in the 1997 NLCS. His second highest strikeout total in the postseason was six—a number he reached in 2002.

Capitalizing on Gregg's generosity, the Marlins emerged with a 2–1 victory. They polished off the Braves in Game 6, battering starter Tom Glavine for seven runs on ten hits. Completing a Cinderella story, they became the first Wild Card team to win the World Series, defeating the Indians in seven games.

Hernandez stuck around the majors for portions of three decades, winning 185 games (including the postseason) and appearing on two All-Star teams. From 2003–2005, he logged more innings of work than any pitcher in baseball. In addition to capturing MVP honors in the 1997 NLCS and World Series, he was named Pitcher of the Month in July of 2003 and Player of the Week during that same span. A competent batsman, he gathered fifty extra-base hits (including ten homers) during his career with 85 RBIs. His record for most strikeouts in an NL postseason game was broken by Kevin Brown of the Padres in 1998.

Though Gregg entered a weight program in 1996 following the on-field death of his colleague and friend, John McSherry, he ended up being fined in 1999 for exceeding the three-hundred-pound limit. He was among the many umpires who lost their jobs in an ill-fated labor dispute that year. He found employment at a Phillies ballpark restaurant, where he was regarded as a celebrity. The dispute between umpires and MLB dragged on until December of 2004, when Gregg accepted a $400,000 settlement. He died two years later of a massive stroke. Gregg's memoirs, written with Marty Appel, were released in 1990.

The 1998 ALCS Disaster
Yankees vs. Indians, October 6–October 13, 1998

In the late-'90s, postseason controversy seemed to follow the Yankees wherever they went. The 1998 ALCS was particularly chaotic as three games were affected by the errant calls of umpires. In a familiar pattern, it was the Bombers who benefited the most.

During the 1998 regular season, the Yankees set a franchise record for wins with 114. There was hardly a weakness to be found in the New York lineup. Centerfielder Bernie Williams captured a batting title with a .339 mark and shortstop Derek Jeter wasn't far behind at .324. Aging veterans Tim Raines, Darryl Strawberry, and Chili Davis made significant offensive contributions while the pitching staff handcuffed opponents all season long, posting the lowest ERA and the best WHIP average in the American League. On May 17, left-hander David Wells set the tone for the Yankees' historic run with a perfect game against the Twins. By the end of September, George Steinbrenner's indomitable crew had built a twenty-two-game lead in the standings.

Elsewhere in the American League, the Cleveland Indians finished first in the AL Central, where all four of their division rivals posted records below .500. They owed much of their success to an offense packed with speed and power. Kenny Lofton and Omar Vizquel combined for 91 stolen bases at the top of the order. Hitting behind them, Manny Ramirez, Jim Thome and Travis Fryman all exceeded the 25-homer mark. Four of five Cleveland starters finished with double digit win totals as right-handed closer Michael Jackson enjoyed the finest season of his career, collecting forty saves and posting a magnificent 1.55 ERA.

After polishing off their Division Series challengers, the Yankees and Indians met for the second consecutive October. The results were different this time around as the Yankees avenged their 1997 ALDS loss. Though they were helped tremendously by an umpiring miscue in the series finale, they came out on the short end of a questionable decision in Game 2.

On the heels of a 7–2 win in the opener, the Bombers failed to generate much offense in the second meeting. More than fifty-seven thousand fans at Yankee Stadium witnessed a tense pitching duel that lasted for four and a half hours. The game remained scoreless until the top of the fourth, when David Justice hit a solo homer off starter David Cone. The Yankees answered in the seventh as Scott Brosius delivered an RBI double off Cleveland ace Charles Nagy. The score remained tied at one until the top of the twelfth.

Jim Thome opened the frame with a single off reliever Jeff Nelson. Employing a "small-ball" strategy, Cleveland manager Mike Hargrove inserted the much speedier Enrique Wilson as a pinch-runner and instructed slugger Travis Fryman to lay down a bunt. Fryman's sacrifice was fielded cleanly by Tino Martinez, but the Yankee first baseman was unable to make an accurate throw since Fryman was running out of the baseline. Martinez's relay hit Fryman squarely in the back and rolled to the edge of the outfield grass. Instead of chasing after it, second baseman Chuck Knoblauch (who was covering first on the play) stood there arguing with umpire Ted Hendry for an interference call. Knoblauch's mental lapse allowed Wilson to stumble home (literally) with what would hold up as the winning run. Subjected to a barrage of criticism afterward, Knoblauch admitted to being stunned by Hendry's non-call.

Though the Yankee second baseman clearly should have chased down Martinez's wayward throw, his objection was reasonable. According to Rule 6.05(k), Fryman could have (and probably *should* have) been called out for running on the infield side of the grass and interfering with the throw. Yankee manager Joe Torre pointed this out after the game, griping to reporters: "It was so blatant. It was a terrible call." Taking things one step further, Torre complained that Hendry's strike zone also "stunk."[7] He was not alone in this assessment. A writer from the *Denver Post* remarked sarcastically: "Hendry's strike zone was so huge, it now has its own zoning laws."[8]

In Game 4, it was umpire Jim McKean's turn to generate controversy. In the fourth inning, Yankee right fielder Paul O'Neill walked and stole second. Bernie Williams worked another free pass off Cleveland starter Dwight Gooden, who appeared to be tiring. Designated hitter Chili Davis followed with a double, scoring O'Neill and sending Williams to third. With a chance to inflict more damage, Tino Martinez lifted a fly ball to Kenny Lofton in center field. Lofton clearly made the catch, but lost control of the ball while transferring it to his throwing hand. McKean, a veteran of twenty-five major league seasons, blew the call, ruling a no-catch. Lofton was charged with an error as the Yankees opened up a 3–0 lead.

McKean's follies continued in the top of the fifth inning, when Brosius singled and Jeter reached on a fielder's choice. With O'Neill at the plate, Jeter broke for second base. Indians catcher Sandy Alomar delivered a throw, but McKean got in the way. The ball hit the umpire's leg, allowing Jeter to advance to third. Aside from Alomar being charged with an error, there were no further repercussions as O'Neill struck out, stranding Jeter. The 4–0 Yankee victory evened the series at two games apiece.

Interestingly, the Canadian-born McKean had turned down scholarship offers from more than thirty colleges to play in the Canadian Football League. He had hoped to become a starting quarterback, but when he was forced into a punter's role, he attended NHL referee school. He officiated at the college level before completing his umpire certification course and landing a job in the big leagues. During the 1998 ALCS, he may have wondered if he had chosen the wrong sport.

With the Yankees on the verge of clinching the AL pennant, arbiter Ted Hendry made another mistake that had lasting consequences. Bernie Williams opened the third inning of Game 6 with a single off Charles Nagy. Chili Davis followed with a routine grounder to second baseman Enrique Wilson. Wilson made a serviceable throw to shortstop Omar Vizquel for the force, but Hendry called Williams safe, believing that Vizquel's foot had come off the bag. Replays proved that he was wrong. Later in the inning, Scott Brosius delivered a two-out homer, staking the Yankees to a 6–0 lead. Hendry's erroneous call loomed large when the Indians rallied for five runs in the fifth off David Cone. The Yankees tacked on a few insurance runs in the sixth, eliminating the Indians with a 9–5 victory.

Asked about Hendry's dubious third-inning decision, Bernie Williams was hesitant to express his opinion. "I don't know," said the soft-spoken outfielder. "I'd rather not comment about that. It will stir a lot of controversy."[9]

After breezing through all three rounds of the 1998 playoffs, the Yankees emerged with the all-time record for total victories in a season with 125. Hendry, who had begun his major league career in 1977, worked one more year before retiring with close to three thousand games of experience. In a poll conducted by the Major League Players Association at the end of the 1998 campaign, he was ranked among the worst AL umpires in multiple categories.

Aside from the playoff debacle of 1998, Hendry had several other stressful moments on the field. In 1979, he had an epic run-in with Orioles manager Earl Weaver after he failed to call interference in the wake of a collision at home plate. The explosive Weaver went into a tirade that lasted for nearly ten minutes. It ended with Weaver tearing up pieces of a rulebook he had shoved in Hendry's face. On another occasion, the arbiter was accidentally hit by catcher Joe Girardi's mask, forcing him out of a game between the Yankees and Rangers. Hendry sustained a wound on his forehead that required several stitches.

Over the course of twenty-two seasons, Hendry's extracurricular assignments included four League Championship Series and two All-Star Games in addition to one World Series (in 1990). He was behind the plate for Bret Saberhagen's no-hitter in 1991 and Jim Abbott's in 1993.

1999 ALCS: The Phantom Tag and Other Issues

*Yankees vs. Red Sox,
October 13–October 18, 1999*

Of all the ailments that can negatively impact the performance of athletes, "The Yips" are perhaps the most mysterious and poorly understood. The term is said to have originated during the 1920s in reference to a pro golfer named Tommy Armour, who developed a puzzling inability to sink short putts. In baseball, the disorder is also known as "Steve Blass Disease" or "Steve Sax Syndrome," taking its name from the two players who most famously suffered from it. Blass was an All-Star pitcher who inexplicably became incapable of throwing strikes. Sax was a talented infielder who could not produce accurate relays to first base. The strange ailment, which affects muscle memory and is accompanied by anxiety, can bring misery to the athletes who are afflicted with it. Such was the case with Chuck Knoblauch.

A gifted second baseman with remarkable speed, Knoblauch came up through the Twins farm system. He was named Rookie of the Year in 1991. Typically used as a lead-off hitter, he had an excellent feel for the strike zone, accruing an on-base percentage of .380 or better during seven of his twelve major league seasons. Before his trade to the Yankees, he had never experienced difficulty making throws to first. In fact, he captured a Gold Glove in 1997. But at some point during the 1999 campaign, he contracted a serious case of "The Yips," committing more errors than any player at his position—a majority of them on throws to first base. Though Knoblauch's fielding woes would intensify the following year, he muddled through the 1999 ALDS without a miscue. In the League Championship Series, his sloppy defense was neutralized on two occasions by the flawed judgments of umpires.

Facing the Red Sox in New York, the Yankees overcame a three-run deficit to send Game 1 into extra innings. Hall of Fame closer Mariano

Rivera was on the mound in the tenth, when Jose Offerman led off with a single. John Valentin, who had hit .303 against the Yankees during the regular season, rapped a grounder to Scott Brosius at third base. The sure-handed Brosius fielded it smoothly and threw to second, but the ball popped out of Knoblauch's glove. This was exactly the sort of thing that had been happening to the Yankee second baseman all year, but on this occasion, he received a gift from umpire Rick Reed.

Instead of rightfully awarding Offerman second base, Reed called him out on the grounds that Knoblauch had caught Brosius's relay then dropped it while transferring it to his throwing hand. Replays proved that this assumption was incorrect. With one out and Valentin at first, Rivera induced an inning-ending double play. Reed's mistake ended up being costly as Bernie Williams led off the bottom of the tenth with a homer, lifting the Yankees to a dramatic 4–3 win.

Asked about the disputed call at second base, Knoblauch smiled slyly and said: "You never say never, but I have rarely seen that call made where the guy is called safe. Rick Reed is a good umpire. If he wasn't, he wouldn't be umpiring in this situation."[10]

After reviewing the game footage, Reed was less confident in his abilities. "I thought [Knoblauch] had possession before he dropped the ball," the arbiter told reporters. "After we went in and looked at the tape, we decided that wasn't the case. As an umpire, it was my job to get it right and I didn't.... I feel awful."[11]

The Series continued without any major controversy until Game 4, when Knoblauch got a helping hand from umpire Tim Tschida. The Yankees were clinging to a tenuous 3–2 lead at Fenway Park, when starter Andy Pettitte surrendered a one-out single to Jose Offerman in the bottom of the eighth. Taking no chances, manager Joe Torre summoned Rivera from the Yankee bullpen. John Valentin hit a check-swing grounder to second base, where Knoblauch fielded the ball and waved his glove half-heartedly in Offerman's direction. Though Offerman evaded Knoblauch's "phantom tag" by a wide margin, Tschida called him out. Knoblauch, in spite of his ongoing battle with "The Yips," managed an accurate relay to first, completing the double play. Red Sox skipper Jimy Williams came out to argue, but Tschida's decision stuck. Since then, it has appeared on nearly every compiled list of baseball's worst umpiring decisions.

Incensed by Tschida's blunder, Red Sox fans treated the umpiring crew to a symphony of jeers. A six-run Yankee outburst in the top of the ninth inning put fans even more on edge. When umpire Dale Scott called Boston's All-Star shortstop Nomar Garciaparra out on a close play at first in the bottom of the frame, an embittered Williams came out to argue. Immediately following his ejection, fans littered the field with trash. The Yankees won, 9–2, taking a commanding three-games-to-one lead in the series. The Bombers polished off the Sox the following day, moving on to a World Series victory over the Atlanta Braves.

The Yankee-Red Sox rivalry is one of the most intense in all of sports. During the late–'90s and early–2000s, Sox fans were disappointed more often than not as Boston finished behind New York in the standings for eleven consecutive seasons. From 1998 through 2005, the Red Sox placed second to the Yankees in the AL East every year.

Aside from his embarrassingly bad call in the 1999 ALCS, umpire Tim Tschida generated very little controversy during his twenty-eight seasons in the majors. The only other incident of note occurred in 1987, when he removed Minnesota pitcher Joe Niekro from a game for scuffing up baseballs. Tschida told a writer that he didn't want to embarrass Niekro but had been forced to act when he caught the hurler red-handed with an emery board in his pocket. Tschida's notoriously small strike zone won him no favor with pitchers over the years but did not prevent him from aspiring to the position of crew chief in 2007.

Umpire Rick Reed suffered a stroke in 2008 but continued to call plays at the major league level through the 2009 campaign. A small-time actor in the offseason, he had bit-parts in a handful of movies. He is best known for his appearance in the 1999 Kevin Costner film, *For the Love of the Game,* in which he played a home plate umpire. He claimed to have been hit more than a dozen times during dress rehearsals due to actor John C. Reilly's inability to catch Costner's throws from the mound. At the time of his retirement from baseball, Reed had more than 3,400 games to his credit including the postseason.

Chuck Knoblauch's fielding difficulties continued in 2000 as he committed fifteen errors in 82 defensive assignments. Things came to a head during a game against the White Sox, when he made three throwing errors in a six-inning span—one of which hit an elderly woman in the stands. After the third miscue, he requested a meeting with Joe Torre between innings. The two men disappeared into the runway leading to the clubhouse. Torre returned, but Knoblauch did not. The four-time All-Star never appeared at second base again, finishing his career as a DH and left fielder. Curiously, he had no trouble throwing from the outfield to other stations, recording thirteen assists and four double plays in 182 appearances—numbers that were on par with the league average.

Pierzynski and the Uncaught Third Strike
White Sox vs. Angels, October 12, 2005

The official MLB website provides a list of some essential requirements for aspiring umpires. In addition to quick reflexes and 20/20 vision, good communication skills are cited as a prerequisite for a job in professional baseball. Sometimes, during complicated plays, the most basic skills are neglected by arbiters. During Game 2 of the 2005 ALCS, umpire Doug Eddings failed to effectively communicate one of his decisions while White Sox catcher A.J. Pierzynski was at the plate. As a result, the Angels ended up losing the game.

Entering the 2005 campaign, the White Sox had not won a championship in more than eight decades. Playing in the shadow of the 1919 World Series scandal, the ChiSox placed no higher than third every year from 1921 through 1956. A string of four consecutive postseason losses beginning in 1959 served only to bolster the legend of a "Black Sox Curse."

Breaking with tradition, the White Sox grabbed the AL Central lead on the first day of the 2005 campaign and hung on until season's end. Nine Chicago players clubbed twelve or more home runs as Paul Konerko led the team with forty. Run production was evenly distributed with five players gathering no fewer than seventy RBIs. Strong pitching helped galvanize the White Sox surprising pennant bid. Right-hander Jon Garland led the staff with eighteen wins and Mark Buehrle, Chicago's most consistent hurler for more than a decade, added sixteen wins while compiling a handsome 3.13 ERA.

In the AL West, the Angels posted the best record in their division for the second straight season. Thirty-two-year-old Bartolo Colon reached the pinnacle of his career, capturing the Cy Young Award with a league-high twenty-one victories. Staff mate John Lackey—a victim of fourteen no-decisions—posted an impressive 14–5 record. In the bullpen, closer Frankie Rodriguez (a.k.a. "K-Rod") saved forty-five games and averaged 12.2 strikeouts per nine innings. On the offensive side, Hall of Famer Vladimir Guerrero led the team with thirty-two homers, 108 ribbies and a .317 batting average. In the ALDS, the Angels succeeded where many other teams had failed, knocking off the Yankees in five games. It would end up being the high point of the season as they dropped four straight to the White Sox in the ALCS.

The Angels looked good in the series opener, winning a close game in which no runs were scored beyond the fourth inning. In the second meeting, the White Sox caught a major break on the final out of the game. The ChiSox manufactured a run in the first on a throwing error by Angels starter Jarrod Washburn. They led, 1–0, until the top of the fifth, when Robb Quinlan launched a solo homer off Buehrle. The score remained tied at one until the bottom of the ninth.

Facing reliever Kelvim Escobar, Carl Everett grounded out and Aaron Rowand went down on strikes. With a full count, Sox catcher A.J. Pierzynski swung through Escobar's signature splitter. Believing he had caught the pitch cleanly, Angels catcher Josh Paul rolled the ball toward the mound and headed off the field. Stationed behind home plate, Eddings signaled for the out, but gave no verbal indication that the play was dead. Remembering a similar situation from the previous year, Pierzynski bolted toward first base.

The rule that set Pierzynski in motion is commonly referred to as the uncaught third strike rule. It states that, when a catcher fails to cleanly handle a pitch on the fly for a third strike with first base open or with a runner on first and two outs, the batter immediately becomes a runner. In that event, a tag or a force out is required to retire the batter-runner. The rule also stipulates that a batter who does not recognize the situation and fails to run to first shall be declared out once he leaves the batting circle. In this case, Pierzynski took full advantage of the opportunity, reaching first base safely and leaving mass confusion in his wake.

Escobar said afterward: "I didn't see the ball hit the dirt, but I saw the umpire point and call him out. That's all I need to see."[12] Asked about the signal he had made, Eddings offered an ambiguous explanation: "My interpretation is that was my 'strike three mechanic' when it's a swinging strike. If you watch, that's what I do the entire game."[13] After reviewing the video, umpire supervisor Rich Reiker conceded that he could not determine conclusively whether or not the ball had hit the dirt. He was confident that the play should have continued, however, since Eddings did not make a verbal ruling on the catch. Josh Paul later griped about the arbiter's failure to vocalize his opinion that the ball had been trapped. But there is no rule obligating an umpire to do so. It's merely a courtesy typically extended to catchers.

Disappointed with the outcome, Mike Scioscia explained the play as follows: "It was a swing. Our catcher caught it. Doug Eddings called him out and, somewhere along the line, because the guy ran to first base, he altered the call."[14] *ESPN* senior writer Jim Caple sympathized with Scioscia, stating in his game report: "The first rule of umpiring is to make your calls clear to everyone and the video plainly shows that [Eddings] did not.... Had [he] given the Angels any indication at all that the pitch had not been caught, they would have had plenty of time to throw out the runner."[15]

The magnitude of Eddings' failure to communicate became painfully evident as Pablo Ozuna, pinch-running for Pierzynski, stole second base. White Sox third baseman Joe Crede then followed with a double, driving Ozuna home and evening the Series at a game apiece. Chicago won the next three meetings by a combined score of 19–7.

Analyzing the controversial play that only slightly detracted from the White Sox long overdue World Series victory, Konerko said: "I think the replay shows the guy caught the ball and it was strike three, but that's sports.... You are always playing as hard as you can outside the play. That means sometimes it's outside the whistle or the play and you force a guy to make a bad call. That's exactly what happened."[16]

After executing a sweep of the Astros in the World Series, the White Sox immediately fell back into a championship drought. As of 2020, the club had not made a postseason appearance in over a decade. Sadly, the glory of 2005 has been virtually forgotten. When the Cubs finally ended their long dry spell in 2016, multiple media outlets either accidentally overlooked or deliberately failed to mention that the Sox had brought a World Series title to Chicago during the twenty-first century. Among the offending parties were *ESPN SportsCenter, CBS This Morning* and *The Washington Post.*

Still active at the time of this writing, Doug Eddings is known for his generous strike zone. Statistics published by *The Hardball Times* in 2011 indicated that it was the largest in the majors that season. Eddings has a low-key style on the field and prides himself on being able to handle player disputes effectively. "As long as they aren't saying anything personal to me, they can pretty much do what they want," he told a reporter. "I don't take most of it personally and I love what I do. After all, it's baseball. It is what it is."[17] Interestingly, Eddings once said that he would have pursued a career as a secret service agent had he not become an umpire.

The uncaught third strike rule has haunted other teams in the past. The Brooklyn Dodgers were one strike away from tying the 1941 World Series at two games apiece when Yankee outfielder Tommy Henrich swung through a 3–2 offering made by reliever Hugh Casey. The pitch eluded Brooklyn catcher Mickey Owen, allowing Henrich to reach first. The Yankees rallied for four runs, taking a commanding three-games-to-one lead. They clinched the Series the following day.

Midges Invade Jacob's Field
Yankees vs. Indians, October 5, 2007

Since a majority of major league stadiums are outdoor venues, players and officials are at the mercy of the elements. Over the course of baseball history, games have been profoundly affected by rain, snow, lightning and other natural factors. In Game 2 of the 2007 ALDS between the Yankees and Indians, the final score was impacted by a massive swarm of insects. During the infestation, which lasted close to an hour, umpires sat idly by allowing play to continue as the game unraveled for New York.

Located along the shores of Lake Erie, the city of Cleveland hosts tiny visitors known as midges or "mayflies" every year. The insects begin their life cycle as larvae at the bottom of lakes, streams or standing water. Though they don't bite or carry disease, they are attracted to moisture on human skin and can be a major nuisance. During the 1960s, Lake Erie was so polluted that the bugs vanished. But a colossal cleanup effort inadvertently brought them back to the metropolitan area during the 1990s.

Typically, midges swarm about three or four times per year and linger for a few days. They appear shortly after dusk and gravitate toward artificial light. Uncommonly warm October temperatures unleashed a new generation of the pests upon Jacobs Field during the game in question.

A Wild Card entry in 2007, the Yankees were making their thirteenth consecutive playoff appearance. The Indians—absent from the postseason since 2001—compiled the best record in the American League then breezed to a 12–3 win against New York in the series opener. A capacity crowd of more than forty-four thousand played witness to the forces of nature in Game 2.

Among the most reliable performers in Yankee history, southpaw Andy Pettitte kept the Cleveland bats quiet until the seventh inning, when reliever Joba Chamberlain was summoned to stifle a one-out rally. Playing in his first season, Chamberlain had been spectacular in nineteen appearances for the Yankees, averaging well over a strikeout per inning while posting a 0.38 ERA. True to form, the hard-throwing right-hander got two quick outs, preserving a fragile 1–0 lead.

And then the swarm appeared.

Cleveland starter Roberto Hernandez got through the top of the eighth uneventfully, but the problem intensified when the Indians came to bat. Soon after taking the mound, Chamberlain was beset by the winged creatures, which are sometimes referred to as "fuzzy bills" on account of their bushy antennae. Reflecting on his experience years later, the former Yankee reliever remarked: "It happened really fast. I didn't really know what was going on.... You can't prepare for it.... Obviously, you have distractions everywhere, but when they're flying in your face and in your ears...."[18]

Yankee trainer Gene Monahan was sent to the mound to spray Chamberlain with insect repellant, inspiring a Cleveland bug expert (who was watching the game on television) to contact the Indians' front office with a warning that the moisture would only attract more pests. As predicted, Chamberlain became a bug magnet. At one point, he looked into the Yankee dugout and complained that he couldn't see. This prompted a second visit from Monahan, who doused the reliever with more insect bait. The results were catastrophic for the Yankees. With midges cavorting all over his face and neck, the rookie hurler game unglued.

After issuing a lead-off walk to Grady Sizemore, Chamberlain uncorked a wild pitch, moving the runner to second. Asdrubal Cabrera sacrificed Sizemore to third, bringing up the dangerous Travis Hafner, who had averaged more than thirty homers per year over the previous three seasons. Hafner lined out to first, but Chamberlain threw another wild pitch with Victor Martinez at the plate, tying the score. Obviously in distress at that point, Chamberlain hit Martinez with a pitch then walked Ryan Garko before recording the final out. The game stretched into the eleventh inning, when Hafner delivered a walk-off single. The Indians eventually eliminated the Yankees in four games.

New York manager Joe Torre later expressed deep regret about not pulling his team off the field. Since there were no bugs in the Yankee dugout, he didn't realize how bad the situation was at the time. Neither did right field umpire Bruce Froemming, who said he never considered stopping the game at any point. "It was just a little irritation," he commented afterward. "I've seen bugs and mosquitoes since I started umpiring. It might not be a perfect scenario, [but] within about forty-five minutes, basically they were gone."[19]

There were plenty who felt that Froemming downplayed the significance of the insect foray. In Boston, where team officials were following the game on television, one executive remarked incredulously: "I can't believe they're playing in that."[20] Indians hitting coach Derek Shelton described the scenario as "shocking."[21] Yankee third base coach, Larry Bowa, asserted: "Hindsight being 20/20, we should have said 'everyone get off the field.' It would have been like a downpour, where you say, 'we can't play in these conditions.'"[22] Home plate umpire Laz Diaz, who was in the thick of things behind home plate, kept swatting at the air and even sprayed himself with repellant, but since Torre did not lodge an official complaint, the veteran arbiter allowed the game to continue.

Unhappy with Torre's failure to handle the situation (and the series loss in general), Yankee owner George Steinbrenner hired Joe Girardi to manage the club in 2008. Chamberlain, on the other hand, never faulted Torre for not requesting a stoppage of play. "It wasn't on him. It was on me," the hurler affirmed. "If I would've said, 'I can't get through this,' it would've been different."[23]

The 2007 "Bug Game" (as it has come to be known) was not the only one disrupted by flying insects. Other infestations have prompted interventions from officials. During a gnat invasion at Ebbets Field in 1946, umpires stopped the game because the waving of scorecards by fans was causing a major distraction to players. A 1959 game at Comiskey Park was temporarily delayed while members of the grounds crew used smoke bombs to ward off a horde of gnats, and a 1972 Texas League game was called off due to a grasshopper incursion.

Midges returned to Cleveland during a 2016 matchup against Houston, wreaking havoc on pitcher Carlos Carasco. One of the pests flew into the hurler's eye as he was delivering a pitch to Astros first baseman Yuli Gurriel. Play was halted briefly while a team trainer extracted the insect. When the game resumed, a distracted Carasco surrendered a single to Gurriel and a two-run homer to outfielder Colby Rasmus. Cleveland weathered the storm with a 6–5 win.

2009 Playoffs: The Fall Guys
October 7–October 26

In August of 2008, Commissioner Bud Selig finally approved the use of video review to challenge questionable home runs. But after a rash of blown calls in multiple rounds of the 2009 playoffs, the argument in favor of using replay for other situations grew even stronger. In an attempt to address the growing problem, MLB fired three umpire supervisors during the offseason.

The trouble began in Game 1 of the American League Division Series, which pitted the Angels against the Red Sox. The Angels had finished ten games ahead of the Rangers in the AL West while the Red Sox had run away with the Wild Card. The game was scoreless in the fourth inning when Boston's Jon Lester induced a two-out grounder off the bat of Howie Kendrick. BoSox shortstop Alex Gonzalez came up with the ball, but his throw pulled Kevin Youkilis off the bag at first. Youkilis, a Gold Glove winner in 2007, tagged Kendrick in front of the base. Though replays proved definitively that Kendrick was out, first base umpire C.B. Bucknor called him safe.

Bucknor's errant fourth inning decision came at no cost to the Red Sox as Lester escaped without any further damage. In the bottom of the fifth, Bucknor was at the center of attention again when he called Angels third baseman Chone Figgins out on a very close play at first. Figgins, who was attempting to sacrifice teammate Erick Aybar to third, appeared to beat the throw though replays were inconclusive. The questionable verdict did not deter the Angels from taking a 3–0 lead on a homer by Torii Hunter.

Completing the hat trick, Bucknor stirred up more controversy in the sixth. Kendrick led off the inning with a ground ball to third. Boston's Mike Lowell handled it and threw off-target to Youkilis at first. The 6-foot-2 Youkilis leaped for the throw and landed on the bag ahead of Kendrick, but in a moment of déjà vu, Bucknor called him safe again. No runs were scored that inning, but Bucknor's multiple lapses invited a stream of scathing comments from the press. The Angels eliminated the Red Sox in three games, moving on to face the Yankees, who got a little boost of their own from the men in blue.

Coming off a convincing 7–2 win in the Division Series opener, the Yankees battled the Twins to a 1–1 tie through seven innings in Game 2. Reliever Phil Hughes retired the first two Minnesota batters he faced in the eighth before surrendering a run on a walk and a pair of singles. Summoned from the bullpen, Mariano Rivera got the third out, but not before yielding an RBI single to right fielder Denard Span. The Twins led, 3–1, until the bottom of the ninth, when Yankee slugger Alex Rodriguez—noted for his inability to deliver clutch hits in the postseason—came through with a game-tying homer. The final outcome was dramatically influenced by umpire Phil Cuzzi's blunder in the eleventh inning.

Joe Mauer, who had captured his third batting title with a .365 mark during the regular season, led off the top of the eleventh with a fly ball that deflected off the glove of Yankee left fielder Melky Cabrera. Mauer's drive landed in fair territory then bounced into the stands. Instead of calling it a ground rule double, Cuzzi mistakenly indicated that the ball had gone foul. The decision ended up being catastrophic. Had Mauer's double counted, he would likely have scored the go-ahead run on subsequent singles by Jason Kubel and Michael Cuddyer. Instead, the Twins ended up stranding all three of their base runners that inning. In the bottom of the frame, Mark Teixeira delivered a walk-off homer, giving the Yankees a 2–0 series lead. The New Yorkers completed the sweep a couple of days later in Minnesota.

Cuzzi felt awful about his mistake, telling one journalist: "There is no excuse. I missed the play.... As badly as many people on that field may have felt, I don't think any of them had a worse night's sleep than I did."[24]

In the American League Championship Series, it was Tim McClelland who was left with some explaining to do. In Game 4 between the Yankees and Angels, he blew two obvious calls. McClelland was not alone in his embarrassment. In the fourth inning, umpire Dale Scott allowed Yankee right fielder Nick Swisher to remain at second base after he was tagged out by shortstop Erick Aybar on a pickoff throw from pitcher Scott Kazmir. It ended up being a no-harm-no-foul situation when McClelland made an even bigger mistake on a play that followed. Swisher made it to third and should have scored on a sacrifice fly by centerfielder Johnny Damon, but McClelland called Swisher out, believing he had left the bag too early. Replays proved decisively that McClelland made the wrong decision.

Before the dust had settled, McClelland made another call that bordered on being ludicrous. With one out in the top of the fifth inning, the Yankees had Jorge Posada on third and Robinson Cano on second. Nick Swisher hit a tapper back to pitcher Darren Oliver. Oliver threw to catcher Mike Napoli, trapping Posada in a rundown. The Yankee backstop scampered to third as Cano arrived at the same station. Both runners were tagged while standing off the bag, but McClelland—in one of the most mystifying judgments in umpiring history—only called Posada out. The ruling had little effect on the Yankees 10–1 blowout win, but it raised serious questions about the competency of the major league umpiring staff.

A writer from *ESPN* sarcastically referred to Game 4 as "the worst umpiring performance at an Angels game since Leslie Nielsen in *The Naked Gun*."[25] McClelland, who had been subjected to harsh criticism in the wake of a terrible call that decided the 2007 NL Wild Card tie-breaker game, owned up to his oversight. "I thought Cano was on the base," he said. "The replay showed that Cano was off the bag when he was tagged. I did not see that for whatever reason. So obviously there were two missed calls."[26]

Derek Jeter tried to smooth things over afterward by commenting: "Umpires are trying their best. Sometimes you get calls and sometimes you don't. I don't think it had any effect on this game."[27] But the Yankee captain's words failed to stifle the ongoing debate.

In addition to the mistakes made by officials in the ALDS and ALCS, Game 3 of the National League Division Series was marred by yet another bad call. Chase Utley of the Phillies reached base safely after a ball he hit bounced off the ground and struck him in the knee. Home plate umpire Jerry Meals completely missed it, but he wasn't the only guilty party. Ron Kulpa blew the ensuing play on Utley, ruling that the foot of Rockies first baseman Todd Helton had come off the bag. This clearly was not the case.

As sportswriters rallied for the implementation of video review, MLB executives scrambled to find a practical solution to the problem. Before the World Series, it was announced that only veteran umpires would be used in the Fall Classic that year. Over the previous twenty-five seasons, introducing at least one "rookie" had been the standard practice.

Carrying things a step further, Major League Baseball dismissed three umpire supervisors before the 2010 campaign. The expelled parties—Marty Springstead, Jim McKean and Rich Garcia—had more than seventy seasons of combined experience. Springstead admitted to being "shocked" by the decision while Garcia reported feeling "sad." MLB executive vice president Rob Manfred gave no direct explanation for the firings, but the rationale was obvious. His official statement to the press was as follows: "The change in supervisors is part of our ongoing effort to make our organization as strong as possible."[28]

Blaming supervisors for the shortcomings of subordinates did not fix the problem. It was extremely short-sighted—especially in the case of C.B. Bucknor. Still active through 2019, Bucknor has been rated baseball's worst umpire in multiple player polls. His mistakes on the field have reinforced the popular belief that he is barely competent.

In April of 2017, Bucknor made one of the worst calls in recent history. Trailing the Nationals, 3–1, in the bottom of the ninth inning at home, the Braves had the bases loaded. Chase d'Arnaud was at the plate facing reliever Shawn Kelley. On a 1–2 pitch, d'Arnaud swung and missed for strike three. Though catcher Matt Wieters failed to catch the ball on the fly, he grabbed it off the ground and stepped on the plate to get the force out. Washington players had begun congratulating one another and were heading off the field when Bucknor—working behind the plate that day—called the umpires together for a conference. After a brief discussion, Bucknor changed the ruling from a game-ending strikeout to a dropped foul ball, thereby entitling d'Arnaud to another chance at the plate. Replays showed conclusively that d'Arnaud had missed Kelley's pitch by five or six inches. Foul tips were not reviewable under the existing rules.

Though the Nationals hung on for the 3–1 win, Bucknor was skewered by the media. TV analyst Ray Knight said "That's ridiculous, you're supposed to be a major league umpire, which means you're one of the best. This guy has struggled forever. I'm just gonna be candid with you—[Bucknor] has never been a good umpire."[29] *Sporting News* correspondent Jason Foster mirrored those thoughts, remarking: "Yes, the derision and disbelief over Bucknor's performance was universal. And yet, it was nothing new—because, again, everyone knows C.B. Bucknor is bad at his job."[30]

Also active through 2019, Phil Cuzzi's credits include seven Division Series, two NLCS and two All-Star Games. Aside from the Joe Mauer controversy, Cuzzi has come under fire on multiple other occasions. In 2010, his blown call at home plate deprived the Giants of a win. In 2011, he mistakenly issued a three-ball walk that went unchallenged and led to the only run in a 1–0 game.

As for the other offending members of the 2009 postseason crew, two of three were still active at the time of this writing. Despite a handful of high-profile mistakes, McClelland left the game in 2013 as one of the most respected arbiters of his era. Both Meals and Kulpa have had their share of troubles on the diamond.

During a 2019 game between the Astros and Rangers, Kulpa caused a major stir after he called a strike on a pitch that was practically in the dirt. The arbiter antagonized players in the Houston dugout by waving his arms and staring them down. This prompted three visits from manager A.J. Hinch, who ended up being ejected along with Astros hitting coach Alex Cintron. Not quite finished instigating trouble, Kulpa later pushed catcher Max Stassi and yelled at Houston starter Gerrit Cole. Recounting the incident, *CBS Boston* correspondent Michael Hurley wrote: "Temper tantrums, typically, are the province of toddlers. They are not supposed to be characteristic of the unbiased, unemotional arbiters of the rules on a sporting field of play."[31] Hinch spoke to MLB's chief baseball officer, Joe Torre, about the incident but no corrective action was taken.

2010 Playoffs: Bad Calls in Multiple Rounds
October 6–October 23, 2010

Sometimes, administrative changes are not the answer to problems within an organization. That fact became glaringly obvious to MLB executives in October of 2010. Despite the presence of three new umpire supervisors, the playoffs were a comedy of errors again.

In Game 1 of the ALDS at Tropicana Field, the Tampa Bay Rays were robbed of a golden scoring opportunity by home plate umpire Tim Welke. The Rays looked as if they would blow things wide open in the bottom of the first, loading the bases off Rangers starter Cliff Lee. With one out, first baseman Carlos Pena was hit in the hand by Lee's 2–1 offering. As Pena headed toward first base, Welke called him back, ruling that the ball had struck Pena's bat. Though video replays were inconclusive, the accompanying audio was quite compelling. Manager Joe Maddon came out to argue, but Welke, who was in his twenty-eighth season of major league service, stood firm on the call. Pena worked the count to 3–2 before striking out. Rocco Baldelli followed with another whiff, ending the inning uneventfully for Tampa Bay. The Rays managed just one run in a discouraging loss. They ended up dropping the series to Texas.

In the opening game of the other American League Division Series, right field umpire Chris Guccione nearly spoiled a happy ending for the Yankees. The Minnesota Twins jumped out to a 3–0 lead through five innings, but the Bombers battled back to carry a 6–4 advantage into the bottom of the ninth. With two out, Minnesota's left fielder Delmon Young hit a blooper to right field. Greg Golson, who had been inserted by Yankee manager Joe Girardi as a defensive replacement, charged after the ball and made a slick game-ending shoestring catch. Unfortunately, the game didn't end as it should have. After a conference with his crewmates, Guccione decided that Golson had trapped the ball. Though replays proved otherwise, the arbiter's glaring mistake brought the tying run to the plate in the form of slugger Jim Thome—a first-ballot Hall of Famer. What could have been a disastrous epilogue for New York ended anticlimactically as Thome popped out to third base. The Yankees ultimately swept the series.

The NLDS between the Giants and Braves was even messier as umpire Paul Emmel created problems on three separate occasions. Game 1 remained scoreless until the bottom of the fourth, when Buster Posey led off with a single. Never noted for his blazing speed, San Francisco's Rookie of the Year catcher attempted to record his first career steal off pitcher Derek Lowe, who had a reputation for being vulnerable to thefts. Posey was out by a mile at second, but Emmel botched the call. His decision was devastating to the Braves as Posey scored the only run of the game on a two-out single by outfielder Cody Ross. In a postgame interview, Posey admitted that Emmel's decision was highly suspect, remarking with tongue-in-cheek: "I guess it's a good thing we don't have instant replay."[32]

In Game 2, Emmel was in the hot seat again for a call he made at first base. With one out in the top of the second, Atlanta's Alex Gonzalez hit a sharp grounder to Giants shortstop Juan Uribe. The veteran infielder made a nice play snaring the ball, but his throw pulled Aubrey Huff off the bag. Emmel called Gonzalez out anyway, inspiring Atlanta skipper Bobby Cox to pad his career ejection record, which he had set three seasons earlier. The crowd at AT&T Park cheered enthusiastically as Cox stalked off the field.

Emmel's disputed call cost Atlanta a two-on, one-out opportunity as Rick Ankiel followed with a single off Matt Cain. Though they failed to score that inning, the Braves had their comeuppance, rallying from a four-run deficit to tie the game. In the eleventh inning, Ankiel delivered the biggest hit of his career with a game-winning homer off Ramon Ramirez, who was the twelfth pitcher to take the mound that evening.

With the series tied at a game apiece, Emmel became public enemy number one in Atlanta with another glaring lapse in judgment. The Braves carried a 2–1 lead into the ninth inning of Game 3 at Turner Field but couldn't hold it as the Giants rallied for a pair of runs. Sabermetric analysis has shown that leadoff batters come around to score roughly fifty percent of the time with a single or walk. Assigned to home plate that evening, Emmel nullified that statistic for Atlanta by ringing up Jason Heyward on five pitches to open the bottom of the ninth. Heyward, who kept the bat on his shoulder through the entire sequence, walked away muttering to himself. During the at-bat, the *Fox Network* displayed a computerized pitch-tracking graphic to evaluate Emmel's calls. The graphic revealed that four of the five pitches thrown by Giants reliever Brian Wilson were outside the strike zone.

Reacting to Emmel's liberal calls, a writer from the popular sports website, *Bleacher Report*, ranted irritably: "When a doctor makes a mistake that kills a patient, he has his performance reviewed and could have his license revoked. Paul Emmel may have killed the Braves' World Series dreams with his terrible umpiring and [commissioner] Bud Selig needs to take action instead of turning a blind eye like he did during the steroids era."[33] The Braves lost the series in four games and, though Emmel encountered a fair share of criticism for his performance, his career continued undaunted.

Putting the finishing touches on an abysmal October, the 2010 ALCS between the Yankees and Rangers was sullied by more controversy. Though the Yankees got the benefit of blown calls in two games, the Rangers persevered, earning their first ever World Series berth.

After a dramatic come-from-behind victory in the opener, the Yankees lost the next two games by a combined score of 15–2. In the second inning of Game 4, they caught a very lucky break on an errant call by umpire Jim Reynolds. With one out and nobody on, second baseman Robinson Cano lifted a fly ball to deep right field. In a scene eerily reminiscent of the Jeffrey Maier incident (described at the beginning of this chapter), a 20-year-old fan named Jared Macchirole reached over the wall and grabbed the ball, preventing Nelson Cruz from making a play. Cruz began shouting at Macchirole as Reynolds signaled for a home run.

Interestingly, with the video replay rule in place for disputed homers, manager Ron Washington could have challenged Reynolds' decision. Had he done so, the video would clearly have indicated fan interference. In fact, game footage suggests that Macchirole actually made contact with Cruz's glove. Reynolds refused to budge despite the protestations of Washington. For whatever reason, the Texas skipper chose not to call for a review. In the end, it mattered very little. The Yankees led 3–2 before a late-inning bullpen implosion gave the Rangers a 10–3 win.

On the brink of elimination in Game 6, the New Yorkers received a helping hand from plate umpire Brian Gorman. Trailing 1–0 in the top of the fifth, slugger Alex Rodriguez led off with a double. He moved to third on a fly ball hit by first baseman Lance Berkman. With a chance to tie the game, switch-hitter Nick Swisher chose to bat left-handed against right-handed starter Colby Lewis. Lewis's first pitch was a low breaking ball that bounced in the dirt before hitting Swisher and evading catcher Bengie Molina. Instead of ruling the ball dead and indicating a hit-by-pitch, Gorman allowed play to continue. Rodriguez scampered home with the tying run. Gorman stuck to his call despite stiff opposition from Molina and Texas manager Ron Washington.

Again, the mistake proved inconsequential as the Rangers exploded for four runs in the bottom of the fifth off Phil Hughes and David Robertson. They tacked on another run in the bottom of the seventh, sending the Yankees home empty-handed. A World Series title was not in the cards for Texas that year as they fell to the Giants in five games.

The performance of the men in blue during the 2010 playoffs invited a host of concerns from the baseball community. One of the most poignant observations came from Joe Posnanski, executive columnist for *MLB Advanced Media*. "Baseball is facing a legitimacy issue," Posnanski wrote. "It's a different kind of legitimacy issue from the gambling problem of the 1910s or the shameful color barrier before Jackie Robinson or even the steroid issue, but it's still dangerous to the sport."[34] A correspondent from Boston.com agreed, asserting that: "MLB needs to explain how it evaluates, assigns and disciplines umpires. Umpires need to be accountable too.... No more hiding behind crew chiefs or locked doors. If some twenty-two-year-old shortstop needs to stand there and explain why he made an error, a fifty-year-old umpire can, too."[35]

Breaking with the previous year's trend, two of six umpires appointed to the 2010 World Series crew were new to the Fall Classic. Refreshingly, there were no major incidents as the Giants claimed their first championship since 1954.

Regarding the five umpires who created issues in the 2010 playoffs—Emmel, Gorman, Guccione, Reynolds and Welke—four were still active at the time of this writing. Welke retired before the 2016 campaign due to ongoing physical concerns that prompted him to undergo surgery on both knees.

2012 NL Wild Card Game: Improperly Invoked Infield Fly Rule
Braves vs. Cardinals, October 5, 2012

Shortly before the 2011 winter meetings, Major League Baseball announced that it would be changing its postseason format. Beginning in 2012, two Wild Card teams from each league were selected to engage in a one-game playoff for the privilege of facing the top-seeded team in the Division Series. The inaugural NL Wild Card game is remembered less for being the first of its kind and more for the controversy generated by an improperly applied infield fly rule.

At the close of the 2012 regular season, the Giants, Nationals and Reds were all sitting on top of their respective divisions. The Braves, who finished four games behind Washington in the East, won the Wild Card race handily, placing six games ahead of their closest competitors—the Cardinals.

Managed by Fredi Gonzalez, the Braves ranked among the top ten in runs per game. Most of the slugging was done by first baseman Freddie Freeman and right fielder Jason Heyward, who combined for fifty homers. Center fielder Michael Bourn provided speed on the basepaths, stealing forty-two bags—second best in the NL. In the pitching department, closer Craig Kimbrel was virtually untouchable, allowing just twenty-seven hits in more than sixty innings of work. He led the NL in saves for the second year in a row.

The Cardinals had entered the 2012 campaign as defending World Champions. Their eleven World Series titles were second only to the New York Yankees. There was plenty of power in the St. Louis lineup as five positional players collected at least twenty homers. Though the Redbirds posted the highest collective on-base percentage in the NL, they stranded more runners than any team in the majors. This factored heavily into their 74 losses. Even so, four Cardinal pitchers finished with double digit win totals and the staff ERA was sixth best in the league.

The Wild Card showdown took place at Turner Field in Atlanta. The Cardinals sent staff ace Kyle Lohse to the mound, a right-hander who had led the league with an .842 winning percentage. The Braves countered with Kris Medlen, a swing-man who had been added to the rotation in late–July. He went 9–0 as a starter with a miserly 0.97 ERA.

Lohse faltered in the bottom of the second, giving up a two-run homer. Medlen was cruising until the fourth inning, when a critical throwing error by Hall of Famer Chipper Jones led to a three-run St. Louis outburst. The Braves trailed the rest of the way, but definitely had their chances. A promising eighth inning rally was squelched by a controversial umpiring decision.

With David Ross on first and Dan Uggla on second, Atlanta's Andrelton Simmons hit a shallow fly to left field. Cardinals shortstop Pete Kozma seemed to lose sight of the ball before giving up on it at the last minute. It dropped between Kozma and left fielder Matt Holliday, who appeared equally perplexed on the play. Had Simmons' pop-up counted as a base hit, the Braves would have had the bases loaded with one out, but left field umpire Sam Holbrook eradicated that scenario by invoking the infield fly rule.

Among the more complicated regulations in baseball, the rule was introduced in 1895 to prevent infielders from intentionally dropping pop flies with runners on base to get multiple outs. In technical terms, the rule states that a batter is out if, when first and second base are occupied or the bases are loaded with less than two outs, he hits a fair fly ball which is not a line drive or a bunt and can be caught by an infielder with ordinary effort. When the rule is invoked and the ball is caught, runners may tag up and advance at their own risk. If the ball is not caught, runners are not obligated to tag up.

After Simmons was declared out by Holbrook, the crowd of 52,000-plus expressed their disapproval by littering the field with trash. This delayed the game for nearly twenty minutes and prompted stadium officials to issue a warning over the PA system that the Braves would be forced to forfeit if the misconduct continued. Asked if he had experienced anything like it before, St. Louis manager Mike Matheny answered: "Not in the United States."[36] Cardinals catcher Yadier Molina remarked: "It was scary."[37]

The Braves failed to score when order was restored and, though they threatened again in the ninth, the Cardinals came out on top, 6–3. A protest issued by the Braves was promptly denied by MLB executive vice president Joe Torre, who stated that Holbrook's decision was a judgment call and could not be overruled.

Questioned about his controversial decision, Holbrook defended his actions, asserting: "Once that fielder established himself, he got ordinary effort. That's when the call was made."[38] There are a number of glaring issues with Holbrook's statement. In the words of broadcaster Ron Darling, whose major league pitching career spanned thirteen seasons: "You cannot call that an infield fly. It's too deep. [Kozma] wasn't camped." Additionally, Kozma admitted to losing sight of the ball. "I was under it. I should have made the play. I took my eyes off it," he told reporters.[39]

Blaming the Atlanta loss entirely on Holbrook's unfortunate ruling would be short-sighted. Though it's true that the Braves were slighted by the call, they committed three errors that led to four unearned St. Louis runs. In a postgame interview, Atlanta's catcher David Ross (who had gone 3-for-4 at the plate with a pair of RBIs) said fittingly: "It stinks, man.... It stinks that the first-ever Wild Card Game is going to be remembered for an infield pop-up blunder. That's not good."[40]

The inaugural NL Wild Card Game was not the first example of an infield fly rule call gone awry, nor would it be the last. According to an article published by the *Baseball Rules Academy* website, roughly half of all major leaguers lack a full understanding of the rule. This was dramatically illustrated in a 2017 game between the Angels and Rangers at Anaheim. The Angels had Mike Trout on first and Kaleb Cowart on second with one out when Albert Pujols hit a pop-up in front of the pitcher's mound. Umpires properly invoked the infield fly rule and Pujols was automatically declared out. When Rangers catcher Robinson Chirinos dropped the ball, things got interesting as both Cowart and Trout took off running. First baseman Mike Napoli recovered the ball and threw accurately to Elvis Andrus at third, but Andrus had obviously not familiarized himself with the rule book. Instead of tagging Cowart, which is a requirement on such a play, the veteran shortstop took Napoli's throw and tagged the bag with his foot as a first baseman would. Remarkably, umpire Stu Scheurwater was equally confused on the play, calling Cowart out. Demonstrating good instincts, Cowart alertly stayed put at third as other members of the umpiring crew reversed Scheurwater's erroneous call.

In addition to his controversial decision in the 2012 Wild Card Game, Holbrook provoked the wrath of fans on at least one other occasion. During the 1998 "Home Run Chase," he ejected St. Louis slugger Mark McGwire and manager Tony LaRussa for arguing a called third strike. Many among the crowd at Busch Stadium went ballistic, tossing garbage onto the field and prompting police intervention. Holbrook later commented: "The farthest thing from my mind of what I wanted to do was eject Mark McGwire.... I did everything I could to keep him in the game and he continued to argue. At some point I had to draw the line."[41]

Since the inception of expanded video review, a significant number of Holbrook's calls have been challenged and overturned. But his appointment to crew chief in 2017 indicated that major league executives had confidence in his abilities. Holbrook has felt the strain of umpiring in an age of rapidly advancing technology. "Today, with the HD television, the lasers, the computers, the pitch counts and things like that, there is just a lot more pressure to be as perfect as you can be," he commented.[42]

2015 ALCS Game 6: A Wet, Wild Finish in Kansas City
Blue Jays vs. Royals, October 23, 2015

Before the 2014 campaign, MLB officials made a long overdue decision, opting to instate video review on plays other than questionable home runs. Though the new system covered a wide variety of sticky situations, there were some scenarios that weren't included, such as checked-swings, balks, infield flies and balls/strikes. Two of the areas deemed unchallengeable created problems in Game 6 of the 2015 ALCS between the Toronto Blue Jays and Kansas City Royals.

The Royals entered the series as defending AL champions. They gathered ninety-five wins during the regular season, finishing twelve games ahead of the second place Twins. Of the six pitchers who shared starting responsibilities for the Royals that year, only two posted ERAs below 4.00. This proved to be no problem for an offense that produced the second-best collective batting average in the AL. Defensively, the Royals were very strong with catcher Salvadore Perez, first baseman Eric Hosmer and shortstop Alcides Escobar all receiving Gold Gloves.

The Blue Jays—winners of ninety-three games—were an offensive powerhouse. Three Toronto players had at least thirty homers and one hundred RBIs. AL MVP Josh Donaldson led the charge with eighty-four extra-base hits and a league-high 123 ribbies. In the pitching department, aging re-treads Mark Buehrle and R.A. Dickey combined for twenty-six wins. David Price, the 2012 Cy Young Award recipient, joined the pitching staff in late–July and went 9–1 down the stretch.

The Royals jumped out to a 3–2 series lead in a quirky affair that included multiple blowouts. Kansas City won the opener by a score of 5–0 then pulverized Toronto in Game 4 by a 14–2 margin. Not to be outdone, the Jays plated eighteen runs in Games 3 and 5, winning both by a combined 9-run advantage. Game 6, which took place at Kauffman Stadium in Kansas City, was the most closely contested of the series.

The Royals scored first on a solo homer by Ben Zobrist. They extended the lead in the second inning with the help of a highly controversial call. With one out and nobody on, infielder Mike Moustakas, who had slammed twenty-two homers during the regular season, hit a deep drive to right-center field. Jose Bautista tracked it to the wall, where a fan reached out and snared it with his glove. The ball appeared to be on a downward trajectory, prompting the Blue Jays to call for a video review. All three members of the *Fox* broadcasting crew—Tom Verducci, Harold Reynolds and Joe Buck—speculated that fan interference had taken place, but after reviewing the play, officials in New York allowed the home run to stand.

Bautista, who was closest to the play, tried to be tactful in his postgame comments. "From where I was looking, from my point of view, it seemed like the ball never left the yard," he said. "But I haven't seen every angle, so it's hard for me to say that they made a mistake."[43]

Trailing, 3–1, after a long rain delay, the Blue Jays tied the game on a two-run homer by Bautista—his second of the evening. But the slugger went from hero to goat in the bottom of the eighth, when his errant throw allowed Lorenzo Cain to score from first base on a single by Eric Hosmer. Snake-bitten by the disputed second inning home run call, the Blue Jays fell prey to more hinky umpiring in the ninth.

Catcher Russell Martin led off with a single. Toronto skipper John Gibbons inserted the much speedier Dalton Pompey as a pinch-runner. With Kevin Pillar at the plate, Pompey stole second and third. Pillar ended up drawing a walk, putting runners at the corners with nobody out. Gibbons called upon Dioner Navarro to pinch-hit for second baseman Ryan Goins. With the count even at 1–1, reliever Wade Davis issued what many Toronto players believed to be a quick-pitch—an illegal offering in which the pitcher does not make a clearly discernible pause in his delivery. Had the infraction been noted by plate umpire Jeff Nelson, a balk would have been in order, allowing Pompey to score and Pillar to move to second. But Nelson ignored it, calling a strike on Davis's offering, which appeared to be outside the strike zone. As Toronto players squawked about it from the bench, Navarro whiffed, setting up another dubious call from the veteran Nelson, who was working in his nineteenth major league season.

A .319 hitter for the Jays that year, left fielder Ben Revere stepped in. With every pitch being of monumental importance, he worked the count to 2–1 before laying off a high and outside offering that Nelson incorrectly ruled a strike. Clearly upset by the call, Revere swung through a 2–2 breaking ball for the second out. After Josh Donaldson grounded out, completing a heart-breaking 4–3 loss for the Jays, Revere mouthed off to reporters. "It wasn't a great call." He said. "I've seen the pitching charts. It was absolutely terrible. It was like six inches off the plate."[44]

Toronto manager John Gibbons was less bitter about the disappointing result. "I'm definitely proud of our team," he said. "It's been a fun group to be around every day. We're all disappointed we're not moving on. That's baseball. We put up our best fight today."[45]

The Royals made the most of the opportunity, claiming their first World Series title since 1985 with a victory over the Mets. The Blue Jays returned to the ALCS in 2016, losing in five games to the Indians.

Generally a reliable performer, Nelson has served as an instructor at various academies organized by major league baseball. As of 2020, his postseason credits included eight Division Series, eight League Championship Series and four World Series. Those assignments featured fifteen home plate appearances. According to an in-depth statistical study, Nelson is slightly pitcher-friendly. He has one of the widest strike zones in the majors on inside pitches to left-handed batters. With right-handers at the plate, he is more likely than most umpires to call strikes on pitches that are up-and-away.

Though the repercussions weren't as serious as his 2015 ALCS gaffe, Nelson made an embarrassing mistake during a Rangers–Mariners game in 2013. The arbiter called Jesus Sucre of the Mariners out at first during a double play sequence despite Rangers pitcher Justin Grimm interfering with the relay to first base. Grimm, whose foot was nowhere near the bag, inadvertently caught the ball, preventing it from reaching first baseman Mitch Moreland. Nelson said after the game that he had never seen a play like that at the major league level. "The pitcher kind of came out of nowhere on that play," he explained. "I didn't pick that up. Obviously, looking at the replays, I wish I had."[46]

2016 NLCS Game 4: Angel Hernandez's Blown Call at Home Plate
Cubs vs. Dodgers, October 19, 2016

Entering the 2016 campaign, the Cubs had not won a World Series in over a century, making them the longest suffering franchise in the majors. The championship drought lasted for so long that generations of fans took to believing there was something supernatural at work in Chicago. As well-weathered tales of a dreaded "curse" continued to circulate widely, the 2016 Cubs posted their highest regular season win total since 1910.

The Cubs were especially strong in the pitching department as five starters combined for a 79–39 record. In late–July, a trade with the Yankees brought Aroldis Chapman to Chicago. Chapman, one of the most effective closers in the majors, was known to regularly exceed one hundred miles per hour on the radar gun. He saved sixteen games in the closing months of the season while compiling an impressive 1.01 ERA.

While the Cubs were busy earning an NLCS berth, the Dodgers were enjoying a successful season of their own, finishing first in the National League West with ninety-one wins. Forty-six of those victories were of the comeback variety—more than any team in the NL. Out for more than two months with an injury, three-time Cy Young Award winner Clayton Kershaw returned in time for the pennant stretch. There was plenty of offense to back him up as eight LA players posted double digit home run totals. Catcher Yasmani Grandal and third baseman Justin Turner tied for the team lead with twenty-seven. Shortstop Corey Seager added twenty-six of his own, capturing Rookie of the Year honors.

After taking out the Washington Nationals in the NLDS, the Dodgers entered the League Championship Series as underdogs. They certainly appeared outmatched in the opener as Chicago exploded for five runs in the bottom of the eighth, handing LA a humbling 8–4 loss. Showing the resiliency that had defined them all season, the Dodgers bounced back to take the next two games by a combined score of 7–0. They were well on their way to grabbing an early lead in the fourth meeting before a controversial call turned the tide in favor of the Cubs.

Facing right-hander John Lackey, LA's clutch-hitting first baseman Adrian Gonzalez led off the bottom of the second with a single. Yasmani Grandal followed with a two-out walk, bringing Andrew Toles—a rookie who had hit .314 in forty-eight games—to the plate. Toles delivered a single to right field. The ball was fielded by Jason Heyward, who made a serviceable throw to home plate, where umpire Angel Hernandez was waiting to render his judgment.

Though Hernandez has received many postseason assignments over the course of his career, he has also gathered a fair share of critics. Writing for a popular Astros fan site in 2019, blogger Brian Cohn remarked bluntly: "Hernandez is absolute garbage as an umpire."[47] Houston manager A.J. Hinch told writers that, in a candid conversation with the arbiter, Hernandez admitted to blowing four calls per game. Commenting on Hernandez's volatile temperament, Hinch added that the arbiter is "known for overreaction."[48]

The questionable call made by Hernandez in Game 4 of the 2016 NLCS did nothing to enhance his reputation. As Adrian Gonzalez dove headfirst into home, Cubs catcher Willson Contreras fielded the throw from Heyward and attempted a sweep tag. From multiple angles, it appeared as if Gonzalez's hand touched the plate before Contreras tagged him on the chin. Hernandez signaled for the out as Gonzalez sprung to his feet and waggled his finger in disagreement. He motioned toward the Dodger dugout for an appeal. The play left plenty of room for doubt and LA manager Dave Roberts issued an official challenge.

After a three-and-a-half-minute delay, a final decision was reached. MLB immediately issued an official statement to the media, which read: "After viewing all relevant angles, the replay official could not definitively determine that the runner's hand contacted home plate prior to the fielder applying the tag. The call stands. The runner is out."[49]

Reacting to the verdict, the Dodger Stadium crowd burst into a hearty round of boos. Social media outlets were instantly abuzz with negative feedback. Hall of Famer Chipper Jones sniped: "I will not watch a game, any game, officiated by Angel Hernandez. His incompetence amazes me and I'm tired of major league baseball doing squat about it!"[50] Washington Nationals slugger Bryce Harper asserted: "He was safe! Replay system still broke.... Same thing all year long!"[51] Ron Cervenka of the popular Dodger fan site, *Think Blue LA*, referred to Hernandez as "the worst umpire in the game today and perhaps ever."[52]

The rest of the evening was an unmitigated disaster for the Dodgers as they ended up losing, 10–2. Bitter about the call at home plate, Gonzalez contended that two of the other umpires on duty told him he was safe. He firmly believed Hernandez's decision mentally affected his team. "Let's be honest," Gonzalez said frankly, "after that, we played a sloppy game."[53] The next two games were equally shoddy as the Dodgers lost by a cumulative nine-run margin.

Erasing over a hundred years of futility, the Cubs came back from a three-games-to-one deficit to defeat the Indians in the World Series. In an oddly touching gesture, thousands of fans wrote the names of loved ones who had not lived long enough to see the Cubs win a championship on the east-facing "Sheffield Wall" outside of Wrigley Field in Chicago. With the Cubs no longer qualifying as baseball's lovable losers, the Cleveland Indians emerged as the most luckless franchise in the majors. The last time Cleveland won a World Series, Harry Truman was President and the average annual American wage was around $3,000 per year.

The Cuban-born Hernandez made trouble for MLB officials in 2017 when he filed a federal lawsuit alleging that racial discrimination had prevented him from earning crew chief promotions and World Series assignments. Justifying those charges, he alleged that MLB's chief officer, Joe Torre, was holding a grudge against him dating back to Torre's days as Yankee manager. According to Hernandez, his performance evaluations had been consistently negative since Torre was appointed chief in 2011. Originally filed in Cincinnati, Hernandez's lawsuit was moved to New York (where MLB is headquartered) in 2019. Unsettled at the time of this writing, the suit officially lists commissioner Rob Manfred and MLB as defendants. The arbiter is seeking back pay and unspecified compensatory damages.

Aside from the 2016 NLCS debacle, Hernandez has been at the center of on-field controversy several times. After Game 3 of the 2018 Division Series between the Yankees and Red Sox (during which three of Hernandez's calls at first base were overturned), *TBS* analyst Pedro Martinez said: "Major league baseball needs to do something about Angel. It doesn't matter how many times he sues major league baseball. He's as bad as there is."⁵⁴ C.C. Sabathia added fuel to the fire after Hernandez's performance behind home plate in Game 4. "I don't think Angel Hernandez should be umpiring playoff games," Sabathia groused. "He's absolutely terrible."⁵⁵ Red Sox pitcher Rick Porcello begged to differ, remarking: "I thought Angel Hernandez called a good game. You've got to put the ball over the white part of the plate and then you get strikes called."⁵⁶ Statistical analysis later proved that Hernandez only missed a handful of pitches by a significant margin.

2017 NLDS Game 5: Nationals Lose on Account of Jerry Layne's Mistakes
Cubs vs. Nationals, October 12, 2017

The year 2016 was filled with major surprises as billionaire capitalist Donald Trump ascended to the U.S. Presidency and the Chicago Cubs ended a prolonged World Series drought. At least one thing remained predictable in the world of baseball the following year: The Washington Nationals were forced to endure yet another crushing postseason series loss. In this particular chapter of the enduring tragedy, the Nats' quest for October glory was impeded by a critical non-call in the NLDS finale.

Among the most star-crossed franchises in baseball history, the Expos failed to win a championship during their entire thirty-six-year tenure in Montreal. Upon moving to Washington and changing their name, they continued the rich tradition of losing, finishing last in five of their first six seasons. Things began to turn around with the gradual addition of some budding stars, but despite four division titles between 2012 and 2017, the Nationals failed to advance beyond the first round of the playoffs.

The 2017 version of the club included precocious slugger Bryce Harper, who had captured an MVP award at the age of twenty-two. Corner infielders Ryan Zimmerman and Anthony Rendon each collected one hundred RBIs. The pitching staff was anchored by three-time Cy Young Award winner Max Scherzer, whose efficiency on the mound was almost scary at times. From May 26 through July 2, he surrendered just six earned runs in sixty-one innings of work. Scherzer was supported in the rotation by Stephen Strasburg and Gio Gonzalez, both of whom were 15-game winners that year.

After capturing the NL East with ninety-seven wins—second most in franchise history—the Nationals faced the Cubs in the Division Series. The Chicago lineup was virtually identical to the previous year with a few minor adjustments in the outfield. Beset by injuries, only three members of the pitching staff made at least thirty starts. John Lackey, Jake Arrieta and Jon Lester were the most durable, combining for thirty-nine wins. Obtained from the White Sox in a mid–July trade, left-hander Jose Quintana won seven of ten decisions while averaging more than ten strikeouts per nine innings.

The Cubs won two of the first three meetings but couldn't get their offense going in a Game 4 shutout loss. In the deciding contest, Washington sent Gonzalez, a left-handed strikeout specialist, to the mound while the Cubs turned to Kyle Hendricks, who had missed most of June and July with a hand injury. Neither pitcher was particularly effective that evening and, by the fifth inning, both had made an early exit.

After reliever Matt Albers pitched a scoreless fourth, Washington manager Dusty Baker turned to Scherzer, who had started Game 3. Baker was hoping to get a couple of innings out of his staff ace before turning the ball over to his set-up men. It seemed like a brilliant strategy on the surface, but as the old proverb states—sometimes even the best laid plans go awry.

The inning began harmlessly enough for Scherzer as Kris Bryant grounded into the Nationals' defensive shift for the first out. Anthony Rizzo, the Cubs' RBI leader, followed with a liner to center field for out number two. It was then that things began to fall apart for the long-suffering Nationals. Catcher Willson Contreras legged out a single on a ball that shortstop Trea Turner made a spectacular diving stop on. Aging utility man Ben Zobrist followed with a bloop single to left field, putting Scherzer in a two-on, two-out jam. Addison Russell then ripped a double down the third baseline, giving the Cubs a 5–4 lead. Things got even worse from there as umpire Jerry Layne blew a critical call at home plate.

Layne, who joined the major league staff in 1989, had worked as an instructor at the Harry Wendelstedt Umpire School for thirty years. Despite his familiarity with the rulebook, he overlooked a basic infraction with Chicago's Javier Baez at the plate. When Scherzer fell behind the clutch-hitting Jason Heyward, the Nationals opted for an intentional walk to get a fresh count. Baez, a .273 hitter during the regular season, struck out to end the inning, but the ball got past catcher Matt Wieters and rolled to the backstop. Baez beat Wieters' throw to first, which sailed into right field, scoring Russell.

There was a glaring problem with this turn of events.

Baez's backswing had struck Wieters in the mask. Had Jerry Layne abided by the major league rules, which state unequivocally that the ball is dead and the pitch is a strike on such occasions, the inning would have been over. But Layne failed to make the ruling despite a visit from Baker. Incredibly, the inning continued to unravel for the Nationals.

Layne had no reservations about calling catcher's interference on Wieters with Tommy LaStella at bat. The infraction loaded the bases. Scherzer, who was trying desperately to maintain his composure, hit Jon Jay with a pitch, extending the Cubs' lead to 7–4. Though many managers would have replaced Scherzer at that point, Baker must have figured things couldn't get much worse. Mercifully, Kris Bryant made the final out, ending an inning that should have been concluded with Baez's plate appearance.

Instead of rolling over, the Nationals climbed back in the game. The score was 9–7 in the bottom of the eighth when Daniel Murphy and Anthony Rendon drew consecutive walks to open the inning. A two-out single by Michael Taylor brought Washington one run closer. Jose Lobaton singled to center field, pushing the tying run to second base. With Trea Turner at the plate, Cubs catcher Willson Contreras delivered a pick-off throw to first. Lobaton appeared to get back in time and was called safe by umpire Will Little. The play was close, however, prompting Cubs manager Joe Maddon to issue an official challenge. A review of the play revealed that Lobaton's body had come off the bag briefly while Anthony Rizzo was applying the tag. The original call was overturned, ending the inning. Both teams went quietly in the ninth as the Cubs prevailed, 9–8.

Interviewed afterward, Scherzer referred to the series-ending loss as a "gut punch" and remarked: "This game's cruel sometimes."[57] There certainly was truth in the statement. Had the proper call been made on Baez's fifth inning backswing, the Nationals would technically have won, 8–7.

Speaking on *Mad Dog Sports* radio two weeks later, MLB chief officer Joe Torre acknowledged Layne's mistake. He pointed out that the Nationals could have asked for a "rule check" from the umpires but speculated that it may not have changed the outcome. Baker, who was in his second season as Nationals manager, ended up being released, prompting Bob Nightengale of *USA Today Sports* to remark sourly: "It's absurd, arrogant really, to think that winning 192 games and back-to-back division titles two years on the job will get you fired." Baker agreed, commenting: "I really thought this was my best year.... It's hard to understand."[58]

Still active through 2019, Jerry Layne's career has been marked by injuries, particularly in 2016, when he was forced to leave three separate games after being struck by balls behind home plate. Additionally, he injured his leg that season while jumping to avoid a foul ball. Wounded in 2006 and 2012 by shards of broken bats, he sustained a concussion in 2008 after being hit with yet another foul.

Over portions of four decades in "The Show," the accident-prone Layne has developed a reputation for having a rather small strike zone. His ejection rate is above the major league average. Commenting on the resentment expressed toward umpires by various sources, he mused: "I don't know what goes through people's minds.... It's basically a game, and it's at high levels, and there's a lot of professionals on the field. Everybody tries to do their best."[59] Unfortunately, Layne's best wasn't good enough in Game 7 of the 2011 World Series—a topic discussed at length in the next chapter.

Though fate was not kind to the Nationals prior to their World Series victory in 2019, things could have been a lot worse. The other Washington franchise, which occupied the nation's capital from 1901 to 1960, posted a cumulative won-loss record well below .500. During the first decade of play, the Senators (also known as the Nationals though the nickname never stuck) finished in seventh place or lower every year. This inspired the enduring maxim: "Washington—first in war, first in peace, and last in the American League."

PART FOUR

Legends of the Fall: Infamous World Series Debates

....

1885 World's Championship Series: Umpire David Sullivan's Hot Mess
Browns vs. White Stockings, October 15, 1885

Though the first official World Series was played in 1903, there were earlier tournaments held to crown the champions of baseball. Beginning in 1884 and continuing through 1890, the pennant winners from the National League squared off against the top American Association teams in an early version of the Fall Classic. The meetings varied from three to fifteen games and were referred to as the "World's Championship Series" (WCS). Since they are not recognized by MLB as being part of the current postseason format, they have been virtually forgotten.

The 1885 WCS pitted the St. Louis Browns against the Chicago White Stockings. Plagued by sloppy defense and bad officiating, the series was shortened from its original twelve game arrangement when attendance figures dwindled significantly. At the conclusion of play, there was no clear victor as the affair ended in a controversial tie.

Baseball was a vastly different sport in 1885. It took six called balls to draw a walk. Hitters could request low or high pitches and flat-sided bats were legal. The pitcher's mound was located a mere fifty feet from home plate. Fans were rowdier, fights were common and, shockingly, umpires worked alone.

The unlucky gentleman assigned to the 1885 WCS was David Sullivan, who had presided over sixty-nine National League games that season. Prior to joining the NL crew full-time, Sullivan had worked in the short-lived

Union Association. With a tendency to panic under fire, his resolve would be tested to the limit in Game 2.

The Browns (later known as the Cardinals) were managed by future White Sox owner Charlie Comiskey, who served a dual role as the club's starting first baseman. Remarkably, the entire St. Louis pitching staff consisted of just three men. There was no such thing as a bullpen in those days and starters were expected to go the distance barring a major injury. Twenty-one-year-old right-hander Bob Caruthers, playing in his first full season, completed all fifty-three of his starts and led the American Association with forty wins as the Browns left the second-place Red Stockings sixteen games behind.

In the National League, Chicago posted a stellar 87–25 record yet barely managed to fend off the Giants, who spent a total of forty-nine days in first place. The White Stockings (later known as the Cubs) carried two of the era's brightest stars on their roster—Adrian "Cap" Anson and Mike "King" Kelly. Though Anson played his last game in 1897, he still ranks among the top ten of all-time in hits and RBIs. When he retired, he held almost every major offensive record. Kelly, who scored a league-leading 124 runs for Chicago in 1885, was one of the game's first matinee idols. Considered rakishly handsome, he was the first ballplayer to have a song written about him and the first to have a successful acting career outside of baseball. In his prime, he was the highest paid player in the majors.

Feeling that his team could easily beat the Browns, Chicago owner A.G. Spalding agreed to a barnstorming format, in which the WCS would travel to cities outside each club's sphere of influence. The gate receipts would be split evenly and, to sweeten the deal, both owners pledged additional prize money to the winning team. The Series opened at the Congress Street Grounds in Chicago. Pre-game festivities went on far longer than necessary, delaying the first pitch considerably. The game was tied at five in the eighth inning when play was suspended on account of darkness. It was just the beginning of much bigger problems.

Game 2 took place at Sportsman's Park in St. Louis. Only 3,000 fans showed up—well below the expected turnout. Incensed by a series of questionable calls in the early innings, the crowd grew restless. In the sixth frame, the White Stockings had a runner on third when Kelly hit a grounder to Bill Gleason at short. Gleason, who had amassed a robust total of sixty-three errors during the regular season, mishandled it before throwing to first base. Anticipating a play at the plate, Sullivan completely lost track of Kelly (one of the many hazards of working alone). Obligated to make a ruling, he called Kelly safe at first. The decision was so bad it was almost comical. In fact, *The Chicago Tribune* reported that Kelly was out by at least ten feet. Comiskey immediately confronted the arbiter, threatening to pull his team off the field. During a raging debate that went on for about fifteen minutes, Sullivan changed his mind repeatedly. In the end, he made the wrong call. Play resumed with Kelly on first and the crowd on the brink of a riot. Inciting them even further, Kelly stole second and scored on an Anson single, tying the game.

Two batters later, the White Stockings pulled ahead on another controversial decision. With Fred Pfeffer on third, infielder Ned Williamson hit a chopper down the first base line. The ball initially went foul then rolled back into fair territory. Comiskey picked it up and flipped it to Sam Barkley covering first as Williamson beat the throw. Though Sullivan initially called him safe, Comiskey pressured the arbiter into making a foul ball ruling. This served to enrage Anson, Kelly and several other Chicago players, who demanded that Sullivan revert to his original call. Incredibly, the embattled official agreed, giving the White Stockings a 5–4 lead. Fans had seen enough at that point and started spilling onto the field in an attempt to get their hands on Sullivan. A sizeable security force was able to usher him to safety.

Sullivan later ruled the game a forfeit in favor of Chicago, alleging that Comiskey had pulled his team off the field. The decision became an immediate point of contention since it was uncertain at what point the Browns had departed. It seems likely that Comiskey's players left the field less in protest and more to evade rampaging fans.

Looking to avoid further trouble, officials from both teams relieved Sullivan of his duties prior to Game 3. His replacement, Harry McCaffery, had played in portions of two seasons for the Browns. After St. Louis won the third meeting, Anson squawked about it, demanding the selection of an umpire with no ties to either club. His protest came shortly before the start of Game 4, prompting a stadium-wide search for a suitable replacement. A local sportsman named William Medart was eventually pulled from the stands and deemed worthy of the task. Unfortunately for the White Stockings, Medart was a diehard St. Louis fan. Most of his calls went in favor of the Browns in a 3–2 Chicago loss.

The umpire controversy was finally settled with the appointment of John O. Kelly. A veteran of both leagues, Kelly had a reputation for impartiality (carrying the nickname of "Honest John"). But despite his sterling character, only five-hundred people showed up on a brisk October day to witness the fifth game of the set. Acknowledging the futility of the original agreement, both owners conceded that Game 7 would be the last.

The White Stockings evened things up with two straight wins, but when the Browns romped to a 13–4 victory in the finale, more controversy arose. Though Comiskey and Anson had initially agreed to ignore the outcome of the second game, Spalding successfully lobbied to reinstate the forfeiture. As a result, the Series was declared a tie and the prize money was returned to both owners.

Any lingering doubt regarding the superiority of either club was settled the following season, when the two teams met again in the WCS. The Browns won four of six meetings, emerging as the undisputed champions of baseball. While the White Stockings never appeared in another World's Championship Series, the Browns did twice. They were defeated by the Detroit Wolverines in 1887 and the New York Giants the following year. When the American Association disbanded before the 1891 campaign, the WCS became defunct.

Out of action in 1886, umpire David Sullivan appeared in just twenty-one games over the next three seasons. He made his last major league appearance in June of 1889. A lifelong Chicago resident, he died of a heart attack before his thirty-fourth birthday. As the story goes, he was playing a game of cards at the time of his passing and had commented just moments before that he was too tough to die.

In 1894, postseason play returned to the majors with the inaugural Temple Cup, which pitted the top two National League teams against each other. When the second-place clubs won three of four annual meetings, the legitimacy of the series was held in question by many. Without a reliable fan base, the tournament was discontinued after the 1897 campaign. Three years later, a local Pittsburgh newspaper sponsored the Chronicle-Telegraph Cup. It was held just once with the Brooklyn Superbas beating the Pittsburgh Pirates. The current incarnation of the World Series began when the Boston Americans (later referred to as the Red Sox) agreed to a best-of-nine showdown against the Pirates in 1903. The last nine-game Series occurred in 1921 between the Giants and Yankees.

1911 World Series Game 5: The Run That Shouldn't Have Counted
Athletics vs. Giants, October 25, 1911

In over a hundred years of play, many World Series games have ended in unusual fashion. Game 5 of the 1911 Fall Classic was definitely among the most peculiar. On the brink of elimination, the Giants pushed the winning run across in the bottom of the tenth. Though an appeal of the play would have been upheld by umpire Bill Klem, Athletics manager Connie Mack accepted the loss to avoid inciting a riot.

A catcher during his playing days, Mack was known for exploiting loopholes in the rulebook. This included tipping the bats of opponents with his glove and deliberately dropping infield pop-ups to turn double plays (strategies that were eventually prohibited). As a manager, Mack had a remarkable eye for talent, often signing players straight off college campuses without a shred of minor league experience. The practice worked well for him and, by 1910, he had built a powerhouse.

Entering the 1911 campaign, the Athletics were defending world champions. Their lineup featured four Hall of Famers and a host of lesser-known deadball stars. The pitching corps were anchored by Cooperstown incumbents Eddie Plank and Charles Bender. A left-hander, Plank became famous for his

No one knew the rulebook better than Bill Klem, who worked as an umpire in portions of five decades. In Game 5 of the 1911 World Series, Klem was obligated to allow the winning run to score under questionable circumstances. Giants infielder Larry Doyle missed home plate, but the A's never lodged a protest (Library of Congress).

stalling tactics, which drove hitters to distraction and helped him win 284 games for Philly over fourteen seasons. Bender, who had Native American roots, ended up being saddled with the nickname of "Chief." He disliked the moniker immensely, always signing autographs as "Charles." A big-game pitcher, Bender compiled a 1.31 ERA in seven World Series starts between 1905 and 1911. Mack once proclaimed that, if he could give the ball to any of the pitchers he ever worked with in a must-win situation, Bender would be his man.

The gentlemanly Mack, who abhorred profanity and always wore a business suit, was particularly enamored with his infield. At the height of the A's deadball success, Mack told a reporter he wouldn't trade his infielders for $100,000 (an enormous sum in those days). The statement became an enduring catchphrase. Mack's so-called "$100,000 Infield" included Hall of Famers Eddie Collins and Frank Baker. A lifetime .333 hitter, Collins possessed numerous qualities that made him the standard by which other second basemen were measured. Baker (a third baseman) hit ninety-nine career homers in an era when they were somewhat rare. The two he slammed during the 1911 World Series earned him his famous nickname. In addition to Baker and Collins, the A's had Stuffy McInnis, an exceptional defensive first baseman and dependable run-producer. Shortstop Jack Barry—the least-heralded of Mack's coveted infield—earned a reputation as a clutch-performer. A writer from the *Philadelphia Press* declared: "If Barry's batting average was only .119 and a hit was needed to win a game for the Athletics, it's a cinch that 99 percent of the fans would rather have Barry at bat than any other man on Mack's payroll."[1]

After leaving the second place Tigers thirteen and a half games behind, the "Mackmen" (as they were sometimes referred to) faced the Giants in the World Series. The pairing was a rematch of the 1905 Fall Classic, which the Giants had won easily on the strength of Christy Mathewson's three complete game shutouts (a record that still stands). "Matty" was still very much in his prime entering the 1911 postseason, and the Giants had strengthened their rotation with the addition of Rube Marquard, who was forging a Hall of Fame career of his own. New York's first place finish was especially impressive considering that they had spent three months in a rented stadium (Hilltop Park) after a massive fire destroyed the Polo Grounds in mid–April.

A record crowd of over thirty-eight thousand witnessed a showdown between Mathewson and Bender in the Series opener. The two had locked horns six years previously to the day. As expected, it was a tight pitcher's duel. Mathewson didn't have command of his fastball that afternoon and relied mostly on curves. Bender struck out eleven batters and yielded just five hits but ended up on the losing end of a 2–1 decision.

The second game took place at Shibe Park in Philadelphia with Plank squaring off against Marquard. The game was knotted at one until the bottom of the sixth, when Baker drove a two-strike fastball into the right field seats. A *Sporting Life* correspondent wrote that Baker's shot "sent the great multitude howling, cheering and stamping for fully five minutes in the conviction that the hit had settled the game."[2] Fans were correct in that assumption as the A's evened the Series with a 3–1 win.

Determined to get all he could out of his staff ace, Giants manager John McGraw sent Mathewson back to the mound in Game 3. The New Yorkers scratched out a run off Philly starter Jack Coombs in the third and held onto the lead until the top of the ninth, when Baker distinguished himself as a hero once again. Determined not to repeat Marquard's mistake from the previous afternoon, Mathewson offered the slugger a two-strike curveball. Anticipating the strategy, Baker drove the pitch over the right field wall, tying the score. From that point forward, he was known as "Home Run" Baker. The game ended on a controversial note when outfielder Fred Snodgrass spiked Baker while sliding into third base. Baker required medical attention (though he stayed in the game) and even the New York crowd treated Snodgrass to a chorus of jeers. The A's prevailed in eleven innings, grabbing a 2–1 Series advantage.

Commenting on Snodgrass's aggressive play, a *New York Times* writer mused: "The endangering of Baker by such a move seemed unsportsmanlike and out of place."[3] Baseball's newly crowned home run king believed the spiking had been intentional and many agreed, including AL president Ban Johnson. But after a series of storms along the East Coast caused the postponement of play for six days, the incident was not as hot a topic.

When action resumed on October 24, the A's beat Mathewson again, 4–2. Facing elimination in Game 5, McGraw handed the ball back to Marquard. The left-hander, who had worked close to 300 innings that year, was nearly out of gas. He lasted through two scoreless frames before yielding a three-run homer to Philly outfielder Rube Oldring. Things looked bleak for the New Yorkers. But the game was far from over.

Swingmen Red Ames and Doc Crandall held the A's scoreless the rest of the way. Giants catcher John Meyers, yet another Native American strapped with the embarrassing handle of "Chief," drove Fred Merkle home with a sacrifice fly in the bottom of the seventh. In the ninth, Crandall chased Art Fletcher across the plate with a double. Left fielder Josh Devore, in his only season of full-time duty, followed with a game-tying single. This set up one of the strangest conclusions in Series history.

As darkness began to descend upon the Polo Grounds, most everyone realized that the tenth inning would be the last. Coombs, who had strained a groin muscle beating out a bunt in the top of the frame, was replaced by Plank. Known to many as "Steady Eddie," the hurler defied his nickname by surrendering a leadoff double to "Laughing Larry" Doyle. Snodgrass then reached on a bunt, sending Doyle to third. Red Murray, who went hitless throughout the Series, lifted a fly ball to right that was too shallow to get the run in. Merkle followed with a shot down the right field line. The ball might have landed in foul territory had Philly's Danny Murphy chosen to let it drop, but it was too close for comfort and he decided to make the catch. Doyle arrived ahead of Murphy's throw to home as fans began piling triumphantly onto the field. Looking to avoid the crush, players headed toward their respective clubhouses.

While all this was transpiring, umpire Bill Klem stood silently at the plate waiting to make a signal. Unbeknownst to many, Doyle had missed home plate. Had the good-natured infielder noticed his mistake and immediately attempted to rectify it, catcher Jack Lapp would have been required to tag him for the out. But the rules clearly state that, when an advancing runner fails to touch home and makes no attempt to return, the defensive team can get the out by simply tagging the base and making an appeal.

After the game, Klem described the play as follows: "When Murphy caught the ball in right field, I set myself to see the plate on Murphy's throw to it. Doyle came in like a streak and made a long, wide slide as he came to the plate. He went across with one leg in back of it and the other over it about eight inches or a foot. He never got any nearer to it than that. I saw it plainly and waited. Usually I run to the dressing room when the game is over, but this time I waited for several seconds, waiting to see if an Athletics player would make an appeal."[4]

None of them did, although several admitted to having noticed Doyle's blunder. Before Klem reached the dressing room, he encountered McGraw, who asked what the arbiter would have done if the Athletics had appealed. Klem said he would have risked a riot to make the right call. "Well," McGraw responded, "I would have protected you."[5]

Interviewed after the game, Mack said he knew that Doyle failed to touch home but had been apprehensive about the consequences of an appeal. He accepted the loss as a matter of principle, remarking: "It was the most pleasing moment of my life when not one of [my players] tried to take advantage of a technicality."[6]

Game 6 was anti-climactic as the A's clinched the Series with a 13–2 blowout. They returned to the October stage twice over the next three seasons. After a sweep at the hands of the Braves in 1914, Mack dismantled his "$100,000 infield." He waited fifteen years for another chance at a World Series title. During his fifty seasons at the Philly helm, he guided the club to a total of nine pennants and five world championships.

Generally regarded as one of the greatest umpires in history, Bill Klem became famous for declaring that he had never missed a call in his life. The statement reportedly originated from a 1912 incident at the Polo Grounds. During a game between the Giants and Cubs, a New York player hit a deep drive that bounced off the scoreboard near the foul line. Klem ruled that the ball had drifted foul—a decision that ultimately cost the Giants the game. McGraw, who hated losing more than any manager who ever lived, ordered a stadium contractor to determine precisely where the ball had struck the scoreboard. After climbing a ladder and measuring the location of the dent, the contractor—a man named Jim Foster—learned that the ball had indeed been foul by three or four inches. When he informed Klem of his findings, the arbiter replied boldly: "You're not telling me a thing, Mr. Foster. I've never missed one of those in my life."[7]

Klem's confidence was evident throughout his career. While deliberating a close play one afternoon, he hesitated before making a signal. When one player impatiently barked: "Well, what is it—safe or out?" Klem famously responded: "It ain't nothing until I call it."[8] Questioned about his failure to draw attention to Doyle's mistake in Game 5 of the 1911 World Series, he said with conviction: "It's not up to the umpire, under the rules, to point out a player's failure to touch a base. The team on defense must spot that lapse. That's why I allowed the tally."[9]

1925 World Series Game 3: Sam Rice's Mystery Catch
Senators vs. Pirates, October 10, 1925

The game of baseball is steeped in controversy. Few if any plays have generated as much discussion as Sam Rice's disputed catch in the 1925 World Series. Though more than a thousand eyewitness accounts were submitted to the commissioner's office afterward, no one is certain to this day whether Rice hung on to the ball or not. The truth about what really happened is a secret the outfielder carried with him to the grave.

A soft-spoken man with a penchant for keeping his personal affairs private, Rice was a remarkable defensive player. Primarily a right fielder, he led the league in putouts six times. He was among the most capable batsmen of the era as well, coming up just short of 3,000 career hits while accruing a lifetime .322 average. He hit .350 in 1925 yet somehow finished a distant eighth in the batting race.

Entering the 1925 campaign as defending world champions, the Washington Senators were well-stocked with capable pitchers, having lured spitball master Stan Coveleski away from Cleveland during the offseason. Coveleski joined a staff anchored by fellow Hall of Famer Walter Johnson, who was reaching the end of a brilliant career highlighted by three triple crowns and more than 400 lifetime victories. Johnson's last great season was 1925 and, though he put up impressive numbers that year, it was Coveleski who led the league in earned run average and winning percentage.

The Senators got off to a decent start but trailed the Athletics through most of the first half. The race remained tight until late–August, when an epic Philadelphia collapse gave Washington some breathing room. Interestingly, the mighty Yankees did not factor into the pennant race, having lost Babe Ruth to a mysterious illness. Described by most sources as a stomach ailment, the Babe may actually have been suffering from venereal disease. Whatever the case, the New Yorkers slumped to seventh place in the standings with Ruth out of action for more than fifty games.

In the National League, the Pirates climbed back on top after a fifteen-year absence. All five of Pittsburgh's primary starters finished with double-digit win totals. The ace of the pitching staff was Lee Meadows, a curveball specialist noted for his durability. Offensively, the Pirates posted the best collective batting average in the NL. Hall of Famer Kiki Cuyler led the team with a career-high .357 mark.

The World Series opened in Pittsburgh with a convincing 4–1 Washington victory. The Pirates bounced back in Game 2, surviving a late Senators rally to win, 3–2. The third meeting took place in the nation's capital, where the sale of more than thirty-six thousand tickets necessitated the construction of temporary bleachers at Griffith Stadium. Braving the elements on a cold, breezy Saturday afternoon, President Calvin Coolidge was among those in attendance.

The two teams pecked away at each other through six innings, scattering runs here and there. Facing right-hander Ray Kremer, the Senators loaded the bases with one out in the bottom of the seventh. First baseman Joe Judge—a fixture in the Washington lineup for over a decade—drove in Earl McNeely with a sacrifice fly. Right fielder Joe Harris followed with a single, putting the Senators up, 4–3.

Looking to protect the lead, Washington player/manager Bucky Harris implemented a defensive switch, moving Rice to right field from center to accommodate McNeely, who had been inserted as a pinch-runner. Firpo Marberry, the game's first prominent relief specialist, was summoned from the bullpen. The Senators appeared to be safe from harm when Marberry struck out shortstop Glenn Wright and first baseman George Grantham in succession. But things got interesting when catcher Earl Smith came to bat.

Smith's .313 average during the regular season was second best in the majors among players with at least ninety-five appearances behind the plate. A spirited brawler who rarely backed down from a challenge, Smith drove Marberry's 2–2 offering to deep right field, where Rice sprang into action. The wide-ranging outfielder sprinted toward the ball and made a back-handed stab in front of the temporary bleachers. Unable to stop his forward momentum, he tumbled over the barrier into the stands and disappeared from view. What happened in the next few seconds remains uncertain.

In those days, umpiring crews consisted of four men with one being assigned to each infield station. Attending to second base that day, veteran arbiter Cy Rigler rushed to the scene to make the call. Several seconds passed before Rice reappeared. Years later, one eyewitness remarked that "it was longer than a TV station break with eight consecutive commercials."[10] Another spectator—a man named Norman Budesheim—claimed that Rice dropped the ball before he landed and then jostled with fans for possession. Whatever the case, Rice had the ball in his glove when he finally rose to his feet. Rigler signaled for the out and, after a lengthy discussion, his decision was supported by the rest of the crew.

Lingering doubts remain about the game-saving catch Sam Rice made in Game 3 of the 1925 World Series. Rice refused to discuss the play during his lifetime, but drafted a letter addressed to the Baseball Hall of Fame with instructions not to open it until after his death (Library of Congress).

On the heels of the Senators' 4–3 win, more than 1,600 fans wrote to commissioner Kenesaw Mountain Landis to relay their side of the story. Some even sent notarized affidavits attesting to the fact that Rice had dropped the ball. Going straight to the source, Landis summoned Rice to his hotel the following day and asked him point-blank if he had made the catch. The tight-lipped Hall of Famer replied guardedly: "Judge, the umpire said I did." Landis mulled this over for a few seconds and responded: "Sam, let's leave it that way."[11]

Rice's defensive gem mattered very little in the final analysis as the Pirates won three straight to take the series in seven games. The controversy endured throughout Rice's lifetime and beyond. Numerous sources pestered the outfielder to come clean about the catch. One magazine reportedly offered him $2,500 for the story, a sizeable chunk of change in those days, but Rice politely refused.

After his induction to Cooperstown, Rice became a regular at Hall of Fame sponsored events. Historian Lee Allen and Hall of Fame president Paul Kerr asked Rice repeatedly about the play, but the former Washington star refused to disclose any new details. Finally, in July of 1965, Rice decided to set the record straight, drafting a letter and handing it to Kerr with instructions not to open it until his death. Rice's final words on the matter were: "At no time did I lose possession of the ball."[12]

Questioned about the infamous World Series catch, Rigler explained that, since Rice already had the ball in his possession, the end of the play was irrelevant. But if that's the case, one can only wonder why the arbiter waited for Rice to reappear with the ball in his glove before making a final decision. In any event, the accuracy of Rigler's call will never be conclusively determined.

A robust man at 6-foot, two-hundred and seventy pounds, Rigler was widely regarded as a peacemaker. Though his size intimidated many, he rarely resorted to profanity and strenuously avoided ejections. He was among the first to raise his right arm to indicate strikes. If his signals were missed, his booming voice served to make the point clear.

At the time of Rigler's retirement in 1935, he had more than four thousand games to his credit, placing him among the all-time leaders. Rigler was appointed National League chief of umpires shortly after his retirement from active duty. Sadly, he held the position for less than a month, succumbing to a brain tumor in December of 1935.

1935 World Series Game 3: Moriarty Defies Landis with 3 Ejections
Tigers vs. Cubs, October 4, 1935

In the wake of the 1919 World Series scandal, Commissioner Landis vowed to clean up the sport. In order to attain that goal, he implemented several restrictive policies and frequently meddled in the affairs of both leagues. One such policy forbade umpires from issuing ejections in the postseason without prior approval. The restriction went unchallenged for well over a decade until baseball maverick George Moriarty enacted several unauthorized expulsions in Game 3 the 1935 World Series. As could only be expected, the Commissioner was none too pleased.

After a succession of dismal showings in the late–'20s/early–'30s, the Detroit Tigers climbed into contention, capturing consecutive pennants in 1934 and 1935. With a trio of Cooperstown greats in the lineup (Hank Greenberg-Charlie Gehringer-Goose Goslin), the Tigers averaged more than six runs per game during those two seasons while posting the highest batting average in the majors. The ace of the pitching staff was right-hander Tommy Bridges, who won no fewer than twenty games every year from 1934–36. Elden Auker and Schoolboy Rowe played strong supporting roles, averaging a collective total of thirty-six victories per season in that same span. Though the Tigers lost to the Cardinals in the 1934 Fall Classic, they redeemed themselves the following year against the Cubs.

Even Ty Cobb, one of the toughest players of the Deadball Era, was said to have backed down from a fight with George Moriarty. This 1911 tobacco card shows Moriarty in his prime with the Detroit Tigers. As an umpire, he provoked the ire of Commissioner Kenesaw Mountain Landis when he ejected three players from Game 3 of the 1935 World Series (a record that still stands) (Library of Congress).

In 1935, no one could have predicted that the Cubs would go more than a century without winning a World Series—especially with five future Hall of Famers on their roster. Among the greatest catchers of all time, Gabby Hartnett foiled fifty-six percent of all attempted steals during his career (the second-highest mark in history behind Roy Campanella). 1935 was Hartnett's signature campaign as he led the league in four defensive categories while hitting .344—a performance that earned him MVP honors. Significant contributions from less celebrated stars such as outfielder Augie Galan and first baseman Phil Cavarretta helped the Cubs assemble a twenty-one-game winning streak (third-longest in modern history) that stretched from September 4 through September 27. It was more than enough to send them back to the World Series for the second time in four years.

After a split in Detroit, the Series moved to Wrigley Field. Game 3 was played on a Friday afternoon with numerous celebrities in attendance, among them heavyweight boxing stars James Braddock and Joe Louis. The Cubs sent 20-game winner Bill Lee to the mound that day while the Tigers countered with Auker, a right-hander with a submarine delivery.

Baseball was a less gentlemanly sport in the 1930s with players frequently heckling one another from the dugout (a practice commonly known as "bench jockeying"). Few players were subjected to more verbal abuse than Detroit's Hank Greenberg. Greenberg was not the first Jewish player in the majors, but he was the first to establish himself as a superstar. Though he wasn't a particularly religious man, he was deeply respectful of the Jewish tradition. When he refused to play on Rosh Hashanah (the Jewish New Year) and Yom Kippur (the Hebrew Day of Atonement) in 1933, he opened himself up to an ongoing barrage of harassment.

The Chicago bench jockeys were particularly hard on Greenberg during Game 1 of the 1935 World Series, riding him mercilessly every time he came to bat. Though no ejections were issued, Moriarty—stationed behind home plate—took exception to the behavior and made a note of who the offenders were. Interestingly, the umpiring crew included Dolly Stark, who was the first Jewish official in major league history.

The abuse of Greenberg continued in Game 2 despite a stern warning issued by Moriarty. Though Greenberg sprained his wrist that day and was out for the rest of the Series, Moriarty grew tired of the relentless chatter coming from the Chicago bench. When Charlie Grimm questioned a call he made on Cavarretta at second base in Game 3, Moriarty treated the Cubs manager to a verbal lashing using colorful language. At some point during the tirade, Grimm accused Moriarty of being a racist, earning a prompt expulsion from the game. As Chicago players continued to sling insults from the bench, Moriarty added Woody English (team captain) and Tuck Stainback to the list of banished parties. One sportswriter quipped: "Mr. Moriarty is quite a pitcher—of ballplayers from dugout to dressing room. He should have been credited as the winning pitcher instead of [Schoolboy] Rowe."[13]

Besieged by reporters after the Tigers' dramatic come from behind victory, Moriarty spouted: "They started it and they can finish it.... I told Grimm at Detroit if I heard any more such profanity as they yelled at Greenberg that I'd chase five of them off the bench with Grimm leading the procession."[14] National League President Ford Frick, who was at the game, refused to endorse the arbiter's behavior, commenting that his actions were "most unbecoming to an umpire."[15]

Upset by Moriarty's disregard of his ejection rule, Commissioner Landis called a conference the following day to sort out the details. Among those present were Chicago infielders Billy Herman and Billy Jurges, who (along with Stainback and English) had baited Moriarty in Game 3. Upon hearing precisely what had been said, Landis issued fines and reprimands to everyone involved, including Moriarity. Speaking to the press at the meeting's conclusion, the Commissioner remarked: "In my time in this world, I have prided myself on a command of lurid expressions. I must confess that I learned from these young men some variations of the language even I didn't know existed."[16]

In what some would call a glaring example of karmic justice, the Tigers won the Series in six games. It was the first championship in franchise history. Moriarty's three ejections are a record that has stood the test of time. To date, there have been only twenty-three ejections in World Series play. The last one occurred in 2019, when Washington Nationals' manager Dave Martinez got tossed from Game 6.

An uncompromising character from baseball's old school, Moriarty was one of the most colorful umpires of the 1920s and '30s. He grew up near the Union Stock Yards on Chicago's South Side and never completed middle school. He began his baseball career at the age of sixteen. Originally signed by the Cubs, he bounced up and down from the majors to the minors for several years before the New York Highlanders purchased his contract in 1906. He reached his peak as a player with the Detroit Tigers.

In 1909, Moriarty became the Tigers' regular third baseman, helping the club to a World Series berth that year. A daring base runner with a penchant for stealing home, he was popular among peers, earning the title of team captain. Like most players of the Deadball Era, Moriarty was rough and always ready to rumble. He squared off against notorious brawlers Hobe Ferris and Bill Carrigan. Interestingly, the ferocious Ty Cobb was said to have backed down from a fight with Moriarty.

By 1917, Moriarty's skills were in decline and he chose a new career path. Remarkably, he was hired as an AL umpire without any prior experience. His contentious nature invited trouble more than once during his career. In 1932, he was provoked into a fight with several White Sox players under the stands at League Park in Cleveland. Though he reportedly laid out one of his opponents, he was left with an assortment of cuts and bruises in addition to a broken hand. Following a full investigation of the incident, Moriarty got off with a stern reprimand.

In 1940, Moriarty decided to put an end to his umpiring career with more than 3,000 games to his credit. He took a job as a traveling lecturer for the American League public relations staff and scouted for the Tigers well into the 1950s. He was seventy-nine years old when he died of kidney cancer in 1964.

1948 World Series Game 1: Bill Stewart's Blown Pickoff Call on Phil Masi
Indians vs. Braves, October 6, 1948

Most anyone who has held a job for any length of time realizes that there are bound to be bad days at the office. Bill Stewart experienced plenty of them during three decades as a multi-sport manager and official. His *New York Times* obituary described him on a professional level as a "melancholy, disillusioned man of icy-hearted integrity, often engaged in brawls, accidents or crowd uproars."[17] Of all the mistakes he made during his professional umpiring career, the most glaring occurred during the 1948 World Series, in which his errant decision directly affected the outcome of Game 1.

The 1948 season is best remembered for the unlikely World Series matchup that took place. Neither the Indians nor the Braves had been to the postseason since Woodrow Wilson's presidency and neither club had finished in the thick of the pennant race in 1947. While the Braves had multiple contenders breathing down their necks into late–September of

1948, the Indians were forced to endure a one-game playoff against the Red Sox to determine the pennant.

The Braves ranked second among NL clubs in runs scored per game. But there were no obvious offensive standouts. Five positional players exceeded the .300 mark at the plate and four drove in at least sixty runs (with only one finishing in triple digits). The stars of the show in Boston were pitchers Warren Spahn and Johnny Sain, who accounted for forty-three percent of the club's total win-share. Their efficiency on the mound inspired a famous poem by *Boston Post* sports editor Gerald V. Hern. It read: "First we'll use Spahn, then we'll use Sain, then an off day followed by rain. Back will come Spahn, followed by Sain, and followed, we hope, by two days of rain."[18] It became the mantra of the 1948 Braves.

Meanwhile, in Cleveland, the Indians led the AL in homers. Hall of Famer Joe Gordon out-slammed his teammates with thirty-two long balls while slick-fielding third baseman Ken Keltner finished right behind him, collecting thirty-one of his own. American League MVP Lou Boudreau stole the spotlight, reaching career-highs in multiple offensive categories, including on-base percentage (.453) and RBIs (106). Additionally, he hit at a vigorous .355 clip while posting the

Bill Stewart made a few faulty decisions during his twenty-two years as a major league umpire. One of his most glaring errors occurred during Game 1 of the 1948 World Series, when he mistakenly called Phil Masi of the Braves safe at second base on a pickoff attempt by Bob Feller. Masi scored the only run of the game, spoiling Feller's two-hitter for the Indians (National Baseball Hall of Fame Library, Cooperstown, N.Y.).

highest fielding percentage among shortstops. In the pitching department, the Indians relied heavily upon the one-two punch of Cooperstown luminaries Bob Lemon and Bob Feller. Southpaw Gene Bearden enjoyed the only spectacular campaign of his brief career with twenty wins and a league-leading 2.43 ERA. Among the most notable sidelights of the season, Negro League legend Satchel Paige made his major league debut with Cleveland in July, posting a 6–1 record down the stretch.

The World Series opened at Braves Field and was the first to be widely televised. The Game 1 pitching match-up featured Sain versus Feller, who said years later: "When the game started, I was as ready as I've ever been in my life."[19] Though Feller tossed a two-hitter that afternoon, he came out on the wrong end of a 1–0 result.

Both pitchers were on point as the game remained scoreless through seven innings. In the bottom of the eighth, Feller issued a leadoff walk to Boston catcher Bill Salkeld. Phil Masi, the Braves' primary backstop, was installed as a pinch-runner. Mike McCormick followed with a successful sacrifice bunt, moving Masi to second. Boudreau, who also served as Cleveland's manager, ordered an intentional walk to Eddie Stanky. The strategy puzzled Feller, who later said: "I thought it was a mistake and I told Lou so. Stanky wasn't a good hitter and I was confident I could get him out."[20] With two on and one out, Feller induced a harmless fly ball off the bat of Sain, bringing up the far more dangerous Tommy Holmes.

Looking to sneak out of trouble, Boudreau signaled to Feller for a pickoff move. According to Feller, he and Boudreau had been using it for years with moderate success. Feller turned and fired accurately to second, catching Masi off guard. Feller described the play as follows: "We caught Masi napping. Unfortunately, we caught the umpire, Bill Stewart of the National League, doing the same thing.... Lou tagged Masi out by two feet. Everybody in the ballpark saw he was out—except one, the umpire."[21] The next day, *Associated Press* photos confirmed the accuracy of Feller's statement.

What should have been the third out of the inning turned sour for the Indians. Holmes—who had hit .325 during the regular season—singled to left field, scoring Masi from second. The Indians went quietly in the ninth, securing a 1–0 victory for the Braves.

Bob Lemon, who started for Cleveland the following day, felt that Stewart's blown call had hidden benefits. Lemon was in a first inning jam with one out, two on and a run already in, when he conspired with Boudreau to try the pickoff play again. This time, it worked. Years later, Lemon pointed out: "All the hell that was raised because everybody thought

Stewart blew the call made the umpires more alert, more aware that we might try it again."[22]

Stewart's misadventures continued throughout the Series. In the first inning of Game 2, he called Braves shortstop Alvin Dark safe on a close play at first base. Multiple witnesses claimed that Stewart made the call before the ball and the runner had even reached the bag. Again, press photos strongly suggested that the arbiter had botched the play.

Booed heartily by fans in Cleveland before the start of Game 4, Stewart generated more first inning controversy when he called Boudreau out while attempting to advance to third on an RBI-double. The ruling could have gone either way and third base coach Bill McKechnie threw his hat on the ground angrily during the ensuing argument. The crowd treated Stewart to a symphony of catcalls, but the Indians came out unscathed, winning the game, 2–1. They clinched the Series two days later.

Asked to share his philosophy on umpiring, Stewart remarked: "the most important thing—and schools can't teach this—is to make decisions quick and to have the guts to stick to them once they're made, come hell or high water."[23] After adhering to those words in the 1948 World Series, Stewart continued as an NL arbiter through the 1954 campaign.

Though Phil Masi claimed for many years that Stewart had made the right decision at second base, he changed his tune shortly before his death in 1990. Masi not only mentioned the play in his will (presumably to clear his conscience), but he also inscribed a baseball sent in the mail to him by a fan: "I was out."[24]

1955 World Series Game 1: Jackie Robinson Steals Home

Yankees vs. Dodgers, September 28, 1955

Entering the 1955 postseason, the Dodgers had never won a World Series. In fact, they had come out on the losing end seven times. In his autobiography, *All My Octobers*, Mickey Mantle accurately described the mood in Flatbush as such: "There was a cloud hanging over the Dodgers that October.... The fans in Brooklyn were always looking forward to next year. They were the most loyal, the most profane, and the most critical of any fans anywhere."[25] They were also the most fortunate that season as

Brooklyn's loveable "Bums" erased decades of failure with an inspiring victory over the New York Yankees. The tone of the Series was set in the eighth inning of Game 1, when Jackie Robinson literally stole a run from Yankee ace Whitey Ford. Stationed behind home plate that day, umpire Bill Summers defended his call on Robinson to the day he died.

Among the most storied clubs in baseball history, the 1955 Dodgers carried five Hall of Famers on their roster (including the young and seldom-used Sandy Koufax). Centerfielder Duke Snider, a.k.a. "The Duke of Flatbush," paced the National League with 136 RBIs. Catcher Roy Campanella and first baseman Gil Hodges chipped in with over a hundred ribbies apiece, adding fifty-nine homers to Snider's impressive total of forty-two. Shortstop Pee Wee Reese provided solid defense and strong leadership while Jackie Robinson—at thirty-six years of age—was still as gritty and determined as ever.

The Yankees had a pretty spectacular club of their own with Mickey Mantle, Yogi Berra and Whitey Ford soaking up most of the attention. The 23-year-old Mantle was just coming into his prime, launching thirty-seven homers before a mid–September injury limited him to a handful of appearances in the final weeks of the season. Berra had been a staple behind the plate in the Bronx since 1947 and was enjoying his second consecutive MVP campaign. Ford, nicknamed "Slick" for his coolness in big-game situations, led the AL with

Yankee icons Yogi Berra and Whitey Ford both contended that Jackie Robinson was out at home on an attempted steal during Game 1 of the 1955 World Series. Umpire Bill Summers did not agree. This picture of Robinson appeared on the back of a 1950s comic book (Library of Congress).

eighteen wins and eighteen complete games. Meanwhile, pitchers Bob Turley and Tommy Byrne quietly contributed thirty-three wins to the Yankee cause.

The NL pennant race was never terribly close. The Dodgers held onto first place from mid–April through the end of the regular season and finished more than thirteen games ahead of the Braves. In sharp contrast, the Yankees shared the lead several times and dropped to second in mid–September before finally outpacing the second place Indians.

The sixth postseason Yankee–Dodger showdown opened at Yankee Stadium. More than sixty-three thousand fans saw Don Newcombe—a twenty game winner that year—square off against Ford, who was making the first of many Game 1 starts for the Yankees. Neither pitcher was effective that afternoon as the Bombers jumped out to a 6–3 lead through six innings.

Ford got into trouble in the eighth, yielding a leadoff single to Carl Furillo. After Hodges flied out, Robinson made it to second on an error by third baseman Gil McDougald. Don Zimmer followed with an RBI sac-fly as Robinson moved to third. Walter Alston called upon utility man Frank Kellert—who had fashioned a .325 average in limited duty—to pinch-hit for relief pitcher Don Bessent. Whitey Ford braced himself for a play at the plate as Robinson tried to bait the All-Star hurler into making a mistake.

"I knew he was going to steal home," Ford said years later. "I almost dared him to by taking a long windup as he danced off the bag. Sure enough, he took off for the plate and I threw the ball to Yogi and got it in there in plenty of time.... Robinson slid right into the tag. [He] was out. There was no question about it."[26] Summers was not of the same mindset, making a decisive call to the contrary. Berra argued his case emphatically, but the arbiter repeatedly turned his back and walked away. Despite the ensuing controversy, the Yankees held on to win, 6–5.

Analyzing the play with existing footage is futile. While the official World Series highlight reel is inconclusive, Robinson appears to be out in multiple photographs. An alternate reverse-angle clip suggests Robinson beat the tag. After examining the more obscure footage, researcher Eric Enders wrote confidently: "Robinson's foot touched the right side of the plate unmolested."[27]

By his own account, Robinson was no longer in peak physical condition at the end of the 1955 campaign. But he was willing to push his limits in order to bring a championship to Brooklyn at long last. Interviewed on Bill Stern's radio show after the game, Pirates manager Fred Haney called Robinson's gambit a "stupid move."[28] Robinson admitted that his actions were risky but reflected: "Whether it was because of my stealing home or not, the team had a new fire."[29]

The Dodgers defended their world championship against the Yankees in 1956, suffering an all-too familiar fate as the Bombers prevailed in seven games. Robinson's steal of home became an enduring symbol of courage and perseverance. In fact, the play continues to resonate even today. In 2015, a cartoon appeared on the official MLB website. The single-panel drawing depicted God, dressed in a baseball hat and equipped with headphones, staring down at Robinson and Berra. God's dialog bubble read: "Jackie tells me you've requested a replay review from the '55 Series."[30]

While Summers contended throughout his lifetime that he made the right call on Jackie Robinson, Yogi Berra insisted the opposite was true. In fact, Summers' grandson once attended an autograph session at Yankee Stadium in which Berra was the guest of honor. Informed of who he was signing for, the retired Yankee icon grew slightly agitated. "Your grandfather was wrong!" he asserted. "Robinson was out at home. [Summers] had no angle to be able to make that call."[31]

Berra, who had been ejected by Summers on multiple occasions, raised a good point. Summers was stationed behind Berra on the infamous play with pinch-hitter Frank Kellert occupying the right-hand side of the batter's box.

A modest man, Summers once said of his own abilities: "I wasn't much of an umpire at first, but I could keep the peace. And that's an umpire's most important and toughest job."[32] Summers did important work with baseball's Rules Committee, assisting with significant revisions that clarified a number of muddled areas in the rulebook. When he retired in 1959, he was the oldest umpire to have worked in the AL at sixty-three years of age.

The Yankee–Dodger rivalry is among the most celebrated in all of sports. The teams first met on the October stage in 1941. To date, there have been a total of eleven postseason showdowns between the two rivals—more than any other teams from opposing leagues. After dropping the first five meetings, the Dodgers won three of the next six. The Yankees have compiled a 37–28 record against the Dodgers in the Fall Classic.

1969 World Series Game 5: The Old Shoe Polish Trick
Orioles vs. Mets, October 16, 1969

In addition to the ground-breaking U.S. moon landing, 1969 was a year of many precedents, particularly in the world of baseball. The New York Mets finished above .500 for the first time in franchise history. They won their first pennant by defeating the Braves in the first National League Championship Series. Though the victory came in the club's eighth season of existence, it must have felt like an eternity to fans.

The Mets joined the National League in 1962 and promptly set a modern record for losses in a season. The team was so bad in those days, even their septuagenarian manager, Casey Stengel, was dumbfounded on occasion. "[I've] been in this game one-hundred years," he joked, "but I see new ways to lose 'em I never knew existed before."[33] The Mets averaged 108 defeats per season from 1962 through 1967. With the arrival of pitchers Tom Seaver and Jerry Koosman, things finally began to improve.

The 1969 Mets were built around solid pitching and strong defense. They posted the third highest fielding percentage in the majors. The Seaver-Koosman tandem—often referred to as the "Tom and Jerry Show"—combined for forty-two regular season wins. As the Mets remained in contention throughout the late summer months, even Stengel (who retired from managing in 1965) became a believer. "This club plays better ball now," he said with tongue-in-cheek. "Some of them look fairly alert."[34]

Considered by many to be a "Super Team," the 1969 Orioles had a power-packed lineup featuring sluggers Frank Robinson and Boog Powell, who jointly blasted sixty-nine homers. On the defensive side, third baseman Brooks Robinson, shortstop Mark Belanger, and centerfielder Paul Blair were among the best at their positions, combining for thirty-two Gold Gloves over the course of their careers. On the mound, the O's had a pair of twenty-game winners in Mike Cuellar and Dave McNally. Hall of Famer Jim Palmer, who was out of the majors in 1968, returned to post sixteen victories as the Orioles finished nineteen games ahead of the defending world champion Tigers.

The odds were heavily stacked against the Mets as the World Series opened in Baltimore. Surprising no one, the Orioles breezed to a 4–1 win. Despite the outcome, the Mets remained upbeat. "I swear, we came into the clubhouse more confident than when we had left it," Seaver recalled years later. "Somebody—I think it was [Donn] Clendenon—yelled out 'Dammit, we can beat these guys!' And we believed it."[35]

That faith grew even stronger as Koosman tossed a two-hitter in Game 2. Gary Gentry and Nolan Ryan followed with a combined shutout. In Game 4, Seaver gave his best performance of the Series, scattering four hits through eight innings. Faltering a little in the ninth, he yielded consecutive singles to Frank Robinson and Boog Powell. Robinson came around to score on a sacrifice fly, tying the game at one. In the bottom of the tenth, the Mets got a helping hand from umpire Lou DiMuro.

Jerry Grote led off with a bloop double that was misjudged by left-fielder Don Buford. Al Weis—a nuisance to Baltimore pitchers throughout the Series—was intentionally walked. Mets skipper Gil Hodges sent J.C. Martin to the plate to bat for Seaver. A .209 hitter during the regular season, Martin bunted the ball toward pitcher Pete Reichert, whose relay to first hit Martin in the wrist. The ball bounced into right field, scoring pinch-runner Rod Gaspar. It was only the second walk-off bunt in World Series history. But there was a glaring problem. Martin had violated major league rule 6.05(k), which prohibits players from interfering with throws to first while running within an allotted distance inside the baseline. For whatever reason, DiMuro chose to ignore the infraction. The Orioles argued to no avail as the Mets took a 3–1 Series advantage.

In Game 5, DiMuro made two more generous contributions to the New York cause. With Baltimore leading, 3–0, in the top of the sixth, Koosman appeared to hit Frank Robinson with a pitch. But DiMuro—stationed behind home plate—ruled that the ball had struck Robinson's bat. He was dead wrong. Replays convincingly showed that the pitch bounced off Robinson's hip before making contact with his bat. Robinson, a Triple Crown winner and two-time MVP, eventually went down on strikes, squandering a subsequent single that might have put him at third base with one out when Brooks Robinson lifted a fly ball to left field.

In the bottom of the sixth, a call reversal by DiMuro became an enduring Series legend. Baltimore's Dave McNally, who had given up just three hits to that point, threw a pitch in the dirt that may or may not have clipped the foot of leadoff batter Cleon Jones. DiMuro was hesitant to make a firm ruling, and as a discussion ensued, Hodges devised a clever strategy. Recalling a nearly identical scenario from the 1957 World Series, Hodges approached DiMuro with the ball and drew the arbiter's attention to a smudge of shoe polish. DiMuro found the evidence compelling enough to give Jones a pass to first base. Clearly rattled by the turn of events, McNally surrendered a two-run homer to Series MVP Donn Clendenon. The Mets tied the score in the seventh on a homer by Al Weis. They tacked on the winning run in the bottom of the eighth, capturing their first World Series title. No expansion team had ever done that before.

The Mets' long-suffering fans were elated. According to *New York Times* sportswriter Arthur Daley: "They came tumbling from the stands by the thousands, lit red flares, brandished signs and whooped it up with unrestrained glee." They also tore the field apart, absconding with all the bases and ripping up the turf until it was (in Daley's words) "as pock-marked as a battlefield."[36]

As the years passed, multiple members of the so-called "Miracle Mets" offered different versions of the smudged ball story. Koosman claimed that Hodges told him to rub the ball on his shoe before presenting it to DiMuro. According to Swoboda, McNally's wild pitch hit a ball-bag underneath the Mets' bench, causing other practice balls to spill out. Since the game ball could not be conveniently located, Swoboda alleged that Hodges randomly grabbed one with a blotch on it. Hall of Famer Frank Robinson acknowledged the ingenuity of Hodges' tactic, remarking more than four decades later: "It's always good planning to have a baseball in the dugout with shoe polish on it just in case."[37]

The incident Hodges took inspiration from occurred during Game 4 of the 1957 Fall Classic. The Yankees were leading the Braves, 5–4, in the bottom of the tenth, when utility man Nippy Jones was called upon to pinch-hit for pitcher Warren Spahn. Jones had played against Yankee hurler Tommy Byrne in the Pacific Coast League and knew that the left-hander habitually started batters off with bad pitches hoping they would chase. True to form, Byrne threw a low pitch that struck Jones in the right foot. It traveled to the backstop then bounced back toward the batting circle, where Jones picked it up and showed it to home plate umpire Augie Donatelli. Sure enough, there was a smudge of shoe polish on the ball, which Jones contended was proof-positive that Byrne's offering had made contact with his foot. Donatelli initially ruled the pitch a ball, but in light of Jones' appeal, changed his decision to a hit-by-pitch. Catcher Yogi Berra argued the call along with Yankee skipper Casey Stengel, but Donatelli refused to budge. Felix Mantilla, who was inserted as a pinch-runner, ended up scoring to tie the game. This set up a two-run walk-off homer by Milwaukee slugger Eddie Mathews. The Braves won the Series in seven games.

1970 World Series Game 1: Ken Burkhart's Miraculous Behind-the-Back Call
Orioles vs. Reds, October 10, 1970

Though baseball's World Series is supposed to represent the highest level of play, there have been many forgettable moments over the years. One such moment occurred during the 1970 Fall Classic, in which Ken Burkhart, Elrod Hendricks and Bernie Carbo combined for a comedy of errors at home plate. The results were less comical to the Reds, who were deprived of a go-ahead run.

In the 1950s, the Baltimore player development scheme came to be known as "The Oriole Way." Created by general manager Paul Richards and farm director Jim McLaughlin, the philosophy was condensed into a manual used by minor league instructors. It emphasized the fundamentals of the game—everything from properly executing a bunt to connecting with the appropriate cut-off man. When Hall of Fame manager Earl Weaver took over in 1968, he felt that the "Oriole Way" was being neglected and brought it back to the forefront. He would later famously describe his strategy as such: "The key to winning ballgames is pitching, fundamentals and three-run homers."[38]

The Orioles had all three of Weaver's indispensable elements working in 1970 as they breezed to another pennant, winning 108 games and leaving the Yankees fifteen games in their wake. Baltimore pitching icon Jim Palmer joined the twenty-win club along with Dave McNally and Mike Cuellar as eight positional players finished with double-digit home run totals. When Gold Gloves were handed out that year, three of them went to members of the Orioles (Paul Blair, Davey Johnson and Brooks Robinson).

In 1969, sportswriter Bob Hertzel of *The Cincinnati Enquirer* coined the phrase "Big Red Machine" in reference to the Reds. Though the nickname would become more applicable in the years that followed, Hertzel's so-called "Machine" was running smoothly in 1970. Construction of a prototype had begun in the 1960s with the addition of superstars Pete Rose, Tony Perez and Johnny Bench to the lineup. Still, the Reds placed no higher than third during the latter half of the decade. Looking to push them over the top, general manager Bob Howsam hired Sparky Anderson to manage the club in 1970. It was the beginning of something wonderful as the Hall of Fame skipper led the Reds to four pennants in a seven-year span. Though he could be dogmatic and overbearing at times, Anderson earned the respect of players by accepting and even welcoming their input.

Perez enjoyed his finest offensive campaign in 1970, reaching career-high marks in home runs (40) and RBIs (129). He finished third in MVP voting behind Bench, who led the majors in both aforementioned categories. Rose, appearing mostly in right field, won a Gold Glove and gathered more than 200 hits for the third consecutive season.

Neither the Reds nor the Orioles had much difficulty with their opponents in the League Championship Series as both teams orchestrated efficient sweeps. The Orioles were on the verge of a World Series sweep before a dramatic eighth inning homer by Cincinnati's Lee May erased a Baltimore lead. It was the only game the Reds would win as the O's clinched the championship with a lopsided victory the following day. Brooks Robinson was a dominant force, hitting .429 and putting on an astounding defensive display. Frustrated by Robinson's work throughout, Anderson quipped sourly: "I'm beginning to see him in my sleep. If I dropped the paper plate I'm holding now, he'd pick it up on one bounce and throw me out."[39]

As crisp as the defensive play was in the Series, Game 1 featured a notoriously sloppy sequence at home plate. The Reds jumped out to an early 3–0 lead, but Boog Powell put the Orioles on the board with a two-run homer in the top of the fourth. Catcher Elrod Hendricks tied the game with a solo shot an inning later. The Reds were pressing to regain the lead in the bottom of the sixth with one out and runners at the corners. Ty Cline, who had collected seven hits and six walks as a pinch-hitter during the regular season, was called upon to bat for light-hitting shortstop Woody Woodward. As Cline hit a high chopper in front of the plate, a combination of miscues followed.

In a glaring lapse of judgment, Burkhart positioned himself on the third base side to make a fair/foul ruling. Believing the ball would elude Hendricks, Bernie Carbo bolted recklessly toward home. Upon reaching the plate, he found Burkhart kneeling directly in his path. Attempting to avoid the roadblock, he executed an awkward, sprawling slide. Hendricks fielded the ball cleanly but was obstructed by Burkhart as he lunged toward Carbo with an empty glove. The umpire, now facing the wrong direction, made a blind call, ruling Carbo out on the play. Completing the farce, Carbo slid around the plate, touching it only accidentally when he rushed over to argue with Burkhart.

Anderson came out of the dugout in a hurry to confront the arbiter. "I'd like to see the picture on that one," he said irately. "So would I," Burkhart replied.[40] The Reds came up empty-handed as pitcher Gary Nolan flied out to end the inning. Brooks Robinson's solo homer in the seventh ended up as the game-winner for the Orioles.

In the next meeting, officials received word that Burkhart was being pelted with objects by fans in right field. Police were dispatched to the scene but found no evidence of any impropriety—aside from a few scattered catcalls. Burkhart finished the Series uneventfully, his presence scarcely figuring into the outcome of the remaining four games.

Though most of his career went off without a hitch, Burkhart's blown call in the 1970 World Series was so flagrant, it was later used in instructional videos to educate umpires on the fundamentals of proper positioning and alertness. Questioned about the play after the game, Burkhart claimed he saw Hendricks apply the tag to Carbo, though he admitted he wasn't sure exactly how he had witnessed it.

Finished as an official after 1973, Burkhart returned in an advisory capacity during the umpire's strike of 1979. The support he provided to replacement officials displeased many of the umpires on strike and he was widely ostracized afterward.

Burkhart was not the only umpire to get caught out of position on a crucial play during the World Series. In Game 2 of the 1973 Fall Classic, Augie Donatelli was at the center of controversy again. The A's and Mets had battled to a 6–6 tie through nine innings. With Bud Harrelson on third in the top of the tenth, New York's second baseman Felix Millan hit a fly ball to shallow left field. Harrelson tagged up and raced home as A's outfielder Joe Rudi caught the ball and fired to catcher Ray Fosse. Believing Harrelson would slide, Donatelli ended up in an awkward spot—behind the play and lying on his stomach. Fosse took the throw a few feet up the line in foul territory and appeared to miss the tag as Harrelson flew by him. After calling Harrelson out from a prone position, Donatelli was besieged by a crowd of angry Mets personnel that included manager Yogi Berra and on-deck hitter Willie Mays. Donatelli stuck to his decision though replays convincingly proved that Harrelson had eluded the tag. The play had no lasting impact as the Mets rallied in the twelfth for a 10–7 win.

1975 World Series Game 3: Armbrister Interferes with Fisk
Red Sox vs. Reds, October 14, 1975

The 1975 World Series was among the most fiercely contested in modern history with five of seven games being decided by a single run. It is best remembered (especially by Red Sox fans) for Carlton Fisk's twelfth inning walk-off homer in Game 6. The footage of Fisk hopping up the first baseline waving his arms in a frantic attempt to steer the ball into fair territory has regularly appeared on World Series highlight reels for decades.

Among the oldest teams in the majors, the Reds made history in 1975 with a franchise record 108 wins. After a few early-season hiccups, the "Big Red Machine" shifted into high gear, building a twenty-game lead over their closest NL West competitors—the Dodgers. The Reds sent five players to the All-Star Game, three of whom ended up in the Hall of Fame.

Johnny Bench—the NL's premier defensive catcher—carried his weight with a bat, smashing twenty-eight homers and gathering a team-leading 110 RBIs. NL MVP Joe Morgan led the league in walks and on-base percentage while finishing second in stolen bases. Tony Perez, a charismatic leader in the clubhouse, drove in 109 runs. Setting the table for Perez, all-time hits leader Pete Rose reached base a total of 310 times—more than any player in the majors.

Renowned for his impatience with pitchers, manager Sparky Anderson sent eight different starters to the mound during the 1975 campaign. In an era when hurlers frequently went the distance, the entire Cincinnati staff combined for just twenty-two complete games—the lowest total in either league.

Whenever discussions regarding the greatest Red Sox teams are raised, the 1975 squad is invariably thrown into the mix. In addition to three Hall of Famers—Fisk, Carl Yastrzemski and Jim Rice—there were several borderline candidates performing at peak efficiency in Boston that year. Rookie sensation Fred Lynn hit .331 while leading the team in doubles and RBIs. Dwight Evans, who was in the early stages of a long, productive BoSox career, provided stellar defense and timely hitting. On the mound, the effervescent Luis Tiant was a delight to fans with his pirouette delivery and kinetic glove waggling. He was far less delightful to opponents, limiting them to a collective .236 batting average over nineteen seasons. Tiant was one of five Red Sox pitchers whose win totals ended up in double digits.

With a strong supporting cast, the Sox climbed into first place for good on June 28, fending off stiff competition from the second place Orioles. In the ALCS, they put an end to the A's bid for a fourth consecutive championship, outscoring Charlie Finley's mustachioed men by a cumulative 18–7 margin.

After making quick work of the Pirates in the NL playoffs, the Reds came out flat in the Series opener at Fenway Park, managing just five hits in a 6–0 loss. They trailed through most of Game 2 before evening the Series with a ninth inning rally. The third contest was characterized by an unsettling round of controversy.

The day was unseasonably warm in Cincinnati with temperatures peaking around eighty degrees. The air was still quite humid at game time, which may at least partially explain the sudden power surge that occurred. A total of six home runs were hit that night—three by each club. By the time the Reds went down in the last of the ninth, the score was tied at five.

In the bottom of the tenth, utility man Ed Armbrister inadvertently created problems for umpire Larry Barnett. A native of the Bahamas, Armbrister lasted just five years in the majors, never making more than seventy-three appearances in any season. After centerfielder Cesar Geronimo opened the inning with a single, the speedy Armbrister was called upon to pinch-hit for reliever Rawly Eastwick. Instructed to bunt, Armbrister produced a high bouncer directly in front of the plate. He described the resulting play as follows: "I really don't know why I stopped. I still can't tell you that. Carlton Fisk, being experienced, should have known what to do. For some reason, I hesitated and he was out there like a cat. I saw him reaching for the ball and I decided to make my way down to first base. My right knee hit his left shin-guard. He then made a [grunting] sound, like he wanted to put everything into the throw."[41] Unfortunately for the Red Sox, Fisk's throw was off the mark, sailing into center field. Geronimo advanced to third and Armbrister motored into second as Fisk appealed to Barnett for an interference call.

Boston manager Darrell Johnson rushed to the scene, but Barnett stood his ground, insisting there had been no infraction on the play. The crowd grew restless, peppering Johnson with boos as he overstayed his welcome on the field. After watching the replay multiple times, *NBC* color analyst Tony Kubek insisted that Barnett should have ruled in favor of the Red Sox. He was mistaken. A section of the MLB rulebook clearly states that: "When a catcher and batter-runner going to first base have contact when the catcher is fielding the ball, there is generally no violation and nothing should be called."[42]

The game unraveled for the Sox after that. Pitcher Jim Willoughby was replaced by Rogelio Moret, who proceeded to intentionally walk Pete Rose. Pinch-hitter Merv Rettenmund struck out. Moret had Morgan in a 1–2 hole before the All-Star second baseman dropped a single into center field, ending the contest in favor of the Reds.

In the locker room, Fisk slammed his mask repeatedly against the wall while several others stomped around and shouted. Asked about the controversial play, Fisk said irritably: "Of course he interfered with me. You all saw it. He stood right under the ball!"[43] *Boston Globe* correspondent Ray Fitzgerald wrote: "I have been in many sullen and snarling locker rooms in the last decade, but never as bitter as the one last night. The Grinch had stolen Christmas from the Red Sox."[44] Always good for a memorable quote, BoSox pitcher Bill "Spaceman" Lee asserted: "If it had been me out there, I would have bitten [Barnett's] ear off. I would have Van Goghed him."[45]

Lee was not alone in his condemnation of Barnett. The arbiter received a stack of death threats from incensed Boston fans and was placed under police protection. He publicly blamed Kubek for the regrettable turn of events, but patched things up with the broadcaster during the off-season.

In the meantime, there was still more than half a World Series left to be played. On the heels of a demoralizing defeat, the resilient Sox bounced back with a 5–4 win. The Reds took Game 5, setting up Fisk's heroics in the next meeting. A rousing come-from-behind victory in the Series finale gave the Reds their first championship since 1940. "Most teams would have quit," said an elated Rose after the game. "This is the happiest moment of my life. I'm scared I'm going to have a coronary."[46] But of course he didn't.

Years later, *Referee Magazine* listed Barnett's call (or non-call in this case) as one of the best decisions in the history of officiating. Barnett stood by the accuracy of his verdict, commenting: "I got the play right, but you could never convince the people in Boston."[47]

Barnett was among several officials who lost their jobs in the failed labor negotiations of 1999. He was named supervisor of umpires the following year, leaving the position in 2001. His postseason credits in thirty-one seasons included seven ALCS and four World Series. Asked about baseball's current state of affairs, Barnett voiced his approval of the replay system. "I think it's better for the game," he contended. "The technology is there, why not use it?"[48]

1978 World Series Game 4: Reggie Jackson Interferes with Infield Throw

Yankees vs. Dodgers, October 14, 1978

The 1978 World Series was the tenth postseason showdown between the Yankees and Dodgers. The Bombers had won seven prior encounters, including the previous year when Reggie Jackson earned the nickname "Mr. October" with an unprecedented display of power. In the 1978 Fall Classic, Jackson not only hurt the Dodgers with his bat, but he used his body as well.

The Yankees' season was marred by turmoil. After clashing repeatedly with Jackson, manager Billy Martin made a snide remark to the press that provoked the fury of owner George Steinbrenner. Facing the prospect of being fired, Martin tearfully resigned on July 24. The Yankees were ten games out of first place when Martin stepped down, leaving replacement manager Bob Lemon with a lot of catching up to do.

The Yankees prospered under Lemon's low-key managerial style, gradually chipping away at the Red Sox lead. The decisive blow came in early–September, when the Yankees swept a four-game series at Fenway Park and moved into a tie for first place. (The disastrous affair came to be known as "The Boston Massacre" among loyal Sox fans.) A one-game playoff in Boston was necessary to decide the division championship. The game featured a clutch homer by light-hitting Yankee shortstop Bucky Dent along with a stellar pitching performance from Cy Young Award winner Ron Guidry. In the ALCS, the Yankees disposed of the Royals in four games.

Among the most powerful teams of the era, the Dodgers were continually suppressed by stronger opponents. During the Reds' era of dominance (1970–1976), the Dodgers finished second in the AL West on six occasions. They finally won a pennant in 1974 but fell prey to the A's in the World Series. It was the third consecutive championship for Oakland.

The 1978 Dodgers were led by Hall of Fame manager Tom Lasorda. Known for his loyalty and passion, he guided the club to four pennants and two World Series titles during his distinguished career. The crop of players at his disposal in the late–'70s/early–'80s would have made almost any manager look good. Don Sutton was as reliable as they came on the mound, posting double digit win totals in seventeen consecutive seasons. Corner infielders Steve Garvey and Ron Cey appeared on six All-Star teams together. Second baseman Davey Lopes provided speed and occasional power at the top of the order while serving as a reliable double-play partner to shortstop Bill Russell. The two worked brilliantly together around second base for portions of ten seasons.

The Dodgers encountered stiff competition from rivals in '78, sharing the division lead numerous times. They built a nine-game lead in mid–September before taking a nosedive during the final week of the season. In the end, they held off the surging Reds by a narrow margin. After disposing of the Phillies in the NLCS, they faced the Yankees in a World Series rematch.

Looking to put an end to the Bombers' postseason mastery, the Dodgers came out swinging in Game 1, battering New York pitchers for eleven runs on fifteen hits. Ron Cey powered L.A. to a Game 2 victory with a three-run homer. The Yankees rebounded in the third meeting and were hoping to pull even in Game 4. Trailing 3–0 in the bottom of the sixth, "Mr. October" stung the Dodgers yet again.

Roy White singled with one out and Thurman Munson drew a walk. Jackson then singled to right field, scoring White and pushing Munson to second. Lou Piniella followed with a sinking line drive to Russell at short. The ball bounced off Russell's glove, but he recovered in plenty of time to tag second and make a throw to first. Jackson scrambled back toward the bag then froze in the middle of the baseline, making no attempt to avoid Russell's relay. In fact, it appeared as if he stuck his hip out deliberately to block the throw, which is a violation of rule 7.09 (f). The ball caromed into right field, allowing the lumbering Munson to score. At the end of the sequence, Jackson retreated to first base and stood on the bag with Piniella, waiting for the umpires to sort things out.

Analyzing the play years later, left field umpire Bill Haller pointed out that Jackson may not have been the only guilty party. Haller suspected that Russell may have purposely bungled Piniella's liner in order to turn a double play, which would not have been allowable under the rules. "I assumed he intentionally dropped the ball," Haller said. "But nothing happened. Nobody said anything about that."[49] Stationed at second base that night, umpire Joe Brinkman saw no obvious infraction and allowed the play to continue as Jackson became the center of attention.

Lasorda came rampaging out of the Dodger dugout, arguing in favor of an interference call. After stating his case to Brinkman, he engaged with first base umpire Frank Pulli, who was not swayed by the Dodger skipper's appeal. "The key to the play was whether it was intentional," Pulli explained. "I knew the ball hit Reggie, but from my angle, it didn't look like he moved to disrupt the throw.... I really believe [Reggie] was confused. If he thought he was out for sure and no longer involved in the play, then why, after it was all over, was he heading back to first base thinking he was safe?"[50]

Plate umpire Marty Springstead stayed out of the argument since he didn't have a good angle on the play. "I will say this," he told a reporter. "I have never seen anybody intentionally get hit by a thrown ball. That thing hurts."[51]

When the dust had settled, third baseman Graig Nettles grounded out to end the inning. The Yankees tied the game in the eighth on an RBI double by Munson. They won it in the tenth, when Piniella drove White home with a single. The rest of the Series was catastrophic for the Dodgers as they lost the remaining two games by a 19–4 margin. Steve Garvey referred to Jackson's interference as "flagrant," and added jokingly that "he should have been banned for the rest of the season."[52]

In 2017, Garvey assembled the "Way We Were Tour," a traveling interview show in which he held candid discussions with former baseball stars in front of live audiences. During a casino appearance in Los Angeles, Garvey prompted Jackson to own up to the deliberateness of his actions in Game 4. Jackson offered a sly smile and said point-blank: "Yeah, I did it."[53] The crowd laughed and cheered as Garvey convinced Jackson to stand up and demonstrate the move he had used to deflect Russell's throw.

Between 1977 and 1981, the Dodgers faced the Yankees in the World Series three times, losing twice. Had Reggie been absent from the proceedings, things could have turned out very differently. The boastful slugger punished L.A. pitchers, gathering eight homers and seventeen RBIs in fifteen games. Additionally, he drew eight walks and scored fifteen runs. His success in the Fall Classic was not limited to his years with the Yankees. Dating back to his time with the A's (which included another appearance against the Dodgers), Reggie was a .357 lifetime hitter in the World Series play. He was named MVP twice—in 1973 and 1977.

Frank Pulli called plays reliably for twenty-eight seasons, appearing in four World Series. He was known for his dramatic strike three calls, which he punctuated with an exaggerated "punch-out" motion. Despite the 1978 World Series incident, his reputation remained largely unblemished until 1989, when he was placed on probation by Commissioner Fay Vincent for associating with illegal bookies. Fellow arbiter Rich Garcia was also implicated.

Pulli is remembered as the first umpire to make use of instant replay. In a 1999 game between the Marlins and Cardinals, Cliff Floyd hit a shot that was initially ruled a home run. Pulli requested a look at the video footage and, after reviewing it, reversed the call to a double. Though this is a common practice nowadays, it was a bold move back then and he was reprimanded for his actions.

1985 World Series Game 6: Don Denkinger's Blown Call at First Base

Royals vs. Cardinals, October 27, 1985

It's a common mistake to blame one man for the fate of an entire team. Rookie first baseman Fred Merkle was held largely responsible for the Giants' failure to win a pennant in 1908. Veteran infielder Bill Buckner assumed a lion's share of the culpability for Boston's 1986 World Series loss. And umpire Don Denkinger became public enemy number one in St. Louis after his blown call turned the tide of Game 6 in favor of Kansas City during the 1985 Fall Classic.

Of course, Denkinger wasn't solely responsible for the Cardinals' World Series loss to the Royals. It took an offensive meltdown, a defensive lapse and a flagrant case of miscommunication to extend the Series to seven games. But few fans in St. Louis remember that. "I was an umpire for more than thirty years in the major leagues," said Denkinger after his retirement. "I know I made a lot of mistakes. That one was just blown out of proportion."[54]

Without a bona fide power hitter in their lineup, the 1985 Cardinals relied heavily on speed, defense and pitching. They stole more bases than any team in the majors by a wide margin. And they posted the highest fielding percentage. On the mound, Cardinal hurlers ranked second among twenty-six teams in the ERA department. Manager Whitey Herzog, who had piloted the Royals for five seasons before signing with St. Louis, was a master at playing to his club's strengths while focusing on the little things that win ballgames. His strategy came to be known as "Whitey Ball."

In the American League West, Hall of Famer George Brett enjoyed a spectacular year at the plate, hitting .335 with 112 RBIs. Aside from that, there were few bright spots in the Royals' lineup. Making up for a listless offense, Kansas City pitchers came through with flying colors, posting the second-best ERA in the AL. Cy Young Award winner Bret Saberhagen was the top starter, gathering twenty victories while finishing among the league leaders in multiple categories. Closer Dan Quisenberry paced the AL for the fourth straight season with thirty-seven saves.

The pennant races were tight. The Royals were stuck in second place from July 23 through September 5, ultimately finishing just one game ahead of the Angels. The Cardinals collected 101 wins yet struggled to hold off the persistent Mets, who captured a World Series title the following year.

In the ALCS, the Royals lost three of the first four games before snatching the pennant from Toronto's grasp. In the National League, St. Louis won four straight over L.A. after dropping the first two meetings. Prior to Game 4, the Cardinals were dealt a serious blow when leadoff man Vince Coleman (who had led the majors with 110 steals) was injured in a bizarre accident. The speedy outfielder was standing on the field at Busch Stadium in St. Louis after pre-game drills when the automatic tarp machine rolled over his leg, chipping a bone in his knee and putting him out of commission for the remainder of the year.

Coleman wasn't the only key player with issues. The strain of close to three-hundred innings of work had taken a toll on 21-game winner Joaquin Andujar. The flashy right-hander posted a 6.44 ERA after September 17, including two shaky appearances in the NLCS. Cardinals second baseman Tom Herr recalled: "We were kind of a wounded team physically going into that Series."[55]

Wounded or not, the Cardinals pushed the Royals to the brink of elimination in Game 5. After putting up a run in the first inning on a pair of doubles by Herr and Jack Clark, St. Louis batters managed just three hits for the rest of the evening. The result was a disappointing 6–1 loss.

Game 6 was a pitcher's duel between Danny Cox—an 18-game winner for St. Louis—and Charlie Leibrandt, who had fashioned the second-lowest ERA in the American League. Through seven innings, only one runner had gotten as far as third base. The Cardinals manufactured a run in the eighth and were nursing the lead when Denkinger made his infamous call.

Summoned from the minors in late–August, 25-year-old right-hander Todd Worrell was selected to pitch the bottom of the ninth. It was an assignment he would have liked to forget. Pinch-hitter Jorge Orta, a fourteen-year veteran who had hit .267 during the regular season, rapped a seemingly harmless grounder to the right side. Stationed at first base, Clark crossed in front of Herr to field the ball. Worrell dutifully hustled over to cover the bag. It was a bang-bang play that was extremely close in real time. Orta tumbled to the ground as Denkinger rendered his verdict.

Safe at first!

Worrell, Clark and Herr confronted Denkinger. They were joined by Herzog soon afterward. In the broadcasting booth, Jim Palmer and Al Michaels analyzed the play in slow-motion. The evidence was indisputable. Denkinger had blown the call.

The rest of the inning was a nightmare for St. Louis. Royals slugger Steve Balboni, who had struck out 166 times during the regular season, hit a catchable pop-up in front of the Kansas City dugout. Clark, a recently converted outfielder, called for it as catcher Darrel Porter hovered nearby. Clark's inexperience proved costly as he misjudged the ball, allowing it to drop behind him untouched. Balboni made the most of the mistake, singling to left field. With two on and no outs, catcher Jim Sundberg came to the plate with instructions to bunt. He failed twice and then tried again with two strikes. Worrell fielded it in front of the mound and fired to third base in time to get the force on Orta. With Hal McRae at the plate, Worrell and Porter got crossed up. Porter was expecting a fastball, but Worrell delivered a slider. The ball got by the veteran catcher, allowing both runners to move up a base. Completing a night of infamy for the Cardinals, pinch-hitter Dane Iorg delivered the biggest hit of his career, blooping a game-winning single into right field.

Interestingly, Denkinger didn't realize he had missed the call at first base until the game was over. Upon encountering Commissioner Peter Ueberroth at the door of the umpire's dressing room, the arbiter asked if he had gotten it right. Ueberroth shook his head and answered in the negative.

With another chance to clinch the title, the Cardinals came up short again, scattering five hits off Saberhagen in an 11–0 Game 7 loss. Frustrated with Denkinger's calls behind home plate in the fifth inning, Herzog shouted from the bench: "If you'd done your damn job last night, we wouldn't be here!" The umpire promptly retorted: "If your team were hitting better than .120, we wouldn't be here either!"⁵⁶ When Herzog's continued taunts became laden with profanity, Denkinger threw him out of the game. Andujar, who had been called upon in relief, lost his composure and got tossed as well. Recounting the Cardinals' experience years later, Herr pointed to Game 6 as the breaking point. "It was important for us to win that night. It was brutal—something we just couldn't recover from."⁵⁷

Making Denkinger's life a living hell, a pair of St. Louis disc jockeys broadcast his address and phone number over the air. Death threats and obscene calls soon followed. Though the chaos eventually subsided, fan resentment of Denkinger lingered for many years in St. Louis. When he announced his retirement after the 1998 campaign, one local newscaster delivered the report accompanied by the "Hallelujah Chorus."

Denkinger's major league career spanned portions of thirty seasons. He developed a reputation for being even-tempered with players and managers, seldom resorting to ejections. However, he had little tolerance for violence on the field. In a 1993 game between the Blue Jays and Angels, he threw a total of six men out for their various roles in a bench clearing brawl.

Denkinger worked in twelve postseason series but is remembered primarily for his mistake in the 1985 Fall Classic. Though he acknowledged his error, he tried very hard not to dwell on it in the years that followed. "It's life and it goes on," he told a reporter.⁵⁸

Asked about the use of instant replay in baseball today, Denkinger said: "The object is to get the call right. That's a good thing. So I'm all for review. And if they had it back then [in '85] no one would even know my name."⁵⁹

1998 World Series Game 1: Rich Garcia Gives Tino Martinez an Extra Pitch to Work With

Yankees vs. Padres, October 17, 1998

The Yankees were a team of destiny during the twentieth century, capturing twenty-five championships. Reflecting on the Padres' Game 4 loss to New York in the 1998 Fall Classic, San Diego pitcher Kevin Brown said: "I can't for the life of me think of one good break we had the whole

Series. They had the talent. And like tonight, they had everything go their way, too."[60] Fortune smiled on the Yankees in Game 1, when home plate umpire Rich Garcia gave Tino Martinez an extra strike to work with during a critical at-bat. It was all Martinez needed to lift the Yankees to an epic come-from-behind victory.

There were so many compelling stories coming out of the Bronx in 1998, it was difficult for writers to keep up. David Cone collected twenty wins for the first time since undergoing surgery to remove a career-threatening aneurysm from his pitching arm. Orlando Hernandez defected from Cuba then won seven of his last eight regular season decisions. And shortly before sweeping the ALDS from the Rangers, the Yankees learned they would be finishing the playoffs without the services of slugger Darryl Strawberry, who was diagnosed with colon cancer.

The Padres' season, though relatively ordinary in comparison, was successful nonetheless. At thirty-eight years of age, Hall of Famer Tony Gwynn proved he could still hit with the best of them, leading the club with a .321 average. Greg Vaughn and Ken Caminiti added some muscle to the lineup with a collective total of seventy-nine homers. Trevor Hoffman, the NL's premier closer, gathered a career-high fifty-three saves while starters Andy Ashby and Kevin Brown combined for thirty-five wins and a 2.83 ERA. In a classic David vs. Goliath scenario, the Padres upset the heavily-favored Astros in the Division Series then marched to an NLCS conquest of the Braves, who had set a franchise record with 106 wins. A World Series victory over the powerful Yankees would have provided a storybook ending to San Diego's astonishing championship bid, but the Bombers were in the midst of their own fairy tale.

Game 1 pitted Brown against David Wells, who had posted a 21–4 record to that point including the postseason. The Yankees struck first with a pair of runs in the second, but the Padres built a 5–2 lead on homers by Vaughn and Gwynn. With one out in the bottom of the seventh, Jorge Posada singled and Ricky Ledee walked, prompting San Diego manager Bruce Bochy to remove Brown from the game. The strategy backfired when Chuck Knoblauch drove reliever Donne Wall's third pitch down the left field line for a game-tying homer.

Things fell apart in a hurry after that.

Derek Jeter followed with a single, ending Wall's brief and unsuccessful appearance. Left-hander Mark Langston, who had been used primarily as a starter during the regular season, was called upon to snuff out the Yankee rally. Paul O'Neill popped out to short right field, bringing AL batting champion Bernie Williams to the plate. After a wild pitch, Williams was intentionally walked. Langston worked the count full to designated hitter Chili Davis but lost him on a slider that was low and inside. With the bases loaded, Langston's 2–2 offering to slugger Tino Martinez appeared to be a knee-high strike from every available camera angle. Unfortunately for the Padres, home plate Rich Garcia disagreed. What should have been an inning-ending strikeout for Langston ended up as ball three.

Garcia had been extremely generous to the Yankees in the past, helping them to a Game 1 ALCS win in 1996 with a blown call on a Derek Jeter homer (details of which appear in the previous chapter). Garcia's latest gift propelled the Yankees to another victory as Martinez drove Langston's 3–2 offering into the upper deck for a grand slam. After the game, which ended in a 9–6 San Diego loss, Padres skipper Bruce Bochy said: "It's obvious that we would have liked to have had that pitch. Langston thought it was there. [Catcher] Carlos Hernandez thought it was there."[61] So did almost every sportswriter in America. In fact, Garcia's decision is widely regarded as one of the costliest mistakes by an umpire in a World Series game.

Interestingly, statistics indicate that Garcia could be extremely generous to pitchers with his calls at times. Asked about his interpretation of the strike zone, Garcia once said: "We don't need a specific definition. We know what the strike zone is. So do hitters and pitchers."[62] Weighing in on the same topic, umpire Joe Brinkman commented: "There are fifty-two different strike zones because there are fifty-two umpires."[63]

After the Yankees completed an efficient sweep, Kevin Brown remarked that the Series was "one break, one pitch away from being a different Series."[64] As of this writing, the Padres were still looking for that one break to give them a shot at redemption.

2006 World Series Game 2: Kenny Rogers and the "Smudgegate" Affair

Tigers vs. Cardinals, October 22, 2006

There's an old maxim which states that no team has gotten terribly far in baseball without cheating a little. Sign-stealing, steroid use, doctoring baseballs—while clearly unethical, all these tactics have been commonly used by players to gain an edge. The key is not to get caught. During

Game 2 of the 2006 Fall Classic, Detroit pitcher Kenny Rogers wasn't fooling anyone with his mound mischief.

The 2006 World Series was highly unusual in that both teams had posted losing records during the second half. The Tigers stumbled at seasons' end, dropping their last five games and handing away the AL Central title after posting the best won-loss percentage prior to the All-Star break. They entered the postseason as a Wild Card team.

Part of the problem in Detroit was closer Todd Jones, who blew three of his last five save opportunities and finished the season with a 3.94 ERA. The Tigers also turned to Fernando Rodney to finish games, but he wasn't spectacular either with a 3.52 earned run average and four blown saves. Detroit starters were far more reliable as Justin Verlander—playing in his first full season—collected seventeen victories, tying for the team lead with the veteran Rogers, who had begun his pro career during the Reagan Presidency.

The Cardinals limped into the playoffs with a 3–9 record over the last two weeks of the season. This included a seven-game losing streak that stretched from September 20 through September 26. The St. Louis offense was led by Albert Pujols, who finished second in MVP voting with a career-high forty-nine homers and 137 RBIs. Chris Carpenter was the top Cardinal starter, compiling a 15–8 record and 3.09 ERA. No one else in the rotation averaged less than four runs per nine innings. Closer Jason Isringhausen was downright awful at times, blowing ten saves.

Though Detroit and St. Louis appeared wobbly at seasons' end, both teams turned things around when the playoffs began. The Tigers took out the Yankees in the Division Series—no mean feat considering that the Bombers had several Hall of Famers on their pitching staff. In the ALCS, the A's proved to be no match for Detroit, losing all four games by a combined score of 22–9. Meanwhile, the Cardinals made quick work of the Padres in the NLDS then stood their ground against the Mets in a hard-fought League Championship Series.

Entering the Fall Classic as underdogs, the Cardinals didn't look the part in Game 1, battering Verlander for seven runs in five innings. Hoping to quiet the St. Louis bats, the Tigers sent Rogers to the mound the following night. The 41-year-old Rogers had started his big league career in the Texas bullpen. Converted to a starter in his fifth season, he won no fewer than twelve decisions during ten campaigns. This included a perfect game against the Angels in 1994. He seemed to get better with age, posting a 75–41 record from 2002 through 2006. On a personal level, he had cemented a reputation as a curmudgeon after a 2005 altercation with cameramen at Ameriquest Field in Arlington. The prickly southpaw was fined and forced to attend anger management classes.

Prior to the 2006 Series, Rogers had been a godsend for the Tigers, winning both of his postseason starts and assembling a 15-inning scoreless streak. His Game 2 appearance took place in appalling weather conditions with steady rain, eighteen mile per hour winds and a temperature of forty-four degrees. During the first inning, television cameras picked up a mysterious brown smudge near the base of Rogers' left thumb. Fox broadcasters Tim McCarver and Joe Buck speculated that it was pine tar.

After Rogers worked a scoreless first inning, umpire supervisor Steve Palermo, who was sitting in the stands, requested a conference with St. Louis manager Tony LaRussa. Standard MLB protocol required a full inspection of Rogers and, in the presence of contraband, an ejection and suspension would have been in order. But plate umpire Alfonso Marquez chose not to go that route. When the meeting with LaRussa was concluded, Marquez politely asked Rogers to remove the substance from his hand. The hurler complied and then shut out the Cardinals for seven more innings, becoming the first pitcher since Christy Mathewson to make three postseason starts without giving up a run. With the Series tied at a game apiece, controversy began to swirl.

In a postgame statement to the press, Palermo announced that Marquez had determined the spot on Rogers' hand was dirt. The hurler claimed it was part of his pre-pitch ritual to rub balls with dirt, resin and sweat. But hardly anyone believed that. Yankee coach Larry Bowa said: "You like to give the guy credit because [he's] been a good pitcher his whole career. But he's dominating now, not just pitching good games, but dominating games. It was obvious last night on TV—that was pine tar. It was shiny. Pine tar is a shiny substance."[65]

The plot thickened when numerous photos were released showing Rogers with the same shiny smudge on his hand during his two previous postseason outings. Tigers' coach Andy Van Slyke believed the substance was residue from Tootsie Rolls—the hurler's favorite candy. "When I shook Kenny's hand, it took me thirty seconds to get it unstuck," he joked.[66] But St. Louis batting coach Hal McRae fueled the fire when he alleged that Rogers was scuffing balls as well. "It's a shame a guy would cheat in a World Series game," McRae remarked sourly. "It hurts the integrity of the game."[67] Described by one reporter as "sarcastic and defensive," Rogers denied the claims made against him. "I think since I wiped the mud off, the last seven innings were pretty good. I'm sure that will get lost in translation."[68]

Asked about why he chose not to pursue the matter further while the game was in progress, LaRussa said: "I decided that I was not going to be part of the B.S. where I was going to go to the mound and undress the pitcher."[69] Instead of causing a major scene, LaRussa and the Cardinals settled the controversy by winning the next three games and claiming their tenth World Series title.

Faced with an ethical dilemma in Game 2 of the 2006 Fall Classic, Alfonso Marquez chose to tread lightly. Though the courteous request he made to Rogers resulted in the removal of whatever forbidden substance the hurler was using at the time, there were many who felt that there should have been more serious consequences. A precedent had been set in Game 3 of the 1988 NLCS, when plate umpire Joe West ejected Dodgers closer Jay Howell for having pine tar on his glove. Howell was later suspended for his actions. But since Tony LaRussa wasn't making a fuss, Marquez let Rogers off with a gentlemanly slap on the wrist. When the Cardinals won the Series anyway, Marquez's leniency became somewhat of a moot point.

Marquez's personal story is quite compelling. He grew up in an impoverished area of Mexico. His home had no running water. In 1979, his father snuck across the border and settled in Fullerton, California. Alfonso (known to his friends and colleagues as "Fonzie") was seven years old when his father arranged to have him transported to the U.S. along with the rest of his immediate family.

Marquez attended the Brinkman Umpire School in 1993 and worked in seven minor leagues before appearing in his first big league game during the 1999 slate. He was the first Mexican-born umpire to reach the majors. Since then, he has appeared in eight Division Series, four League Championship Series and three Fall Classics. Marquez is very grateful for all the lucky breaks he has had in his lifetime. "My Dad has always instilled in us and drilled in our heads that we can't forget where we came from," he said during a 2012 interview. "But I love this country. We've always said it is the country of opportunity. What better example than me?"[70]

It's interesting to note that the practice of doctoring baseballs was once legal (almost). Though nineteenth century rules prohibited players from discoloring or damaging the ball, these restrictions were rarely enforced in the early–1900s. Since the penalty for defacing the ball was relatively mild—a $5 fine—pitchers more or less did as they pleased and umpires almost always ignored their transgressions. There are currently three spitball artists from the deadball era enshrined at Cooperstown—Burleigh Grimes, Stan Coveleski and Red Faber. All were allowed to use the pitch (due to a grandfather clause) after spitballs were officially banned in 1920. Since then, other hurlers have become famous for secretly doctoring baseballs. That list includes Hall of Famers Whitey Ford, Don Drysdale, Gaylord Perry and Don Sutton.

2011 World Series Games 3 and 7: Ron Kulpa and Jerry Layne Make a Mess of Things
Rangers vs. Cardinals, October 22 and 28, 2011

After a series of raging debates in the 2009 and 2010 playoffs, the 2011 postseason got off to a mild start. Cardinals manager Tony LaRussa created a minor stir over Jerry Meals' strike calls in Game 2 of the NLDS, and there was a brief dispute over whether Tigers designated hitter Victor Martinez had been hit by a pitch in Game 2 of the ALCS. Other than that, things remained relatively quiet.

Until the World Series got underway.

Though the Rangers implemented several lineup changes in 2011, the end result was the same as they finished first in the AL West and survived both rounds of the playoffs for the second straight year. In the National League, the Cardinals made the most of a Wild Card berth, returning to baseball's center stage after a five-year absence. St. Louis won the Series opener, 3–2, but the Rangers answered with a 2–1 victory in the second meeting. The third game was marred by controversy.

Kyle Lohse got the start for St. Louis, opposing Rangers left-hander Matt Harrison. It was a rough night for both pitchers as neither lasted into the fifth inning. The Cardinals were leading, 1–0, in the top of the fourth, when Albert Pujols led off with a single. Matt Holliday hit a double play ball to Rangers shortstop Elvis Andrus. Second baseman Ian Kinsler made a high throw to first that pulled Mike Napoli off the bag. Napoli spun and tagged Holliday before he reached the base, but umpire Ron Kulpa blew the call. Texas manager Ron Washington rushed onto the field to argue, contending later: "He missed the play and I knew he missed the play when I went out there."[71] During the ensuing discussion, no appeal was made to any of Kulpa's crewmates to uphold or overturn his decision. Kulpa admitted his mistake after the game and added in his own defense: "On that type of play, I'm not going to ask for help. Ron [Washington] didn't ask for me to get help either."[72]

There were consequences to Kulpa's lapse in judgment as the Cards made the most of a one on, one out situation. Lance Berkman singled, pushing Holliday to second base. David Freese followed with an RBI double. Looking for a force at home plate, Lohse intentionally walked catcher Yadier Molina to load the bases. The Texas hurler got the grounder he needed off the bat of centerfielder Jon Jay, but Napoli made a poor throw to the plate, scoring Berkman and Freese. By the time the last out of the inning was recorded, the Cardinals had opened a 5–0 lead. Plenty of bad pitching followed in a wild 16–7 St. Louis win.

A .297 hitter during the regular season, Cardinals third baseman David Freese compiled a .545 average in the NLCS, capturing MVP honors. He continued his heroics in Game 6 of the World Series. The Rangers were one out away from clinching the first championship in franchise history when Freese smashed a two-run triple, sending the game into extra innings. He added a leadoff homer in the bottom of the eleventh, evening things at three games apiece and securing his eventual status as Series MVP.

Umpire Jerry Layne drew scathing criticism for his work behind home plate in the finale. A meticulous breakdown of Layne's performance revealed that he made close to thirty borderline calls and more than a dozen flagrant errors. Most of his questionable decisions went in favor of the Cardinals.

In the bottom of the first inning, Freese took a first pitch from Harrison that was clearly a strike, but Layne called it a ball. The pitch was ultra-important because Harrison was struggling (having walked the previous two batters) and needed a boost. After Layne's mistake, Freese took two pitches then swung through a change-up, evening the count at 2–2. Had Layne made the correct call on Harrison's first offering, Freese would have been out on strikes and the inning would have been over. Instead, Freese worked the count full then slammed a two-run double to tie the score.

A series of dubious decisions by Layne in the fifth inning helped seal the Rangers' fate. With the bases empty, one out and the Cards ahead, 3–2, leftfielder Allen Craig walked on two errant calls. Then, with the bases loaded, Layne made a highly suspect ball four ruling on Yadier Molina, forcing in a run. The Rangers never recovered, losing the game and the Series.

Interviewed after it was over, Texas third baseman Adrian Beltre said: "It's probably easier to lose four games in a row in a World Series, but being a strike away, it's something that will be hard to forget."[73] As sportswriters pored over the details in the days and weeks that followed, Layne's Game 7 performance coupled with Kulpa's critical mistake in Game 3 factored heavily into discussions. *SB Nation* blogger Robbie Griffin made a valid observation when he wrote: "...Baseball should not be like this. We should not be subjected to human error in officiating that might favor one of the teams—even if not on purpose—on the biggest stage the game has to offer."[74] Perhaps, but it's important to note that the Rangers committed a total of eight errors in the Series—not exactly the kind of play that championships are built upon. And umpires were not solely responsible for the forty-one walks and thirty-two earned runs surrendered to St. Louis hitters. The walk totals were a new team record.

According to data published by Boston University researchers, Jerry Layne had the highest ratio of bad calls in the majors over a ten-year period from 2008 to 2018. Statisticians analyzed close to 46,000 of Layne's ball-strike calls in the aforementioned period and determined that he missed more than 6,000 of them (for a blown call ratio over fourteen percent). Layne was certainly not alone. According to the same study, major league officials collectively missed more than 34,000 calls in 2018—an average of 1.6 per inning. Reflecting on those findings, Boston University researcher and lecturer John T. Williams contended: "Throughout its history, MLB has protected its error-prone umpires, resisted adopting strong performance measurements, and not taken advantage of available technology that could better the game. At a time of autonomous cars and machine learning, MLB needs to embrace useful change."[75] Williams strongly suggested that MLB begin using radar tracking devices to determine the precise location of pitches in relation to the strike zone.

2013 World Series Game 3: Cardinals Score Game-Winner on Obstruction Call at Third Base
Red Sox vs. Cardinals, October 26, 2013

Whoever authored the famous quote: "there's nothing new under the sun" had obviously never seen a World Series. Though baseball's October showcase has been held every year (with two exceptions) since 1903, new precedents are set on an almost annual basis. In Game 3 of the 2013 Fall

Classic, the final score was decided by umpires as St. Louis utility man Allen Craig drew the first walk-off obstruction call in Series history.

The Cardinals pitching staff was especially strong in 2013. Right-hander Adam Wainwright finished second in Cy Young voting while Lance Lynn and Shelby Miller each contributed fifteen wins to the St. Louis cause. Among the best two-way catchers in the majors, Yadier Molina won a Gold Glove while gathering eighty RBIs. Molina was one of four positional players to reach the .300 mark at the plate as the Red Birds finished on top of the NL Central for the first time in four years. Neither the Pirates nor the Dodgers could stop St. Louis from advancing through both rounds of the playoffs.

The Red Sox had a solid offensive core in 2013 led by David Ortiz—one of the greatest clutch performers in baseball history. On the mound, Jon Lester led the staff with fifteen wins. John Lackey deserved much better than his 10–13 record as Boston hitters supported him with two runs or less in nine of his starts. Despite Lackey's plight, the Sox finished first in the AL East and took three of four games from the Rays in the ALDS. A win over the Tigers brought them back to the World Series for the first time since 2007.

Boston outmuscled St. Louis at Fenway Park in Game 1, but the Cardinals bounced right back with a 4–2 win in the second meeting. The third game was an epic struggle as the Sox rallied twice to overcome a pair of two-run deficits. In the bottom of the ninth, the Cardinals scored the winning run in highly unusual fashion.

With Brandon Workman on the mound for Boston, Molina drove a 3–2 pitch to right field for a single. Sox manager John Farrell went to the bullpen, summoning right-hander Koji Uehara, who had led the club with twenty-one saves and a 1.09 ERA. Cardinals pinch-hitter Allen Craig doubled on Uehara's first offering, putting the Sox in a one-out jam. With runners on second and third, Boston infielders moved in on the grass to guard against the bunt. Jon Jay smashed a hard grounder to the first base side, forcing Dustin Pedroia to make a spectacular diving grab. The Gold Glove second baseman sprang to his feet and threw home in time to nab Molina. It happened so quickly that catcher Jarrod Saltalamacchia had a legitimate shot at cutting down Craig as he was advancing to third. Unfortunately, Saltalamacchia's throw dipped under the glove of Will Middlebrooks and bounced into left field. Nursing a painful foot injury that had kept him out of action for over a month, Craig lumbered to his feet and headed for home, tripping over Middlebrooks on the way. Leftfielder Daniel Nava recovered Saltalamacchia's wayward throw and made an off-target relay to the plate. The ball arrived ahead of Craig, who was tagged out.

But he wasn't out.

Home plate umpire Dana DeMuth had seen crewmate Jim Joyce point to Middlebrooks at third base, indicating that there had been obstruction on the play. As Craig slid in, DeMuth made a safe call, confusing everyone in proximity. Saltalamacchia started shouting: "What do you mean safe? He can't be safe. I tagged him out. I'm halfway up the baseline!"[76] Farrell joined the argument as Pedroia stood nearby with his arms outstretched and a bewildered expression on his face.

ESPN writer Jayson Stark offered lavish praise to Joyce and DeMuth, referring to the call as the last great decision of the pre–Instant Replay Era. As shocking as it was to the Red Sox and their fans, the call was completely justified under rule 2.00, which states that a fielder who is not in possession of the ball and not in the act of fielding the ball cannot impede a runner's progress. In such cases, the umpire has a right to take corrective steps to nullify the obstruction. Explaining himself to reporters after the game, DeMuth said: "I could have called him out if the throw from the outfield had gotten [home with] Craig halfway up the baseline.... But here, seeing that obstruction happen, and seeing how close the play was at home ... that's where my judgment is that, had the obstruction not occurred, he would have scored."[77]

Though clearly not pleased with the outcome, Farrell at least accepted it. "That rule is straightforward," he told reporters. "You can't argue that."[78] But in the aftermath of the Red Sox loss, there were plenty of objections raised.

Boston pitcher Jake Peavy referred to the call as "a joke" and said of DeMuth: "He's already proven that he cannot see things correctly in Game 1."[79] Peavy was referring to a mistake the arbiter had made on a double play sequence at second base in the Series opener. DeMuth had called Pedroia out believing that Cardinals shortstop Pete Kozma had caught the relay and then dropped it while transferring it to his throwing hand. Other members of the crew felt that Kozma never had control of the ball. After a brief conference, DeMuth's decision was overturned.

The obstruction call in the third game did not turn the tide of the Series in favor of the Cardinals. In fact, the opposite occurred. Carried by the heroics of MVP David Ortiz, Boston won the next three games by a combined score of 13–4. Fittingly, the Sox clinched the championship at Fenway Park for the first time since 1918, when Babe Ruth had worn a Boston jersey.

Among the most experienced umpires in major league history, DeMuth's extensive career spanned portions of thirty-five major league seasons and included more than 4,200 appearances. He served as crew chief for several years. By the time he worked his last game in 2017, he had been assigned to eleven Division Series, five League Championship Series and five World Series. He was behind the plate for Game 6 of the 1993 Fall Classic, when Blue Jays outfielder Joe Carter hit a memorable Series-ending walk-off homer.

DeMuth was extremely even-tempered on the field, retiring with an ejection rate less than half the major league norm. An extremely private man, he seldom offered comments to reporters after games and even dodged U.S. President Barrack Obama once. Obama visited the umpire's locker room before the start of the 2009 All-Star Game and met each member of the crew—except for DeMuth, who was conspicuously absent.

After their 1918 championship run, the Red Sox experienced one of the longest droughts in major league history, waiting until the new millennium to capture a World Series title. At the time of this writing, they were the winningest team of the twenty-first century with four MLB crowns to their credit since 2004. As of 2020, Boston's nine championships ranked third on the all-time list behind the Yankees and Cardinals.

2017 World Series Game 5: Bill Miller's Oddly Shaped Strike Zone
Astros vs. Dodgers, October 29, 2017

Yasiel Puig grimaced and rolled his eyes in disbelief. Kike Hernandez put his hands on his head and walked away with a smirk on his face. More than half a dozen players had words with home plate umpire Bill Miller during Game 5 of the 2017 World Series, which pitted the Astros against the Dodgers. Through it all, computerized graphics showed that Miller's strike zone resembled a gerrymandered congressional district.

Both clubs had waited a long time to be in the World Series. The Astros had not made it past the first round of the playoffs in twelve years. The Dodgers had been absent from the Fall Classic for nearly three decades. But when Game 5 was over, neither team griped about Miller's questionable judgments. Houston pitcher Collin McHugh said: "I probably got a call or two that went my way and a call or two that didn't go my way. That's baseball and this is the World Series and nobody gets here by making excuses."[80] Dodger manager Dave Roberts was of a similar mindset. "I think for us and I think on the other side, we know Bill Miller's strike zone. So I don't think that at all affected the outcome of the game."[81]

... But of course it did.

During the regular season, Miller had led the majors with 151 called third strikes. He carried that trend to an extreme during his Game 5 appearance with eight called strikeouts—seven of which came at the Dodgers' expense. In all, twelve players from both teams were victimized for a total of eighteen punch-outs. Miller wasn't always generous with his strike calls. He issued eleven walks as well—four more than the combined average of both teams. One social media site comically compared Miller's strike zone to the *Nickelodeon Network* logo.

Controversy aside, the game was immensely entertaining to fans who favor offense. In five hours and seventeen minutes, there were twenty-five runs scored on twenty-eight hits, and an extra inning was required to determine the outcome. By the time third baseman Alex Bregman delivered a walk-off single in the bottom of the tenth, the Astros had rallied twice to erase deficits of three runs or more and squandered a three-run lead of their own.

When the game was over, *Fangraphs* blogger Jeff Sullivan aptly stated: "The game packed in enough astonishing action that there are more interesting and important points to make besides the strike zone having been so weird." But Sullivan wasn't so quick to dismiss Miller's calls as being inconsequential. "The obnoxious reality is that the zone was a factor, because every game changes with every pitch.... We'd prefer not to think about it, but blissful ignorance doesn't acknowledge all that went on."[82]

Anyone who watched the game knows that plenty went on. Sportswriter Mike Lupica referred to it as "baseball's gift to everybody" and remarked: "There is really only one appropriate way to describe what we saw that night, and what we heard in Houston. You do it with these two words: 'Oh my.'"[83]

Miller's decisions could hardly have been perceived as a "gift" to the Dodgers. His dubious strike calls spanned seven consecutive innings. Nine went against L.A. hitters who were eventually retired, representing one-third of the team's allotted outs. Since every run was important, the calls unquestionably changed the complexion of the game.

The 13–12 slugfest was followed by a pitcher's duel, which involved nine different hurlers and was won by Los Angeles. Game 7 was never terribly close as the Astros put up five runs in the first two innings then hung on the rest of the way. It was the first major sports title in Houston since the Dynamo captured back-to-back soccer championships in 2006 and 2007. For the Astros, it was their first World Series victory.

Still active through 2019, Miller's career has been stressful at times. During his rookie year in the International League, he was bound, gagged and robbed at gunpoint by unidentified assailants at a Norfolk hotel. One of the captors kept shouting for the gunman to shoot Miller in the head. The arbiter later remarked that he had never experienced anything so frightening in his entire life.

Though not quite as harrowing, Miller's on-field experiences have also been somewhat taxing. In 2012, he was assaulted by Blue Jays third baseman Brett Lawrie. After being ejected from the game for arguing a strike call, Lawrie threw his helmet, which bounced up and struck the arbiter. Later, as Miller was exiting the field, an unruly fan tossed a beer at him.

Miller was selected to work as an instructor at the MLB umpiring camps held at the Urban Youth Academy in Compton, California. He also worked at MLB sponsored camps for Marines. He was appointed crew chief before the 2014 campaign.

The Astros' 2017 championship could not have been sweeter considering the club's star-crossed history. Joining the National League lineup in 1962, the team was originally known as the Colt .45s. For three seasons, they played in a hastily constructed ballpark that was situated on a reclaimed plot of marshland. Because of its impractical location, Colt Stadium often fell prey to hordes of gnats and thick banks of fog. On occasion, stray rattlesnakes roamed the outfield grass. A name change and new domed stadium did nothing for the club in 1965 as the newly christened Astros lost 97 games and finished 32 games out of the running. The club later suffered ten consecutive postseason failures before finally bringing a championship to Houston.

Notes

Preface

1. John Thorn, "Distant Replays: What If Replay Had Existed Way Back When?" "Distant Replays," Our Game (blog), Dec. 11, 2017 (retrieved June 28, 2018), https://ourgame.mlblogs.com/distant-replays-cff7e4d7bf0d.
2. Christy Mathewson Page, Brainyquote.com/authors/christy_mathewson.
3. Billy Evans Page, Brainyquote.com/authors/billy_evans.

Introduction

1. Paul Sullivan, "Rise of the Machine? Automated Strike Zones a Concept Worth Considering," *Chicago Tribune*, May 7, 2017.
2. Gil Lebreton, "Umps Get One in Three Close Pitches Wrong, HBO Story Shows," *Star-Telegram*, Oct. 1, 2016.
3. Joe Giglio, "End of Umpires? Electronic Strike Zone Could Be Coming to MLB in 2018," NJAdvanceMedia.com, Aug. 23, 2017.
4. *Ibid.*
5. Nestor Chylak Page, quotetab.com/quotes/by-nestor-chylak#qZB51FK4G5Ll CocQ.97.
6. Umpire Quote Page, baseball-almanac.com/quotes/umpire_quotes.shtml.
7. *Ibid.*
8. Julianne Escobedo-Shepherd, "A Brief History of Why Umpires Wear Suits," pictorial.jezebel.com, Nov. 1, 2016.
9. *Ibid.*
10. Phil Rogers, "Umpires Pay Heavy Dues on Way to Majors," *Chicago Tribune*, July 18, 1999.
11. Umpire Quote Page, baseball-almanac.com/quotes/umpire_quotes.shtml.

Part One

1. Earl Gustkey, "50th Anniversary of Twin No-Hitters: Vander Meer's Un-Matched Pair," *LA Times*, June 15, 1988 (retrieved Feb. 4, 2018).
2. *Ibid.*
3. *Ibid.*
4. "Tough, Honest Ump Dies in VA Hospital," *United Press International*, Feb. 19, 1964 (retrieved Feb. 7, 2018).
5. baseball-almanac.com/feats/featsjv.shtml.
6. James W. Johnson, "Johnny Vander Meer," sabr.org/bioproj/person/14ff1abe.
7. "Bill Stewart, 69, Ex-Umpire, Dead, In National League 1933–55—Also a Hockey Referee," *New York Times*, Feb. 19, 1964 (retrieved Feb. 7, 2018).
8. Lawrence Baldassaro, "Joe DiMaggio, sabr.org/bioproj/person/a48f1830.
9. *Ibid.*
10. *Ibid.*
11. Richard Ben Cramer, *Joe DiMaggio: The Hero's Life* (New York: Simon & Schuster, 2000), p.161.
12. Larry R. Gerlach, *The Men in Blue: Conversations with Umpires* (Lincoln: University of Nebraska Press, 1980), p. 71.
13. Harvey Frommer, "Summer of '41: Joe DiMaggio's Epic 56-Game Hitting Streak," baseballguru.com/hfrommer/

analysishfrommer271.html (retrieved Feb. 11, 2018).

14. Joel Sherman, "Stats Say Joe DiMaggio's Record Tougher Now," *New York Post*, May 11, 2014 (retrieved Feb. 11, 2018).

15. Ken Schultz, "Ted Williams Underappreciated On-Base Streak," baseballprospectus.com, Mar. 2, 2017 (retrieved Mar. 27, 2019).

16. David Pietrusza, et al., *Baseball: The Biographical Encyclopedia* (Toronto: Sport Classic Book, 2003), p. 292.

17. Charles F. Faber, "Don Larsen," sabr.org/bioproj/person2b1a1fee.

18. *Ibid.*

19. David Pietrusza et al., *Baseball: The Biographical Encyclopedia* (Toronto: Sport Classic Book, 2003), p. 643.

20. Charles F. Faber, "Don Larsen," sabr.org/bioproj/person2b1a1fee.

21. *Ibid.*

22. John Derringer, "Larsen Beats Dodgers in Perfect Game, Yanks Lead, 3–2, on First Series No-Hitter," *New York Times*, Oct. 9, 1956.

23. Scott Ostler, "Dale Mitchell Watched Big One Go By," *LA Times*, Jan. 7, 1987 (retrieved Feb. 17, 2018).

24. Charles F. Faber, "Don Larsen," sabr.org/bioproj/person2b1a1fee.

25. John Derringer, "Larsen Beats Dodgers in Perfect Game, Yanks Lead, 3–2, on First Series No-Hitter," *New York Times*, Oct. 9, 1956.

26. Larry Gerlach, "Babe Pinelli," sabr.org/bioproj/person/8dbf8c1c.

27. probaseballinsider.com/baseball-instruction/what-is-a-balk/.

28. Jordan Zim, "7 Really Bad Sports Records That Will Never Be Broken," stack.com/a/worst-sports-records, Dec. 23, 2012 (retrieved Mar. 28, 2018).

29. David Vincent, "Al Barlick," sabr.org/bioproj/person/70fbe802.

30. Theron Schulz, "Balks: The Story of the 1988 Major League Season," recondite-baseball.blogspot.com, Aug. 11, 2008 (retrieved Mar. 29, 2019).

31. Don Drysdale Page, baseball-almanac.com/quotes/quodrys.shtml.

32. Richard D. Lyons, "Don Drysdale, Hall of Fame Pitcher, Dies at 56," *New York Times*, July 5, 1993.

33. Tony Favia, "Umpire/Batter Debate, 1968 Drysdale Pitch," *United Press International*, Jan. 21, 1981.

34. Larry Schwartz, "Drysdale Sets Consecutive Scoreless Innings Streak," espn.com/moment/010608drysdalerecord.html, Nov. 19, 2003 (retrieved Mar. 12, 2018).

35. *Ibid.*

36. *Ibid.*

37. Lance Pugmire, "Harry Wendelstedt Dies at 73, Baseball Umpire Also Ran School," *LA Times*, Mar. 10, 2012 (retrieved Dec. 22, 2018).

38. *Ibid.*

39. "Drysdale Gets 58.2 Shutout Innings Before Skein Ends," *Associated Press*, June 9, 1968.

40. *Ibid.*

41. "He Made a Name for Himself," *LA Times*, Oct. 18, 1988 (retrieved Mar. 17, 2018).

42. *Ibid.*

43. Sam McManis, "49 and Counting: With Title Clinched, Hershiser Focuses on Matching Drysdale's Streak," *LA Times*, Sept. 28, 1988 (retrieved Mar. 17, 2018).

44. Eric Stephen, "Today in Dodger History: Hershiser Breaks Drysdale's Scoreless Inning Record," SB Nation-True Blue LA, trueblue.com, Sept. 28, 2013 (retrieved Mar. 18 2018).

45. *Ibid.*

46. Bill Plaschke, "Orel Hershiser's Streak Was a Different Ballgame," *LA Times*, July 5, 1993.

47. "1994 Strike Was a Low Point for Baseball," *Associated Press*, Aug. 10, 2004.

48. Bob Nightengale, "1994 Strike Most Embarrassing Moment in Major League Baseball History," *USA Today*, Aug. 11, 2014.

49. "1994 Strike Was a Low Point for Baseball," *Associated Press*, Aug. 10, 2004.

50. Tom Verducci, "The Greatest Season Ever," *Sports Illustrated*, Oct. 5, 1998.

51. Mark McGwire Page, baseball-almanac.com/players/player.php?p=mcgwima01.

52. "McGwire Is King, but Sosa Is Prince," *New York Times*, Sept. 9, 1998.

53. Chris Broussard, "McGwire Gets One but Loses Another," *New York Times*, Sept. 21, 1998.

54. *Ibid.*

55. *Ibid.*

56. Bob Davidson Page, baseball-reference.com/bullpen/Bob_Davidson_ (umpire).
57. "Fan Sues to Get McGwire Ball Back," *Associated Press*, Sept. 26, 1998.
58. Jon Wertheim, "Flame Thrower: Cubs Phenom Kerry Wood Strikes Out 20 Astros," *Sports Illustrated*, May 6, 2015.
59. Sam Miller, "Baseball's Seven Wonders: Kerry Wood's 20 Strikeout Game," baseballprospectus.com, Mar. 18, 2014 (retrieved Dec. 24, 2018).
60. *Ibid.*
61. Mark Strotman, "Kerry Wood Ends the Debate: 20 Strikeout Game's Hit Was Legit," nbcsports.com/Chicago, May 19, 2017 (retrieved Dec. 24, 2018).
62. Paul Sullivan, "Kerry Wood Makes It Look Easy in Fanning 20 Astros," *Chicago Tribune*, May 7, 1998.
63. Amy R. Nelson, "Searching for Meaning in the Mistake," espn.com, Jan. 9, 2011 (retrieved Dec. 24, 2018).
64. *Ibid.*
65. Dave Hogg, "Armando Galarraga Deliver Lineup Card to Jim Joyce One Day After Blown Call Costs Him Perfect Game," *Daily News*, June 3, 2010.
66. Amy R. Nelson, "Searching for Meaning in the Mistake," espn.com, Jan. 9, 2011 (retrieved Dec. 24, 2018).
67. Tracy Ringolsby, "Q&A: Joyce Reflects on Memorable Career: 30-Year Umpiring Veteran Relives His Most Noteworthy Moments," mlb.com, Feb. 25, 2017 (retrieved Dec. 24, 2018).
68. James Schmehl, "Armando Galarraga Awarded Corvette for Near-Perfect Game," mlive.com, June 3, 2010 (retrieved Mar. 31, 2019).
69. Grant Brisbee, "The Unwritten Rules of Sticking an Elbow Out to Ruin a Perfect Game," SBNation.com, June 22, 2015.
70. Cliff Corcoran, "Blame Umpires, Not Tabata for Scherzer's Lost Chance at Perfection," *Sports Illustrated*, June 20, 2015.
71. Clinton Yates, "Jose Tabata's Infamous At-Bat Ended Max Scherzer's Perfect Game Was Actually Impressive," *Washington Post*, June 20, 2015.
72. Grant Brisbee, "The Unwritten Rules of Sticking an Elbow Out to Ruin a Perfect Game, SBNation.com, June 22, 2015.

Part Two

1. Brian McKenna, "Bob Ferguson," sabr.org/bioproj/person/df8e7d29.
2. *Ibid.*
3. Baseball-History-Daily Archives, Tim Hurst, baseballhistorydaily.com/tag/tim-hurst/ (retrieved Apr. 4, 2019).
4. *Ibid.*
5. "Hot-Headed Hurst, His Quick Temper Gets Him in Trouble," *Sporting Life*, Aug. 14, 1897.
6. Rich Huhn, "Tim Hurst's Last Call," sabr.org/research/tim-hurst-s-last-call-0 (retrieved Apr. 4, 2019).
7. Society for American Baseball Research, *Deadball Stars of the National League* (Washington, D.C.: Brassey's, 2004), p. 20.
8. Mike Lynch, "Who's on First? The Farce That Helped the Pirates Set a Record," thenationalpastimemuseum.com, Apr. 17, 2014 (retrieved Apr. 20, 2018).
9. *Ibid.*
10. *Ibid.*
11. *Ibid.*
12. Cait Murphy, *Crazy '08: How a Cast of Cranks, Rogues, Boneheads and Magnates Created the Greatest Year in Baseball History* (New York: Smithsonian, 2008), p. xiv.
13. Trey Strecker, "Fred Merkle," sabr.org/bioproj/person/37264391.
14. Don Jensen, "John McGraw," sabr.org/bioproj/person/fef5035f.
15. Italie Hillel, "Fred Merkle's Bonehead Play Forced Giant-Cub Playoff Game in 1908," *Associated Press*, Oct. 8, 1989 (retrieved Dec. 26, 2018).
16. Society for American Baseball Research, *Deadball Stars of the National League* (Washington, D.C.: Brassey's, 2004), p. 20.
17. Cait Murphy, *Crazy '08: How a Cast of Cranks, Rogues, Boneheads and Magnates Created the Greatest Year in Baseball History* (New York: Smithsonian, 2008), p. 191.
18. Italie Hillel, "Fred Merkle's Bonehead Play Forced Giant-Cub Playoff Game in 1908," *Associated Press*, Oct. 8, 1989 (retrieved Dec. 26, 2018).
19. Trey Strecker, "Fred Merkle," sabr.org/bioproj/person/37264391.

20. Society for American Baseball Research, *Deadball Stars of the National League* (Washington, D.C.: Brassey's, 2004), p. 20.
21. Joe Santry and Cindy Thomson, "Ban Johnson," sabr.org/bioproj/person/dabf79f8.
22. Lawrence S. Ritter, *The Glory of Their Times* (New York: Macmillan, 1966), p. 35.
23. Richard Bak, "The Madcap Life of Germany Schaefer, Baseball's Clown Prince," detroitathlete.com, Aug. 23, 2012 (retrieved May 21, 2018).
24. "There Once Was a Major League Baseball Player Who Stole First Base," todayifoundout.com, Aug. 18, 2012 (retrieved May 21, 2018).
25. Dan Holmes, "Germany Schaefer," sabr.org/bioproj/person/2594238c.
26. Society for American Baseball Research, *Deadball Stars of the National League* (Washington, D.C.: Brassey's, 2004), p. 389.
27. "Herman Schaefer Is Dead," *New York Times*, May 17, 1919.
28. *Ibid.*
29. Official Major League Rules, mlb.com/mlb/official_info/official_rules/official_rules.jsp.
30. "Bill Brennan versus Philadelphia," baseballhistorydaily.com/tag/bill-brennan/.
31. brainyquote.com/topics/Yankees.
32. John Branch, "60 Years and 1,000 Tales Since 14 Were Ejected," *New York Times*, July 6, 2006.
33. Ted Williams and John Underwood, *My Turn at Bat: The Story of My Life* (New York: Pocket Books, 1970), p. 81.
34. John Branch, "60 Years and 1,000 Tales Since 14 Were Ejected," *New York Times*, July 6, 2006.
35. *Ibid.*
36. *Ibid.*
37. George Castle, "If Two Balls in Play at Once Seems Weird, Then 3 Must Be a Crowd," chicagobaseballmuseum.org, June 23, 2014 (retrieved May 22, 2018).
38. John C. Skipper, *Take Me Out to the Ballgame: 35 Former Ballplayers Speak of Losing at Wrigley* (Jefferson, NC: McFarland, 2000), p. 110.
39. "Vic Delmore, 43, Former Umpire," *New York Times*, June 11, 1960.
40. Stew Thornley, "April 8, 1976: Hammerin' Hank Aaron Knocks in Three in His Final Opening Day," sabr.org/gamesproj/game/april-8-1976-hammerin-hank-knocks-three-his-last-opening-day.
41. Earl McKean, "All Managers Are Maniacs," *The Calgary Herald*, Sept. 11, 1976.
42. *Ibid.*
43. Bill Traughter, "Sounds Manager Don Money Looks Back on His Career," mlb.com, May 10, 2010 (retrieved Apr. 3, 2019).
44. Earl McKean, "All Managers Are Maniacs," *The Calgary Herald*, Sept. 11, 1976.
45. Murray Chass, "The Pine Tar Rule is Clarified," *New York Times*, Dec. 10, 1983.
46. Phil Pepe, *The Ballad of Billy and George* (Guilford, CT: The Lyons Press. 2008), p. 179.
47. *Ibid.*, p. 179.
48. *Ibid.*, p. 180.
49. Patrick Saunders, "Game 163: In 2007 the Rockies Shocked the Padres in Rocktober Fashion," *The Denver Post*, Oct. 1, 2017 (retrieved June 14, 2018).
50. *Ibid.*
51. *Ibid.*
52. *Ibid.*
53. *Ibid.*
54. Jeffrey Marcus, "Rockies Win with Sleight of Hand," *New York Times*, Oct. 2, 2007.
55. Patrick Saunders, "Game 163: In 2007 the Rockies Shocked the Padres in Rocktober Fashion," *The Denver Post*, Oct. 1, 2017 (retrieved June 14, 2018).
56. Bruce Miller, "Baseball: Rockies' Ump Says He'd Make the Same Call Again," *The DesMoines Register*, Oct. 2, 2007.
57. "How to Become an Umpire," mlb.com/mlb/official_info/umpires/how_to_become.jsp.
58. Tom Layberger, = "A Trip Through Time with Former MLB Umpire Bill Hohn," *The Times Herald*, Aug. 17, 2013.
59. "2009/07/29 Cox, McCann Ejected," youtube.com/watch?v=7WPzRoXBVS0.
60. David O'Brien, "Chipper Jones Rips Umpire Over Fist Bump, Ejections," *The Atlanta Journal-Constitution*, July 31, 2009.
61. Ray Kelsey, "Bill Hohn Should Be Suspended Immediately," tomahawktake.com, July 30, 2009 (retrieved July 2, 2018).

62. Tom Layberger, "A Trip Through Time with Former MLB Umpire Bill Hohn," *The Times Herald*, Aug. 17, 2013.
63. Matt Brooks, "Pirates Fall to Braves in 19 Innings on Controversial Call at Home Plate," *The Washington Post*, July 27, 2011.
64. *Ibid.*
65. "Joe Torre Talks About Blown Call in Pirates–Braves Game," www.youtube.com/watch?v=6x-BXAfuLMA.
66. "Umpire Jerry Meals, MLB Admit Blown Call Ended 19-inning Marathon," *The Sporting News*, July 27, 2011.

Part Three

1. Joe Henderson, "Been There, Done That: Rich Garcia Feels Ump's Pain," *Tampa Bay Times*, June 3, 2010.
2. Mickey Bradley and Dan Gordon, *Haunted Baseball* (Guilford, CT: The Lyons Press, 2007), p. 29.
3. Jeff Sullivan, "Let's Consider Eric Gregg and Livan Hernandez in the 1997 NLCS," fangraphs.com/blogs, Jan. 17, 2013 (retrieved Jan. 1, 2019).
4. *Ibid.*
5. *Ibid.*
6. *Ibid.*
7. Bill Madden, "Pastime Faces Crucial Call," *New York Daily News*, Oct. 12, 1998.
8. *Ibid.*
9. Murray Chass, "For Umps It's Not a Perfect World," *New York Times*, Oct. 17, 1998.
10. Jack Curry, "One That Got Away Draws Smile From Knoublach," *New York Times*, Oct. 15, 1999.
11. George A. King III, "Ump Admits Blown Call at Second Base," *New York Post*, Oct. 14, 1999.
12. Jim Caple, "Mr. Eddings ... You're Guilty," espn.com, Oct. 12, 2005 (retrieved Jan. 29, 2019).
13. Scott Merkin, "White Sox Look Back, Part 1: Dropped Third Strike," mlb.com, June 29, 2015 (retrieved Jan. 29, 2019).
14. *Ibid.*
15. Jim Caple, "Mr. Eddings ... You're Guilty," espn.com, Oct. 12, 2005 (retrieved Jan. 29, 2019).
16. Scott Merkin, "White Sox Look Back, Part 1: Dropped Third Strike," mlb.com, June 29, 2015 (retrieved Jan. 29, 2019).
17. Jeff Berg, "Calling 'Em as He Sees 'Em," desertexposure.com, Apr. 2012 (retrieved Jan. 29, 2019).
18. "Joba Chamberlain Recalls His Bout with Midges," youtube.com/watch?v=AVOG34uht_y.
19. "The Bugs Who Ate the Yankees," cbsnews.com, Oct. 7, 2007 (retrieved Apr. 27, 2019).
20. Joe Torre and Tom Verducci, *The Yankee Years* (New York: Doubleday, 2009), p. 438.
21. Ken Davidoff and George A. King III, "The Night When Bugs Changed the Course of Yankee History," *New York Post*, Oct. 4, 2017.
22. Joe Torre and Tom Verducci, *The Yankee Years* (New York: Doubleday, 2009), p. 440.
23. Ken Davidoff and George A. King III, "The Night When Bugs Changed the Course of Yankee History," *New York Post*, Oct. 4, 2017.
24. Kristie Ackert, "Umps Call Selves Out on Foul Ball Mistake in ALDS Game 2," *Daily News*, Oct. 10, 2009.
25. Jim Caple, "Umpire Errors a Real Embarrassment," espn.com, Oct. 20, 2009 (retrieved June 29, 2018).
26. "Umpires Miss More Calls in Game 4 of ALCS," foxsports.com, Oct. 21, 2009 (retrieved June 29, 2018).
27. Jim Caple, "Umpire Errors a Real Embarrassment," espn.com, Oct. 20, 2009 (retrieved June 29, 2018).
28. Jerry Crasnick, "MLB Changes Umpire Supervisors," espn.com, Mar. 6, 2000 (retrieved June 29, 2018).
29. Liz Roscher, "This Call from Umpire CB Bucknor Might Be One of the Worst in History," yahoosports.com, Apr. 18, 2017 (retrieved Apr. 9, 2019).
30. Jason Foster, "CB Bucknor Proves That MLB Umpires Are Essentially Employed for Life," sportingnews.com, Apr. 19, 2017 (retrieved Apr. 9, 2019).
31. Michael Hurley, "MLB Simply Has to Discipline Umpire Ron Kulpa for Incident with Astros," boston.cbslocal.com, Apr. 4, 2019 (retrieved Apr. 10, 2019).
32. Edward Glazarev "Tim Lincecum Sets San Francisco Giants Record with 14 Strikeouts in 1–0 NLDS Win Over Atlanta Braves," *Daily News*, Oct. 8, 2010.

33. Brett Keltyle, "2010 MLB Playoffs: It's Time for Paul Emmel to Own Up to His Mistakes," bleacherreport.com, Oct. 10, 2010 (retrieved July 3, 2018).
34. Joe Posnanski, "Bad Calls in Baseball," joeposnanski.com, Oct. 8, 2010 (retrieved July 3, 2018).
35. Peter Abraham, "MLB Needs to Fix Its Umpire Problem," boston.com, Oct. 8, 2010 (retrieved July 3, 2019).
36. "Cards Win NL Wild Card Playoff After Controversial Call Turns to Chaos," Associated Press, Oct. 5, 2012.
37. Ibid.
38. Ibid.
39. Jayson Stark, "The Pop-Up Heard 'Round the World," espn.com, Oct. 7, 2012.
40. Ibid.
41. Erik Malinowski, "Better Know an Umpire: Sam Holbrook," deadspin.com, June 14, 2012 (retrieved Jan. 7, 2019).
42. Ibid.
43. Jorge L. Ortiz, "Royals Win in Wet, Wild Game 6 Over Blue Jays, Advance to World Series Again," USA Today, Oct. 25, 2015 (retrieved June 17, 2018).
44. Ibid.
45. Neil Davidson, "Blue Jays Eliminated With Game 6 Loss in ALCS," The Canadian Press, Oct. 24, 2015 (retrieved June 17, 2018).
46. "Umpire Jeff Nelson Expressed Regret of Botched Call," Associated Press, May 25, 2013 (retrieved Jan. 7, 2019).
47. Brian Cohn, "Angel Hernandez, the Worst Umpire in Baseball," crawfishboxes.com (retrieved Apr. 11, 2019).
48. Ibid.
49. Tom Gatto, "Umpires Uphold Out Call on Adrian Gonzalez. Were They Right?" The Sporting News, Oct. 20, 2016.
50. Ron Cervenka, "Baseball's Worst Umpire Lives up to Reputation ... Again," thinkblueLA.com, Oct. 20, 2016 (retrieved June 17, 2018).
51. Ibid.
52. Ibid.
53. Tom Gatto, "Umpires Uphold Out Call on Adrian Gonzalez. Were They Right?" The Sporting News, Oct. 20, 2016.
54. Adam Kilgore, "Under-Fire Umpire Angel Hernandez Likely Done for the Playoffs, but Not for the Reason You Think," The Washington Post, Oct. 10, 2018.
55. Ibid.
56. Ibid.
57. Sam Belden, "The Nationals Lost the NLDS Thanks in Part to a Controversial Overturned Call in the 8th Inning," Insider.com, Oct. 13, 2017 (retrieved June 23, 2018).
58. Bob Nightengale, "In Firing Baker, Nationals' Gutless Arrogance Is on Display," USA Today, Oct. 20, 2017.
59. Erik Malinowski, "Better Know an Umpire: Jerry Layne," deadspin.com, Apr. 17, 2012 (retrieved Jan. 7, 2019).

Part Four

1. Norman Macht, "Jack Barry," sabr.org/bioproj/person/0a842468.
2. 1911 World Series Page, baseball-reference.com/bullpen/1911_World_Series.
3. Ibid.
4. Ibid.
5. Ibid.
6. Eric Enders, The Fall Classic: The Definitive History of the World Series (New York: Sterling Publishing Co., 2007), p. 33.
7. David Pietrusza, et al., Baseball: The Biographical Encyclopedia (Toronto: Sport Classic Book, 2003), p. 613.
8. Ibid., p. 614.
9. "The More Things Change," mlblogsbbbb.wordpress.com, Oct. 3, 2019 (retrieved Apr. 12, 2019).
10. Eric Enders, The Fall Classic: The Definitive History of the World Series (New York: Sterling Publishing Co., 2007), p. 66.
11. Steve Wulf, "The Secrets of Sam," Sports Illustrated, July 19, 1993.
12. Able, Stephen, "Sam Rice," sabr.org/bioproj/person593ed95f.
13. Francis E. Stan, "Sports Scope: Tame Bruins and Tigers of Regular Season Now Berserk," Evening Star, Oct. 5, 1935.
14. Paul Mickelson, "Umpire's Tired Abusive Charge," Associated Press, Oct. 5, 1935.
15. Ibid.
16. David Pietrusza, Judge and Jury: The Life and Times of Judge Kenesaw Mountain Landis (South Bend: Diamond Communications, 1998), Kindle edition.
17. "Bill Stewart, 69, Ex-Umpire, Dead, in National League 1933–55—Also a

Hockey Referee," *New York Times*, Feb. 19, 1964.

18. "Spahn and Sain by Gerald V. Hearn," baseball-almanac.com/poetry/po_rain.shtml.

19. Eric Enders, *The Fall Classic: The Definitive History of the World Series* (New York: Sterling Publishing Co., 2007), p. 119.

20. *Ibid*.

21. *Ibid*.

22. Russell Schneider, *The Cleveland Indians Encyclopedia* (Champaign, IL: Sports Publishing, 2004), p. 463.

23. "Bill Stewart, 69, Ex-Umpire, Dead, in NL 1934–55—Also a Hockey Referee," *New York Times*, Feb. 19, 1964.

24. John McMurray, "Phil Masi," sabr.org/bioproj/person/7981dd4f.

25. Mickey Mantle with Mickey Herskowitz, *All My Octobers* (New York: Harper Collins, 1994), p. 49.

26. Eric Enders, Eric, *The Fall Classic: The Definitive History of the World Series* (New York: Sterling Publishing Co., 2007), p. 136.

27. *Ibid*.

28. Stephen C. Weiner, "October 4, 1955: Brooklyn Dodgers Win First World Series as 'Next Year' Finally Arrives," sabr.org/gamesproj/game/october-4-1955-brooklyn-dodgers-win-first-world-series-next-year-finally-arrives.

29. *Ibid*.

30. Joey Nowak, "Jackie Safe at Home? Not According to Yogi," mlb.com, Sept. 24, 2015.

31. Bill Ballou, "Upton's Summers Was One of Baseball's Best Umpires," *Worcester Telegram*, Sept. 15, 2013.

32. Bill Summers Page, revolvy.com/page/Bill-Summers-(umpire).

33. Casey Stengel Quote Page, baseball-almanac.com/quotes/quosteng.shtml.

34. *Ibid*.

35. Donald Honig, *The New York Mets: The First Quarter Century* (New York: Crown, 1987), p. 61.

36. Thomas J. Brown, Jr., "October 16, 1969: Miracle Mets Become First Expansion Team to Win a World Series," sabr.org/gamesproj.

37. *Ibid*.

38. Warren Corbett, "The 1970 Orioles: The Oriole Way," sabr.org/latest/1970-baltimore-orioles-oriole-way.

39. Eric Enders, *The Fall Classic: The Definitive History of the World Series* (New York: Sterling Publishing Co., 2007), p. 175.

40. Chris Jaffe, "15,000 Days Since a Botched World Series Play," fangraphs.com, Nov. 4, 2011 (retrieved Jan. 21, 2019).

41. Rory Costello, "Ed Armbrister," sabr.org/bioproj/person/917df0fa.

42. Bruce Weber, "Game 3's Decisive Play: Why Call Was Obstruction," *New York Times*, Oct. 27, 2013.

43. CJ Kelly, "The Bunt That Changed History," howtheyplay.com, Jan. 16, 2019 (retrieved Jan. 20, 2019).

44. Rory Costello, "Ed Armbrister," sabr.org/bioproj/person/917df0fa.

45. *Ibid*.

46. Scott Miller, "Forgotten Game 7 of Reds–Red Sox '75 World Series Still Haunts Players, Coaches," bleacherreport.com, Oct. 29, 2015 (retrieved Jan. 20, 2019).

47. Mitch Vingle, "Ex-MLB Umpire Larry Barnett Returns Home," *Charleston Gazette-Mail*, Aug. 19, 2015.

48. *Ibid*.

49. "Hip-Hip, No Way: Yankees versus Dodgers 1978 World Series," referee.com, July 1, 2017 (retrieved Jan. 22, 2019).

50. *Ibid*.

51. *Ibid*.

52. "Steve Garvey on Reggie Jackson's Infamous '78 World Series Interference Play," *The Rich Eisen Show*, youtube.com/watch?v=tbyfq76MQUw.

53. *Ibid*.

54. Doug Miller, "Denkinger Cool with Reminders of Mistaken Call in '85 Series," mlb.com, Oct. 20, 2014 (retrieved Jan. 24, 2019).

55. *Ibid*.

56. Dan Greene, "After the Call," si.com/longform/2015/1985/world-series-cardinals-royals/index.html (retrieved Jan. 25, 2019).

57. Doug Miller, "Denkinger Cool with Reminders of Mistaken Call in '85 Series," mlb.com, Oct. 20, 2014 (retrieved Jan. 24, 2019).

58. *Ibid*.

59. *Ibid*.

60. Jason Diamos, "1998 World Series:

Yankees vs. Padres, Losers, Yes, but to a Winsome Ovation," *New York Times*, Oct. 22, 1998.

61. Peter Schmuck, "Yankees Roar Back in 9–6 Win," *Baltimore Sun*, Oct. 18, 1998.

62. Peter Gammons, "Whatever Happened to the Strike Zone," *Sports Illustrated*, Apr. 6, 1987.

63. *Ibid.*

64. Jason Diamos, "1998 World Series: Yankees vs. Padres, Losers, Yes, but to a Winsome Ovation," *New York Times*, Oct. 22, 1998.

65. Tyler Kepner, "With Smudge and Streak, Rogers Has Left an Imprint," *New York Times*, Oct. 24, 2006.

66. Eric Enders, *The Fall Classic: The Definitive History of the World Series* (New York: Sterling Publishing Co., 2007), p. 281.

67. *Ibid.*

68. Tyler Kepner, "With Smudge and Streak, Rogers Has Left an Imprint," *New York Times*, Oct. 24, 2006.

69. Eric Enders, *The Fall Classic: The Definitive History of the World Series* (New York: Sterling Publishing Co., 2007), p. 279.

70. Lou Ponsi, "Umpire Blazes Trail," *Orange County Register*, July 8, 2007.

71. Jerry Crasnick, "Ron Kulpa's Name Now Notorious," espn.com, Oct. 23, 2011 (retrieved Feb. 2, 2019).

72. *Ibid.*

73. "World Series Capsules: Cards Win World Series, Beat Texas 6–2 in Game 7," *Associated Press*, Oct. 28, 2011.

74. Robbie Griffin, "2011 World Series Game 7 Recap—Cardinals Win," dallas.sbnation.com, Oct. 28, 2011 (retrieved Feb. 2, 2019).

75. Mark T. Williams, "MLB Umpires Missed 34,294 Ball-Strike Calls in 2018. Bring on Robo-Umps?" *BU Today*, Apr. 8, 2019 (retrieved Apr. 18, 2019).

76. Jayson Stark, "The Last Great Calls," espn.com, Mar. 24, 2014.

77. *Ibid.*

78. *Ibid.*

79. Bryan Kilpatrick, "Reactions to Obstruction Call in World Series Game 3," sbnation.com, Oct. 27, 2013 (retrieved Feb. 4, 2019).

80. J.P. Hoornstra, "Bill Miller's Large, Imperfect Strike Zone Favored Hitters in World Series Game 5," *The Orange County Register*, Oct. 30, 2014.

81. *Ibid.*

82. Jeff Sullivan, "Incredulous Responses to Bill Miller's Strike Zone," Oct. 30, 2017 (retrieved Feb. 10, 2019).

83. Mike Lupica, "A World Series Game 5 for the Ages," sportsoneearth.com, Dec. 22, 2017 (retrieved Feb. 11, 2019).

Bibliography

Able, Stephen. "Sam Rice." SABR BioProject. https://sabr.org/Bioproj/Person593ed75f.

Abraham, Peter. "MLB Needs to Fix Its Umpire Problem." Boston.com, Oct. 8, 2010 (retrieved June 16, 2018).

Ackert, Kristie. "Umps Call Selves Out on Foul Ball Mistake in ALDS Game 2." *Daily News*, Oct. 10, 2009.

"Al Barlick Is Colorful Umpire, but Never Got Far as a Player." *Milwaukee Journal*, Aug. 8, 1942.

Anderson, Dave. "Sports of the Times: Hershiser's Best Pitch Is His Brainball." *New York Times*, July 4, 1999.

Anderson, David W. "Bill Klem." SABR BioProject. https://sabr.org/Bioproj/Person/31461b94.

____. "Tommy Connolly." SABR BioProject. https://sabr.org/Bioproj/Person/E99149e7.

Arnold, Perry. "Do Yankee Ghosts Haunt the New Yankee Stadium?" Bleacherreport.com, Apr. 23, 2009 (retrieved May 22, 2018).

Axisa, Mike. "Max Scherzer Loses Perfect Game in Ninth, Throws No-Hitter Against Pirates." Cbssports.com, June 20, 2015 (retrieved Apr. 14, 2018).

____. "Possible Blown Call Highlights Fifth Inning Meltdown by Nats in Game 5 vs. Cubs." Cbssports.com, Oct. 13, 2017 (retrieved June 23, 2018).

Baldassaro, Lawrence. "Joe DiMaggio." SABR BioProject. https://sabr.org/Bioproj/Person/A48f1830.

Ballou, Bill. "Upton's Summers Was One of Baseball's Best Umpires." *Worcester Telegram*, Sept. 15, 2013.

Belden, Sam. "The Nationals Lost the NLDS Thanks in Part to a Controversial Overturned Call in the 8th Inning." Insider.com, Oct. 13, 2017 (retrieved June 23, 2018).

Berg, Jeff. "Calling 'Em as He Sees 'Em." Desertexposure.com, Apr. 2012 (retrieved Jan. 29, 2019).

"The Big List of Umpire Heckles." Heckle Depot, https://www.heckledepot.com/umpire-heckles/.

"Bill Brennan Versus Philadelphia." Baseballhistorydaily.com/Tag/Bill-Brennan/.

"Bill Klem." National Baseball Hall of Fame. https://Baseballhall.org/Hall-Of-Famers/Klem-Bill.

"Bill Klem, 77, Dies, Dean of Umpires." *New York Times*, Sept. 17, 1951.

"Bill Stewart, 69, Ex-Umpire, Dead, in National League 1933–55—Also a Hockey Referee." *New York Times*, Feb. 19, 1964.

Bingham, Dennis. "Hank O'Day." SABR BioProject. https://sabr.org/Bioproj/Person/94b47a84.

"Biology and Control of Non-Biting Aquatic Midges." NC State Extension Publications. https://content.ces.ncsu.edu/biology-and-control-of-non-biting-aquatic-midges.

Bois, Jon. "Bobby Cox Ejected Perhaps for Last Time." Sbnation.com, Oct. 8, 2010 (retrieved June 15, 2018).

Bradley, Mickey, and Dan Gordon. *Haunted Baseball*. Guilford, CT: Lyons Press, 2007.

Branan, John. "60 Years and 1,000 Tales Since 14 Were Ejected." *New York Times*, July 6, 2006.

"Braves Protest Denied by MLB." Espn.com, Oct. 5, 2012 (retrieved June 18, 2018).

Brisbee, Grant. "The Unwritten Rules of Sticking an Elbow Out to Ruin a Perfect Game." Sbnation.com, June 22, 2015 (retrieved Apr. 14, 2018).

Brooks, Matt. "Pirates Fall to Braves in 19 Innings on Controversial Call at Home Plate." *The Washington Post*, July 27, 2011.

Broussard, Chris. "McGwire Gets One but Loses Another." *New York Times*, Sept. 21, 1998.

Brown, Larry. "Umpire Angel Hernandez Ripped for Terrible Strike Zone." Larrybrownsports.com, May 22, 2018.

Brown, Thomas J., Jr. "October 16, 1969: Miracle Mets Become First Expansion Team to Win a World Series." SABR Games Project. https://sabr.org/gamesproj/game/october-16-1969-miracle-mets-become-first-expansion-team-win-world-series.

Brubaker, Bill. "In Postseason, Calls Are Going Against Umpires." *The Washington Post*, Oct. 16, 1998.

"The Bugs Who Ate the Yankees." Cbsnews.com, Oct. 7, 2007 (retrieved Apr. 27, 2019).

Caple, Jim. "Mr. Eddings … You're Guilty." Espn.com, Oct. 12, 2005 (retrieved Jan. 29, 2019).

_____. "Umpire Errors a Real Embarrassment." Espn.com, Oct. 20, 2009 (retrieved June 3, 2018).

"Cardinals Win NL Wild Card Playoff After Controversial Call Leads to Chaos." *Associated Press*, Oct. 5, 2012.

Castle, George. "If Two Balls in Play at Once Seems Weird, Then Three Must Be a Crowd." Chicagobaseballmuseum.org, June 23, 2014 (retrieved Apr. 27, 2018).

Cervenka, Ron. "Baseball's Worst Umpire Lives Up to Reputation … Again." Thinkbluela.com, Oct. 20, 2018.

Chass, Murray. "On Baseball: For Umps It's Not a Perfect World." *New York Times*, Oct. 17, 1998.

_____. "The Pine Tar Rule Is Clarified." *New York Times*, Dec. 10, 1983.

"Chicago White Sox Multiple Media Outlets Forget 2005 World Series Title." Foxsports.com, June 30, 2017 (retrieved Apr. 9, 2019).

"Chipper Jones Rips Umpire Over Fist-Bump, Ejections." Baseballthinkfactory.org, July 31, 2009 (retrieved May 3, 2018).

Cicotello, David. "Bob Emslie." SABR BioProject. https://sabr.org/Bioproj/Person/D8dafeb2.

_____. "Cy Rigler." SABR BioProject. https://sabr.org/Bioproj/Person/2c639453.

Cooper, J.J. "Atlantic League Expected to Add Robo-Umps, Other Changes from New MLB Agreement." Baseballamerica.com, Feb. 26, 2019.

Corbett, Warren. "The 1970 Orioles: The Oriole Way." SABR BioProject. https://sabr.org/Latest/1970-Baltimore-Orioles-Oriole-Way.

Corcoran, Cliff. "Blame Umpires, Not Tabata for Scherzer's Lost Chance at Perfection." Sportsillustrated.com, June 20, 2015 (retrieved Apr. 14, 2018).

_____. "Royals Top Blue Jays in ALCS Game 6 to Reach Second Straight World Series." Si.com, Oct. 24, 2015 (retrieved June 17, 2018).

Costello, Rory. "Ed Armbrister." SABR BioProject. https://sabr.org/Bioproj/Person/917df0fa.

Cox, Zack. "Jerry Meals Admits to Blowing Call at Home Plate, Says Daniel Nava Should Have Been Safe." Nesn.com, July 29, 2013 (retrieved May 9, 2018).

Cramer, Richard Ben. *Joe DiMaggio: The Hero's Life*. New York: Simon & Schuster, 2000.

Crasnick, Jerry. "MLB Changes Ump Supervisors." Espn.com, Mar. 6, 2010 (retrieved June 6, 2018).

_____. "Ron Kulpa's Name Now Notorious." Espn.com, Oct. 23, 2011 (retrieved Feb. 1, 2019).

Curry, Jack. "One That Got Away Draws Smile from Knoblauch." *New York Times*, Oct. 15, 1999.

Davidoff, Ken, and George A. King III. "The Night When Bugs Changed the Course of Yankee History." *New York Post*, Oct. 4, 2017.

Davidson, Neil. "Blue Jays Eliminated with Game 6 Loss in ALCS." *The Canadian Press*, Oct. 24, 2015 (retrieved June 17, 2018).

Derringer, John. "Larsen Beats Dodgers in Perfect Game, Yanks Lead, 3–2, on First Series No-Hitter." *New York Times*, Oct. 9, 1956.
Dewan, John. "The Dreaded Leadoff Walk." Billjamesonline.com (retrieved June 16, 2018).
Diamos, Jason. "1998 World Series: Yankees Vs. Padres, Losers, Yes, but to a Winsome Ovation." *New York Times*, Oct. 22, 1998.
Dittmar, Joseph J. *Baseball's Benchmark Boxscores*. Jefferson, NC: McFarland, 1990.
Doutrich, Paul F. "Champions, Tantrums and Bad Umps: The 1885 World Series." *SABR Baseball Research Journal*, Vol. 46, Number 2 (Fall 2017).
Einstein, Charles. *The Second Fireside Book of Baseball*. New York: Simon & Schuster, 1958.
Enders, Eric. *The Fall Classic: The Definitive History of the World Series*. New York: Sterling Publishing, Co., 2007.
_____. "George Moriarty." SABR BioProject. https://sabr.org/Bioproj/Person/44c82f26.
Epstein, Samuel. *The Game of Baseball*. Champaign, IL: Garrand Publishing Co., 1965.
Escobedo Shepherd, Julianne. "A Brief History of Why Umpires Wear Suits." Pictorial/Jezebel.com, Nov. 1, 2016 (retrieved Mar. 2, 2018).
Events of 1948. Thepeoplehistory.com/1948.Html.
"Everything Goes Foul for Cubs in Loss." *Associated Press*, May 25, 1997 (retrieved Apr. 4, 2019).
Faber, Charles. "Don Larsen." SABR BioProject. https://sabr.org/Bioproj/Person/2b1a1fee.
Fallstrom, R.B. "McGwire Ejected, Fans Litter Field." *Associated Press*, Aug. 30, 1998.
"Fan Sues to Get McGwire Ball Back." *Associated Press*, Sept. 26, 1998.
Favia, Tony. "Umpire/Batter Debate 1968 Drysdale Pitch." *UPI*, Jan. 24, 1981.
Fehler, Gene. *When Baseball Was Still King: Major League Players Remember the 1950s*. Jefferson, NC: McFarland, 2012.
Felber, Bill. "Misjudgment Calls." National Pastime Museum, May 31, 2016 (retrieved Apr. 27, 2018). https://www.thenationalpastimemuseum.com/?s=Felber.
Ford, John. "Goodbye Balkin' Bob." *SB Nation*, Draysbay.com, Feb. 22, 2017 (retrieved Dec. 24, 2018).
Forster, Terry. *100 Things Tiger Fans Should Know and Do Before They Die*. Chicago: Triumph Books, 2013.
"Frank Pulli First Umpire to Use Replay, Dies at 78." *New York Times*, Aug. 29, 2013.
Frommer, Harvey. "Summer of '41: Joe Dimaggio's Epic 56-Game Hitting Streak." Baseballguru.com/Hfrommer/Analysishfrommer271.Html.
"Frustrated Oswalt Denies He Was Showing Up Ump." *Houston Chronicle*, May 31, 2010.
Gammons, Peter. "Whatever Happened to the Strike Zone." *Sports Illustrated*, Apr. 6, 1987.
Garrity, John. "How Bugs Drive Baseball Batty." *Sports Illustrated*, Aug. 18, 1986.
Garro, Adrian. "34 Years Ago Today, the Iconic George Brett Pine Tar Incident Happened at Yankee Stadium." MLB.com/Cut4, July 24, 2017 (retrieved May 1, 2018).
Gatto, Tom. "Angel Hernandez Shows Why He's a Bad Major League Umpire." *Sporting News*, May 23, 2018.
Gerlach, Larry. "Babe Pinelli." SABR BioProject. https://sabr.org/Bioproj/Person/8dbf8c1c.
Gerlach, Larry R. *The Men in Blue: Conversations with Umpires*. Lincoln: University of Nebraska Press, 1980.
"Get to Know an Umpire: Chris Guccione." Umpscare.com, Dec. 1, 2015.
Giglio, Joe. "End of Umpires? Electronic Strike Zone Could Be Coming to MLB in 2018." NJAdvanceMedia.com, Aug. 23, 2017 (retrieved May 7, 2018).
Glazarev, Edward. "Tim Lincecum Sets San Francisco Giant Record with 14 Strikeouts in 1–0 NLDS Win Over Atlanta Braves." *Daily News*, Oct. 8, 2010.
Goldstein, Richard. "Eric Gregg, Umpire Who Battled Weight Problems, Dies at 55." *New York Times*, June 6, 2006.
Gordon, Peter M. "King Kelly." SABR BioProject. https://sabr.org/Bioproj/Person/Ffc40dac.
Greene, Dan. "After the Call." Si.com/Long

form/2015/1985/World-Series-Cardinals-Royals/Index.Html (retrieved Jan. 25, 2019).

Griffin, Robbie. "2011 World Series Game 7 Recap—Cardinals Win." Dallas.Sbnation.com, Oct. 28, 2011 (retrieved Feb. 2, 2019).

Gurnick, Ken. "Career Years, Comebacks Highlight Dodgers Clutch '16." MLB.com, Dec. 28, 2016 (retrieved June 20, 2018).

Gustkey, Earl. "50th Anniversary of Twin No-Hitter: Vander Meer's Unmatched Pair." *LA Times*, June 15, 1988.

Haynes, Paul. "Cleveland Indians Welcome Back Midges with Open Eyes (Ouch), Arms in Win Over Astros." Cleveland.com, Sept. 8, 2016 (retrieved Apr. 28, 2019).

"He Made a Name for Himself." *Los Angeles Times*, Oct. 18, 1988.

Henderson, Joe. "Been There, Done That: Rich Garcia Feels Ump's Pain." TBO.com, June 3, 2010 (retrieved May 22, 2018).

"Here's the Call on Umps." *Hartford Courant*, Apr. 4, 1999.

"Herman Schaefer Is Dead." *New York Times*, May 17, 1919.

Herzog, Bob. "A Look Back at 1968: The Year of the Pitcher." *Newsday*, Mar. 27, 2018.

Hillel, Italie. "Fred Merkle's Bonehead Play Forced Giant-Cub Playoff Game in 1908." *Associated Press*, Oct. 8, 1989.

"Hip-Hip, No Way: Yankees Versus Dodgers 1978 World Series." Referee.com, July 1, 2017 (retrieved Jan. 22, 2019).

Hiro, Brian. "Padres: Blow-By-Blow Account of Ugly 1984 Brawl with Braves." *San Diego Union Tribune*, Aug. 8, 2009.

Hogg, Dave. "Armando Galarraga Delivers Lineup Card to Jim Joyce One Day After Blown Call Costs Him Perfect Game." *Daily News*, June 3, 2010.

Holmes, Dan. "Germany Schaefer." SABR BioProject. https://sabr.org/Bioproj/Person/2594238c.

Honig, Donald. *The New York Mets: The First Quarter Century*. New York: Crown, 1987.

Hoornstra, J.P. "Bill Miller's Large, Imperfect Strike Zone Favored Hitters in World Series Game 5." *Orange County Register*, Oct. 30, 2014.

"How Did a So-Called 'Farce Game' Ruin a Record for Walter Johnson?" legendsrevealed.com, Aug. 15, 2012 (retrieved Apr. 2, 2019).

"How Do Ballpark Factors Affect Batters for MLB DFS?" *DFS Strategy*, retrieved May 2, 2018. http://www.dfsstrategy.com/ballparks-effect-batters-mlb-dfs-part-1/.

Huhn, Rick. "Tim Hurst's Last Call." SABR BioProject. https://sabr.org/Research/Tim-Hurst-S-Last-Call-0 (retrieved Apr. 4, 2019).

Huss, Mike. "Hey! Somebody's Gotta Like the Guy!" *St. Louis Sports Online*, Nov. 6, 1998 (retrieved Jan. 26, 2018). http://www.stlsports.com/archives/archives98/hussondenkinger.html.

"In Memoriam: Remembering NL Umpire Frank Pulli." Closecallsports.com, Aug. 30, 2013 (retrieved Jan. 22, 2019).

Irish Baseball Hall of Fame Members Listing. Irishbaseballhall.Net/Inductees.

Jacobsen, Lenny. "Joe Tinker." SABR BioProject. https://sabr.org/Bioproj/Person/Bc0df648.

Jaffe, Chris. "15,000 Days Since a Botched World Series Play." *Hardball Times*, Nov. 4, 2011 (retrieved Jan. 21, 2019). https://tht.fangraphs.com/tht-live/15000-days-since-a-botched-world-series-play/.

James, Bill. *The New Bill James Historical Baseball Abstract*. New York: Free Press, 2003.

Jansen, Larry, et al. *How to Play Baseball*. St. Louis: Charles C. Spink & Son, 1951.

"Joba Chamberlain Recalls His Bout with Midges." Youtube.com/Watch?V=AVOG34uht_Y.

Johnson, Bill. "Bob Shaw." SABR BioProject. https://sabr.org/Bioproj/Person/208a41d7.

Jones, David, ed. *Deadball Stars of the American League*. Dulles, VA: Potomac Books, 2006.

Joseph, Andrew. "Umpire Bob Davidson Stopped Game to Eject Phillies Fan for Heckling Him." *USA Today*, Aug. 2, 2016.

Judge, Lee. "Want to Know Why Umpires Miss Pitches? Here's Part of the Answer." *The Kansas City Star*, Sept. 4, 2017.

Kansas City Royals Team History and Encyclopedia. Baseball-Reference.com/Teams/KCR/Index.Shtml.

Kashatus, William C. *Diamonds in the Coalfields: 21 Remarkable Baseball Players, Managers and Umpires from Northeastern Pennsylvania.* Jefferson, NC: McFarland, 2002.

Kelly, CJ. "The Bunt That Changed History." Howtheyplay.com, Jan. 16, 2019 (retrieved Jan. 20, 2019).

Kelsey, Ray. "Bill Hohn Should Be Suspended Immediately." Tomahawktake.com (retrieved May 3, 2018).

Kepner, Tyler. "With Smudge and Streak, Rogers Has Left an Imprint." *New York Times,* Oct. 24, 2006.

"Kerry Wood." https://www.jockbio.com/Bios/Wood/Wood_bio.html.

Kettyle, Brett. "2010 MLB Playoffs: It's Time for Paul Emmel to Own Up to His Mistakes." Bleacherreport.com, Oct. 10, 2010 (retrieved June 15, 2018).

Kilpatrick, Bryan. "Reactions to Obstruction Call in World Series Game 3." Sbnation.com, Oct. 27, 2013 (retrieved Feb. 4, 2019).

Kurkijan, Tim "Match Vander Meer? Ryan Tried." Espn.com, June 15, 2013 (retrieved Mar. 27, 2019).

Lango, Sarah. "By the Numbers: Remembering Joe Dimaggio's Hitting Streak." Espn.com/Blog, May 15, 2017 (retrieved Mar. 18, 2018).

Layberger, Tom. "Backyard Ball Instead of Ball Yard Suits Ex-Ump Bill Hohn Just Fine." *Norristown Times Herald,* Aug. 17, 2013.

Lebreton, Gil. "Umps Get 1 in 3 Close Pitches Wrong, Hbo Story Claims." *Star-Telegram,* Oct. 1, 2016.

Ledewski, Paul. "Pittsburgh Pirates: Don't Blame Only Meals, MLB Blew This Call." Bleacherreport.com, July 27, 2011 (retrieved Dec. 24, 2018).

Litsky, Frank. "Ed Runge, 87, Veteran Umpire Who Was Partial to Pitchers." *New York Times,* July 30, 2002.

Lomonico, Dave. "The 15: Fights Between Managers and Umpires." *Press Box* (online), Issue #189, Sept. 2013 (retrieved Jan. 2, 2019) https://Pressboxonline.com/Story/10623/The-15-Fights-Between-Managers-And-Umpires.

"Looking Back at the Crazy Ending to Royals–Blue Jays ALCS Game 6." Cbssports.com, Oct. 24, 2015 (retrieved June 17, 2018).

Lopez, Michael, and Saide Lewis. "An Exploration of MLB Umpire's Strike Zones." Fangraphs.com/Tht/An-Exploration-of-MLB-Umpires-Strike-Zones, May 4, 2018 (retrieved Dec. 31, 2018).

Lucas, Scott. "Jerry Layne's Strike Zone." Rangers.Scottlucas.com, Oct. 21, 2011 (retrieved Feb. 2, 2019).

Lynch, John. "Umpire Answers Calling: Gorman Follows Legendary Dad." *LA Times,* Mar. 11, 1995.

Lynch, Mike. "Who's on First? The Farce That Helped the Pirates Set a Record." Thenationalpastimemuseum.com, Apr. 17, 2014 (retrieved Apr. 20, 2018).

Lyons, Richard D. "Don Drysdale, Hall of Fame Pitcher, Dies at 56." *New York Times,* July 5, 1993.

Madden, Bill. "Pastime Faces Crucial Call." *New York Daily News,* Oct. 12, 1998.

"Major League Baseball Career Lengths in 20th Century." Ncbi.Nlm.Nih.Gov (Retrieved May 23, 2018).

Malinowski, Erik. "Better Know an Umpire: Alfonso Marquez." Deadspin.com, May 15, 2012.

_____. "Better Know an Umpire: Brian Gorman." Deadspin.com, Apr. 6, 2012 (retrieved June 16, 2018).

_____. "Better Know an Umpire: Dana Demuth." Deadspin.com, May 18, 2012 (retrieved Feb. 6, 2019).

_____. "Better Know an Umpire: Jerry Layne." Deadspin.com, Apr. 17, 2012 (retrieved Jan. 7, 2019).

_____. "Better Know an Umpire: Jim Reynolds." Deadspin.com, May 7, 2012.

_____. "Better Know an Umpire: Sam Holbrook." Deadspin.com, June 14, 2012 (retrieved Jan. 7, 2019).

Mantle, Mickey, with Mickey Herskowitz. *All My Octobers: My Memories of 12 World Series When the Yankees Ruled Baseball.* New York: HarperCollins, 1994.

Marchand, Andrew, and Ian Begley. "Cano Home Run Conjures Jeffrey Maier." Espn.com, Oct. 20, 2010 (retrieved June 16, 2018).

Marcus, Jeffrey. "Rockies Win with Sleight of Hand." *New York Times,* Oct. 2, 2017.

Markusen, Bruce. "Cooperstown Confidential: Resurrecting the Houston Colt .45s." *The Hardball Times,* Mar. 16, 2012 (retrieved Apr. 19, 2019).

"McGwire Is King, but Sosa Is Prince." *New York Times*, Sept. 9, 1998.

McKenna, Brian. "Bob Ferguson." SABR BioProject. https://sabr.org/Bioproj/Person/Df8e7d29.

McManus, Sam. "49 and Counting: With Title Clinched, Hershiser Focuses on Matching Drysdale's Scoreless Streak." *Los Angeles Times*, Sept. 28, 1988.

McMurray, John. "Phil Masi." SABR Bio-Project. https://sabr.org/Bioproj/Person/7981dd4f.

McRae, Earl. "All Managers Are Maniacs." *Calgary Herald*, Sept. 11, 1976.

Meisel, Zack. "The Yips: Difficult to Understand, Difficult to Cure." MLB.com, May 10, 2013 (retrieved June 3, 2018).

Mickelson, Paul. "Umpire's Tired Abusive Charge." *Associated Press*, Oct. 5, 1935.

Miller, Bryce "Baseball: Rockies' Ump Says He'd Make Call Again." *The DeMoines Register*, Oct. 2, 2017.

Miller, Doug. "Denkinger Cool with Reminders of Mistaken Call in '85 Series." MLB.com, Oct. 20, 2014 (retrieved Jan. 24, 2019).

Miller, Sam. "Baseball's Seven Wonders: Kerry Wood's 20-K Game." Baseballprospectus.com, Mar. 18, 2014 (retrieved Apr. 9, 2018).

———. "Obstruction Obfuscation." Slate.com, Oct. 27, 2013 (retrieved Feb. 6, 2019).

Miller, Scott. "Umpire Jim Joyce Makes the Best Call of the Year—Before the Game." CBSsports.com (retrieved Apr. 12, 2018).

"MLB Acknowledges Blown Call." *Associated Press*, July 28, 2011.

"MLB Team Walks Per Game." Teamrankings.com, Mlb/Stat/Walks-Per-Game (retrieved Feb. 11, 2019).

Muder, Craig. "Dysdale Makes Shutout History." Baseballhall.org.

Murphy, Cait. *Crazy '08: How a Cast of Cranks, Rogues, Boneheads and Magnates Created the Greatest Year in Baseball History*. Washington, D.C.: Smithsonian, 2008.

Mushnick, Phil. "Ump's Passing Deserved Bigger." *New York Post*, June 11, 2006.

Nash, Bruce, and Allan Zullo. *The Baseball Hall of Shame*. New York: Pocket Books, 1985.

———, and ———. *The Baseball Hall of Shame 2*. New York: Pocket Books, 1986.

Nash, Earl. "Illegal Warm-Up Pitch Hit for Home Run." Bosoxinjection.com (retrieved Apr. 6, 2019).

The National Baseball Hall of Fame and Museum. *The Hall: A Celebration of Baseball's Greats*. Boston: Little, Brown, 2014.

Nelson, Amy R. "Searching for Meaning in the Mistake." Espn.com, Jan. 9, 2011 (retrieved Apr. 12, 2018).

Nemec, David, ed. *Major League Baseball Profiles, Volume 2, 1871–1900*. Lincoln: University of Nebraska Press, 2011.

New York Yankee Team History and Encyclopedia. Baseball-Reference.com/Teams/NYY/Index.Shtml.

Newham, Ross. "16 Suspended for 82 Games for Roles in Chicago Brawl." *LA Times*, Apr. 28, 2000.

Nightengale, Bob. "In Firing Baker, Nationals' Gutless Arrogance Is on Display." *USA Today*, Oct. 20, 2017.

———. "1994 Strike Most Embarrassing Moment in MLB History." *USA Today*, Aug. 11, 2014.

———. "Yer Out! Three Umpire Bosses Fired Over Blown 2009 Playoffs Calls. *USA Today*, Mar. 8, 2010.

"1994 Strike Was a Low Point for Baseball." *Associated Press*, Aug. 10, 2004.

Nowak, Joey. "Jackie Safe at Home? Not According to Yogi." MLB.com, Sept. 24, 2015 (retrieved Jan. 14, 2019).

Okrent, Daniel, and Harris Lewine, eds. *The Ultimate Baseball Book*. Boston: Houghton Mifflin, 2000.

Olney, Buster. "Change Artist: How Did Trevor Hoffman Go from a Scrawny Minor League Shortstop with One Kidney to a Hall of Fame Closer? He Got a Grip." *ESPN the Magazine*, Jan. 24, 2011.

"Only Memories and Ghosts Remain." *Associated Press*, Sept. 23, 2008.

Ortiz, Jorge L. "Royals Win in Wet, Wild Game 6 Over Blue Jays, Advance to World Series Again." *USA Today*, Oct. 25, 2015.

Ostler, Scott. "Dale Mitchell Watched Big One Go By." *LA Times*, Jan. 7, 1987.

Pepe, Phil. *The Ballad of Billy and George*. Guilford, CT: Lyons Press, 2008.

Perez, A.J. "Umpire Angel Hernandez

Who's Suing MLB for Alleged Discrimination, to Work All-Star Game." *USA Today,* July 6, 2017.

____, et al. *Baseball: The Biographical Encyclopedia.* Toronto: Sport Classic Book, 2003.

____. *Judge and Fury: The Life and Times of Judge Kenesaw Mountain Landis.* South Bend: Diamond Communications, 1998.

Politi, Steve. "Umpire Who Blew Call in Ny Yankees Victory Over Twins Says 'There Is No Excuse.'" Nj.com, Oct. 11, 2009 (retrieved June 3, 2018).

Ponsi, Lou. "Umpire Blazes Trail." *Orange County Register,* July 8, 2007.

Posnanski, Joe. "Bad Calls in Baseball." Joeposnanski.com, Oct. 8, 2010 (retrieved June 16, 2018).

Pridge, Mathew. "The 1976 Game-Winning Grand Slam That Wasn't: When Billy Martin Shouted Down a Brewers' Comeback Win." Shepherdexpress.com, July 17, 2017 (retrieved Apr. 28, 2018).

Pugmire, Lance. "Harry Wendelstedt Dies at 73, Baseball Umpire Also Ran School." *LA Times,* Mar. 10, 2012.

Randhawa, Manny. "Perfect Games Broken Up in the Ninth Inning or Later." MLB.com, Mar. 11, 2019.

The Retro Sheet (newsletter for Retrosheet.org), June 1, 2000. Retrosheet.org/News/121.Pdf.

Ringolsby, Tracy. "Q&A: Joyce Reflects on Memorable Career: 30-Year Umpiring Veteran Relives His Most Noteworthy Moments." MLB.com, Feb. 25, 2017 (retrieved Dec. 24, 2018).

Ritter, Lawrence. *The Glory of Their Times.* New York: Macmillan, 1966.

Rosen, Ron. "Al Umpire Dimuro Struck, Killed by Auto After Texas Game." *Washington Post,* June 8, 1982.

Rosencrans, C. Trent. "MLB Suspends Umpire Bob Davidson and Phillies Manuel. Cbssports.com, May 18, 2012 (Retrieved Apr. 8, 2018).

Rothenberg, Matt. "Bill Stewart's Career as an Official Swept Through MLB, NHL." Baseballhall.org (retrieved Dec. 17, 2018).

Sandamir, Richard. "An Electronic Umpire? Baseball Tried It (In the 1950s)." *New York Times,* Apr. 30, 2016.

Santry, Joe, and Cindy Thomson. "Ban Johnson." SABR BioProject. https://sabr.org/Bioproj/Person/Dabf79f8.

Saunders, Patrick. "Game 163: In 2007 Rockies Shocked the Padres in Rocktober Fashion." *Denver Post,* Oct. 1, 2017.

Schechter, Gabriel. "Babe Pinelli: Far from a One-Pitch Posterity." http://www.thenationalpastimemuseum.com/article/babe-pinelli-far-one-pitch-posterity.

Schimler, Stuart. "Jack Pfiester." SABR BioProject. https://sabr.org/Bioproj/Person/35db06a1.

Schmehl, James. "Tigers Armando Galarraga Awarded Corvette for Near-Perfect Game." Mlive.com, June 3, 2010 (retrieved Mar. 31, 2019).

Schmuck, Peter. "Yankees Roar Back in 9–6 Win." *Baltimore Sun,* Oct. 18, 1998.

Schneider, Russell. *The Cleveland Indians Encyclopedia.* Champaign, IL: Sports Publishing, 2004.

Schulz, Theron. "Balks: The Story of the 1988 Major League Season." Reconditebaseball.Blogspot.com, Aug. 11, 2008 (retrieved Mar. 29, 2019).

Schwartz, Larry. "Drysdale Sets Consecutive Scoreless Innings Mark." Espn.com/Classic, Nov. 19, 2003 (retrieved Mar. 27, 2018).

Simon, Mark. "Inside Hershiser's Scoreless Streak." Espn.com, Sept. 30, 2013 (retrieved May 30, 2018).

Simon, Tom, ed. *Deadball Stars of the National League.* Dulles, VA: Brassey's, 2004.

Skipper, John C. *Umpires: Classic Baseball Stories from the Men Who Made the Calls.* Jefferson, NC: McFarland, 1997.

Snow, Chris. "Plan Is to Lower a Steal Curtain." *Boston Globe,* Feb. 26, 2005.

Spalding Official Baseball Guide. New York: American Sports, 1919.

Stan, Francis E. "Sports Scope: Tame Bruins and Tigers of Regular Season Now Berserk." *Washington (DC) Evening Star,* Oct. 5, 1935.

Stark, Jayson. "The Last Great Calls." Espn.com, Mar. 24, 2014.

____. "The Pop-Up Heard 'Round the World." Espn.com, Oct. 7, 2012 (retrieved June 17, 2018).

Stellini, Nicholas. "The C.B. Bucknor Experience." Fangraphs.com, Apr. 19, 2017 (retrieved Jan. 4, 2019). https://blogs.fangraphs.com/the-cb-bucknor-experience/.

Stephen, Eric. "Today in History: Orel Hershiser Breaks Don Drysdale's Scoreless Inning Record." Truebluela.com, Sept. 28, 2013 (retrieved Apr. 8, 2018).

Steve Basil Umpire Card. Retrosheet.org/TSNUmpireCards/Basil_Stephen.Jpg.

"Steve Garvey on Reggie Jackson's Infamous '78 World Series Interference Play." *Rich Eisen Show*, Youtube.com/Watch?V=Tbyfq76MQUw.

Strecker, Trey. *"Fred Merkle."* SABR BioProject. https://sabr.org/Bioproj/Person/37264391.

Strotman, Mark. "Kerry Wood Ends the Debate: 20 Strikeout Game's Hit Was Legit." NBCsports.com/Chicago, May 19, 2017 (retrieved Apr. 9, 2018).

Sullivan, Jeff. "Incredulous Responses to Bill Miller's Strike Zone." Fangraphs.com, Oct. 30, 2017 (retrieved Feb. 10, 2019). https://blogs.fangraphs.com/incredulous-responses-to-bill-millers-strike-zone/.

____. "Let's Consider Eric Gregg and Livan Hernandez in the 1997 NLCS." Fangraphs.com, Jan. 17, 2013 (retrieved May 24, 2018). https://blogs.fangraphs.com/lets-consider-eric-gregg-and-livan-hernandez-in-the-1997-nlcs/.

____. "Umpire Brian Gorman's Mistake Leads to Tie Game." Sbnation.com, Oct. 22, 2010 (retrieved June 16, 2018).

Sullivan, Paul. "Kerry Wood Makes It Look Easy in Fanning 20 Astros." *Chicago Tribune*, May 7, 1998.

____. "Rise of the Machines? Automated Strike Zones a Concept Worth Considering." *Chicago Tribune*, May 7, 2017.

____. "Umpire Phil Cuzzi Stuck by His Call and Ejection of Ben Zobrist." *Chicago Tribune*, Aug. 15, 2018.

"There Once Was a Major League Baseball Player Who Stole First Base." Todayifoundout.com, Aug. 18, 2012 (retrieved Apr. 22, 2018).

Thomason, Mac. "Bill Hohn Is Cheating on Bobby Cox." Awfulumpiring.Wordpress.com, Aug. 11, 2009 (retrieved May 3, 2018).

Thorn, John. "Distant Replay: What If Replay Had Existed Way Back When?" Our game.MLBblogs.com, Dec. 11, 2017 (retrieved Apr. 2, 2018).

___, ed. *The Complete Armchair Book of Baseball.* New York: Galahad Books, 1997.

___. "October 1845: The First Baseball Games in New York." SABR Games Project. https://www.SABR BioProject. https://sabr.org/gameproj.com.

___, et al. *Total Baseball: The Official Encyclopedia of Major League Baseball.* Kingston, NY: Total Sports Publishing, 1989.

Thornley, Stew. "April 8: Hammerin' Hank Knocks in Three in His Final Opening Day." SABR Games Project. SABR BioProject. https://sabr.org/gameproj (retrieved Apr. 28, 2018).

"Tides' Umpire Robbed at Hotel." *Virginia Pilot*, June 11, 1995 (retrieved Feb. 11, 2019).

"Tim Hurst." Baseball History Daily Archives, retrieved Apr. 4, 2019. https://baseballhistorydaily.com/Tag/Tim-Hurst/.

Torre, Joe, and Tom Verducci. *The Yankee Years.* New York: Doubleday, 2009.

"Tough, Honest Ump Dies in Va Hospital." *United Press International*, Feb. 19, 1964.

Traughter, Bill. "Sounds Manager Don Money Looks Back on His Career." MLB.com, May 10, 2010 (retrieved Apr. 3, 2019).

"Umpire Delmore Dies in Scranton." *Toledo Blade*, June 10, 1960.

"Umpire Jeff Nelson Expressed Regret of Botched Call." *Associated Press*, May 25, 2013 (retrieved Jan. 7, 2019).

"Umpire Moves Up." *Associated Press*, Apr. 12, 1989.

"Umpire Tendencies Vs. the Shrinking Strike Zone." Closescallsprts.com, Feb. 10, 2017 (retrieved Feb. 2, 2019).

"Umpires Miss More Calls in Game 4 of ALCS." Foxsports.com, Oct. 21, 2009 (retrieved June 3, 2018).

Vecsey, George. "Sports of the Times: Lou Dimuro, Umpire." *New York Times*, June 9, 1982.

Venturi, David. "Balks: An Illustrative and Qualitative History." Davidventuri.com/Blog/Balks, May 9, 2016 (retrieved February 24, 2018).

Verducci, Tom. "The Greatest Season Ever." *Sports Illustrated*, Oct. 5, 1998.

"Veteran Ump Mcclelland Retires." *Associated Press*, Feb. 20. 2015.

Vincent, David. "Al Barlick." SABR Bio Project. https://sabr.org/bioproj/person/70fbe802.

Waddel, Levi. "Former Umpire Bob Davidson Discusses Career and What Needs to Change." Milehighsports.com, Feb. 24, 2017 (retrieved Dec. 24, 2018).

Wade, David. "Inside the Rules: It's Not a Dropped Third Strike." *Hardball Times*, Nov. 16, 2010 (retrieved May 5, 2019).

Wagner, John. "10 Questions with Rick Reed." *Toledo Blade*, July 4, 2010.

Weber, Bruce. "Game 3's Decisive Play: Why Call Was Obstruction." *New York Times*, Oct. 27, 2013.

Weber, Scott. "Bob Davidson and the God Complex of Major League Umpires." SB Nation. Lookoutlanding.com, July 13, 2014 (retrieved Dec. 24, 2018).

Weinbaum, Willie. "Vander Meer's Feat Stands the Test of Time." ESPN.com, June 13, 2003 (retrieved Mar. 17, 2018). http://www.espn.com/mlb/s/2003/0610/1565923.html.

Weiner, Stephen C. "October 4, 1955: Brooklyn Dodgers Win First World Series as 'Next Year' Finally Arrives." SABR Games Project. https://sabr.org/gamesproj/game/october-4-1955-Brooklyn-Dodgers-Win-First-World-Series-Next-Year-Finally-Arrives.

Weinstock, Josh. "Which Umpire Has the Largest Strike Zone." *Hardball Times*, Jan. 11, 2012 (retrieved Feb. 2, 2019). https://tht.fangraphs.com/which-umpire-has-the-largest-strikezone/.

Welsh, Chris. "Major League Coach Estimates Only Fifty Percent of Big Leaguers Know the Infield Fly Rule." Baseballrulesacademy.com (retrieved Apr. 10, 2019).

Wertheim, Jon. "Flame Thrower: Cubs Phenom Kerry Wood Strikes Out 20 Astros." *Sports Illustrated*, May 6, 2015.

"What Percentage of Minor League Ballplayers Ever Reach the Majors?" Quora.com (retrieved May 23, 2018).

"Where Are They Now? Tim Tschida Is a Bartender." Closecallsports.com, July 19, 2018 (retrieved Jan. 3, 2019).

Williams, Mark T. "MLB Umpires Missed 34,294 Ball-Strike Calls in 2018. Bring on Robo-Umps?" Bu.Edu/Today/MLB-Umpire-Strike-Zone-Accuracy, Apr. 8, 2019 (retrieved Apr. 18, 2019).

Williams, Ted, and John Underwood. *My Turn at Bat: The Story of My Life*. New York: Pocket Books, 1970.

Wolf, Gregory H. "Ken Burkhart." SABR BioProject. https://sabr.org/Bioproj/Person/854e5db9.

"World Series Capsules: Cards Win World Series, Beat Texas 6–2 in Game 7." *Associated Press*, Oct. 28, 2011.

"Wrigley Field Message Wall Grows as End of World Series Draws Near." Chicago.cbs.local.com, Nov. 1, 2016 (retrieved June 21, 2018).

Wulf, Steve. "The Secrets of Sam." *Sports Illustrated*, July 19, 1993.

Yates, Clinton. "Infamous At-Bat That Ended Max Scherzer's Perfect Game Was Actually Impressive." *Washington Post*, June 20, 2015.

"The Year of the Pitcher." Thisgreatgame.com/1969-Baseball-History.html (retrieved Mar. 26, 2018).

Zim, Jordan. "7 Really Bad Sports Records That Will Never Be Broken." Stack.com/A/Worst-Sports-Records, Dec. 23, 2012 (retrieved Mar. 20, 2018).

Index

Aaron, Hank 76
Abbaticchio, Ed 57
Abbot, Jim 98
Adams, Franklin Pierce 53
Ainsmith, Eddie 52
Albers, Matt 124
ALCS: (1996 Game 1) 89–91, 166; (1998) 95–98; (1999) 98–100; (2005 Game 3) 101–103; (2009 Game 4) 108–109; (2010 Game 4) 113; (2010 Game 6) 114; (2015 Game 6) 117–120; (2016 Game 4) 120–123
ALDS: (2007 Game 2) 104–106; (2009 Game 1, Angels vs. Red Sox) 106–107; (2009 Game 2, Yankees vs. Twins) 107–108; (2010 Game 1, Rays vs. Rangers) 111; (2010 Game 1, Yankees vs. Twins) 111
Alexander, Pete 65
All-Star Game: (1961) 23
Allen, Lee 138
Alomar, Roberto 89
Alomar, Sandy 96, 97
Alou, Moises 35
Alston, Walter 18, 24, 147
Alvarez, Pedro 87
Ameriquest Field (home of the Rangers) 167
Ames, Red 133
Amoros, Sandy 18
Anderson, Bob 73
Anderson, Sparky 1, 152, 153, 154, 156
Andrus, Elvis 117, 170
Andujar, Joaquin 162
Ankiel, Rick 112
Anson, Adrian "Cap," 128, 129, 130
Appel, Marty 94
Armbrister, Ed 156
Armour, Tommy (golfer) 98
Arnold, Dorothy (first wife of DiMaggio) 14

Arrieta, Jake 124
Ashford, Emmet (first black umpire) 7, 93
AT&T Park (home of the Giants) 112
Atlantic League Experiment ("robo umps") 4
Auker, Elden 139
Averill, Earl 68
Aybar, Erick 107, 108

Baer, Bill 41
Baez, Javier 124, 125
Bagwell, Jeff 35
Baker, Del 18
Baker, Dusty 124, 125, 126
Baker, Frank "Home Run" 132, 133
Baker, John 85
Baker Bowl (home of the Phillies) 65
Balboni, Steve 163
Baldelli, Rocco 111
balk rule 20–22
Ballafant, Lee (umpire) 7
balloon protectors 6
ban on warm-up pitches 60–61
Banks, Ernie 21, 72, 73
Barber, Red 91
Barkley, Sam 129
Barlick, Al (umpire) 21, 22
Barnett, Larry (umpire) 156, 157
Barr, George (umpire) 6
Barrett, Michael 83
Barry, Jack 132
base runner interference 29, 96, 150, 156–157, 159
Basil, Steve (umpire) 13, 15
Bauer, Hank 18
Bautista, Jose 118, 119
batter interference with catcher 125
Bearden, Gene 144
Beckley, Jake 50
Bedell, Howie 26

Bee Hive (home of Boston Bees) 12
Belanger, Mark 12, 149
Bell, Derek 35
Beltre, Adrian 171
Bench, Johnny 152, 153, 155
bench jockeying 140
Bender, Charles "Chief" 60, 131, 132
Benitez, Armando 90
Berkman, Lance 114, 171
Berra, Yogi 19, 146, 147, 148, 151, 154
Bessent, Don 147
"The Big Red Machine" 77, 152, 155
Biggio, Craig 35
Bingay, Malcolm 64
Bittman, Red (umpire) 46
Black, Bud 78, 82, 83
"Black Sox Curse" 101
Blair, Paul 149, 152
Blauser, Jeff 35
Bochy, Bruce 165, 166
Bonds, Barry 33, 34
Bonin, Greg 80
Boone, Aaron 89
"The Boston Massacre" (1978 Yankees–Red Sox) 158
Boudreau, Lou 143, 144, 145
Bourn, Michael 115
Bowa, Larry 105, 168
Braddock, James 140
Braden, Dallas 38, 39
Bragan, Bobby 22
Bregman, Alex 176
Bremigan, Nick (umpire) 76
Brennan, Bill (umpire) 64, 65, 66
Bresnahan, Roger 53
Brett, George 78–80, 162
Bridges, Tommy 139
Bridwell, Al 1, 55
Brinkman, Joe 160
Brisbee, Grant 41
Brosius, Scott 96, 97, 99
Brown, Kevin 31, 94, 164, 165, 166
Brown, Mordecai "Three Finger" 53, 58
Bruce, Jay 20
Bryant, Kris 124, 125
Buck, Joe 118, 167
Buckner, Bill 161
Bucknor, C.B. (umpire) 107, 109, 110
Budig, Gene 90
Buehrle, Mark 101, 118
Buford, Don 150
Burkhart, Ken (umpire) 152, 153, 154
Busch Stadium (home of the Cardinals) 117, 162
Butler, Brett 28
Byrne, Bobby 65
Byrne, Tommy 146, 151

Byrnes, Eric 4
Byron, Bill "Lord" (umpire) 19

Cabrera, Asdrubal 105
Cabrera, Melky 107
Cabrera, Miguel 38
Cain, Lorenzo 119
Cain, Matt 112
Camilli, Dolph 10
Caminiti, Ken 165
Campanella, Roy 18, 140, 146
Candlestick Park (home of the Giants) 23, 27
Cano, Robinson 108, 109, 113
Canseco, Jose 32
Caple, Jim 102–103
Caraco, Carlos 106
Carbo, Bernie 152, 153, 154
Carey, Andy 18
Carlton, Steve 23
Carpenter, Chris 167
Carrigan, Bill 142
Carroll, Jamey 82, 83
Cartuyvelles, James 46
Caruthers, Bob 128
Casey, Hugh 103
Cash, Norm 12, 23
catcher's interference 125
Cavarretta, Phil 140
Cepeda, Orlando 24
Cey, Ron 159
Chalmers, George 65
Chamberlain, Joba (the bug game) 104–106
Chambliss, Chris 76, 77
Chance, Frank 53, 58
Chapman, Jack 45
Chirinos, Robinson 117
Chronicle-Telegraph Cup 130
Chylak, Nestor (umpire) 5
Cintron, Alex 110
Clark, Jack 162
Clarke, Fred 49, 50, 57
Clemens, Roger 36, 41
Clendenon, Donn 150, 151
Clift, Harlond 14
Cline, Ty 26, 153
Cobb, Ty 142
Colavito, Rocky 79
Cole, Gerrit 110
Coleman, Vince 162
Collins, Eddie 47, 60, 70, 131
Colon, Bartolo 101
Colt Stadium (home of the Colt .45's) 177
Comerica Park (home of the Tigers) 38
Comiskey, Charlie 128, 129, 130

Index

Comiskey Park (home of White Sox) 15, 69, 106
Cone, David 95, 97, 165
Congress Street Grounds (home of the White Stockings) 128
Connolly, Tommy (umpire and supervisor) 15, 49, 61, 63, 64
Contreras, Wilson 124, 125
Coolidge, Calvin (U.S. president) 136
Coombs, Jack 133
Coors Field (home of the Rockies) 81
Corcoran, Cliff 41
Costas, Bob 33
County Stadium (home of the Brewers) 75
Coveleski, Stan 136, 169
Cowart, Kaleb 116–117
Cox, Bobby 1, 84, 85, 112
Cox, Danny 162
Craig, Allan 171, 173, 174
Craig, Roger 29
Cramer, Richard Ben 14
Crandall, Doc 133
Cravath, Gavvy 65
Creamer, Joseph 57, 58
Crede, Joe 103
Crowe, Trevor 38
Cruz, Nelson 113
Cubas, Joe 92
Cuddyer, Michael 108
Cuellar, Mike 149, 152
Cultural diversity among umpires 7
Cuyler, Kiki 10, 136
Cuzzi, Phil (umpire) 107, 108, 110

Daley, Arthur 71, 151
Damon, Johnny 108
Daniel, Dan (official scorer) 14
Dark, Alvin 73, 145
Darling, Ron 116
d'Arnaud, Chase 109–110
Darvish, Yu 42
Darwin, Bobby 76
Davidson, Bob (umpire) 32, 33, 34
Davis, Chili 95, 96, 97, 166
Davis, Wade 119
Dean, Dizzy 24
Delmore, Vic (umpire) 72–74
Demaree, Al 67
DeMuth, Dana (umpire) 174, 175
Denkinger, Don (umpire) 2, 161, 163, 164
Dent, Bucky 158
Devlin, Art 55
Devore, Josh 133
DeWitt, William Jr. 33
Diaz, Laz (umpire) 106
Dickey, R.A. 118
Dietz, Dick 25–26, 29

DiMaggio, Dominic 70
DiMaggio, Joe 13–16, 67, 68
DiMuro, Lou (umpire) 150, 151
disputed home runs: A-Rod 1; Cliff Floyd 161; Derek Jeter 90; Don Money 76–77; Ed Abbaticchio 57; George Brett 78–79; John Mayberry 79; Mark McGwire 32–33; Mike Moustakas 118; Robinson Cano 113; Sammy Sosa 80; Stuffy McInnis 60–61
doctoring baseballs 169–170
Dolan, Cozy 49
Donald, Jason 38
Donaldson, Josh 118, 119
Donatelli, Augie (umpire) 26, 151, 154
Donlin, "Turkey Mike" 51, 53, 55, 58
Donovan, Patsy 61
Doolin, Mike 66
Doyle, "Laughing Larry" 133, 134, 135
Drew, J.D. 84
Dreyfuss, Barney 48, 50, 51, 57
Drysdale, Don: consecutive scoreless innings streak 23–27; doctoring baseballs 169; reaction to Hershiser's streak 29
Duffy, Hugh 63
Durocher, Leo 11
Dwyer, Frank 46
Dykes, Jimmy 69

Eason, Mal (umpire) 65
Eastwick, Rawley 156
Ebbets Field (home of the Dodgers) 106
Eddings, Doug (umpire) 101, 102, 103
Egan, Charles "Rip," (umpire) 60
Eggler, Dave 44
ejection records for umpires (in a single-game) 70, 72
ejections in World Series 139, 141
Elberfeld, Kid 63
Emmel, Paul (umpire) 112, 113
Emslie, Bob (umpire) 47, 48, 49, 55, 56
Enders, Eric 147
English, Woody 141
Escobar, Alcides 118
Escobar, Kelvim 102
Evans, Billy (umpire) 2, 60
Everett, Carl 42, 102
Everett, Mike 72
Evers, Johnny 53, 55, 56
exception to the hit batsman rule 25, 40–41
Exposition Park (home of the Pirates) 47

fair-foul controversies 57, 68–69, 80, 129, 107–108
farcical games: 1902 Reds–Pirates 50–51; 1913 Senators–Red Sox 52

Farrell, John 173, 174
Feller, Bob 13, 68, 144
Fenway Park (home of the Red Sox) 72, 84, 156, 173
Ferguson, Bob 43–45, 70
Ferris, Hobe 142
Figgins, Chone 107
Figueroa, Ed 76
Finely, Charlie 156
Fisk, Carlton 155, 156, 157
Fitzgerald, Ray 157
Fitzpatrick, Mike 84
Fletcher, Art 133
flood at Exposition Park in Pittsburgh 47–49
Floyd, Cliff 161
Fogel, Horace 65
Fogg, Josh 82
For The Love of the Game (Kevin Costner film) 100
Force, Davey 44
Ford, Whitey 17, 146, 147, 169
Forsythe, Logan 42
Fosse, Ray 154
Foster, Marty (umpire) 3
Foulke, Kieth 72
Frankel, John 3
Franks, Herman 26
Frazier, George 79
Freeman, Freddie 115
Freese, David 171
Fregosi, Jim 86
Frick, Ford 24, 141
Froemming, Bruce (umpire) 30, 77, 105
Fryman, Travis 95, 96
Fulton County Stadium (home of the Braves) 84
Furillo, Carl 147

Galan, Augie 140
Galarraga, Armando (near-perfect game) 2, 37–39
Gallego, Mike 83
Garcia, Pedro 76
Garcia, Rich (umpire) 7, 77, 90, 91, 109, 165, 166
Garciaparra, Nomar 99
Garko, Ryan 105
Garland, Jon 101
Garms, Debs 12
Garvey, Steve 159, 160
Gaspar, Rod 150
Gedney, Count 44
Gehrig, Lou 14, 67, 91
Gehringer, Charlie 139
Gentile, Jim 23
Gentry, Gary 150

Geronimo, Cesar 156
ghosts of Yankee Stadium 89, 90, 91
Giamatti, Bartlett A. 5
Giambi, Jason 91
Gibbons, John 119
Gibson, Bob 24, 52
Giglio, Joe 4
Gil, Warren 56
Giles, Brian 83
Giles, Warren 20, 22, 74
Girardi, Joe 97, 106, 111
Glavine, Tom 92, 94
Gleason, Bill 128
Goins, Ryan 119
Golson, Greg 111
Gomez, Lefty 15, 16
Gonzalez, Adrian 81, 82
Gonzalez, Alex 107, 112
Gonzalez, Fredi 115
Gonzalez, Gio 124
Gonzalez, Marwin 42
Gooden, Dwight 96
Gorman, Brian (umpire) 114, 115
Gordon, Joe: as manager 20; as player 143
Goslin, Goose 139
Gossage, Goose 78
Grant, Eddie 67
Grantham, George 136
Greenberg, Hank 139, 140, 141
Gregg, Eric (umpire) 92, 93, 94
Greinke, Zack 30
Griffin, Alfredo 28, 29
Griffin, Robbie 172
Griffith, Clark 52
Griffith Stadium (home of the Senators) 136
Grimes, Burleigh: as manager 10; as player 169
Grimm, Charlie 140, 141
Grimm, Justin 120
Grote, Jerry 150
Grudzielanek, Mark 38
Guccione, Chris (umpire) 111, 115
Guerrero, Vladimir 101
Guidry, Ron 79, 158
Gurriel, Yuli 106
Gutierrez, Ricky 36
Gwyn, Tony 30

Haas, Moose 71
Hadley, Bump 68
Hafner, Travis 105
Hairston, Scott 82
Hale, Odell 68, 69
Halladay, Roy 20, 38
Haller, Bill (umpire) 160
Hammaker, Atlee 28

Index

Haney, Fred 148
Hanlon, Ned 48
Hanson, Tommy 87
Hargrove, Mike 96
Harper, Bryce 123
Harrelson, Bud 154
Harridge, William 15, 69
Harris, Bucky 136
Harris, Joe 136
Harrison, Josh 41, 42
Harrison, Matt 170, 171
Hart, Jim Ray 25
Hartnett, Gabby 140
Hasset, Buddy 11
Hatfield, John 44
Hawkins, Andy 29
Hawpe, Brad 81
Haynes, Joe 70
Heinz 57 Ketchup 16
Helton, Todd 81, 82, 109
Hemingway, Ernest 13
Hemus, Solly 74
Hendricks, Elrod 152, 153, 154
Hendricks, Kyle 124
Hendry, Ted 96, 97, 98
Henrich, Tommy 103
Herman, Billy 141
Hern, Gerald V. 143
Hernandez, Kike 175
Hernandez, Livan 92–94
Hernandez, Orlando "El Duque" 165
Hernandez, Roberto 104
Herr, Tom 162, 164
Hershiser, Orel 27–30
Hertzel, Bob 152
Herzog, Buck 55
Herzog, Whitey 162, 163, 164
Heyward, Jason 87, 112, 115, 124
Hiatt, Jack 26
Hicks, Nat 44, 70
Higham, Dick 6
Hill, Rich 42
Hilltop Park (temporary home of the Giants in 1911) 132
Hinch, A.J. 110
Hodges, Gil 18, 146, 150, 151
Hodgin, Ralph 71
Hoffman, Trevor 81, 82, 83, 165
Hofman, Solly 56
Hohn, Bill (umpire) 84–86
Holbrook, Sam (umpire) 115, 116, 117
Holliday, Bug 46
Holliday, Matt 81, 82, 83, 115, 170
Holmes, Tommy 144
Home Run Chase (1998; McGwire and Sosa) 30–34, 117
Hosmer, Eric 118, 119

Howell, Jay 168
Howsam, Bob 152
Howser, Dick 79
Hubbell, Carl 25, 27, 30
Hudson, Marvin (umpire) 38
Huff, Aubrey 112
Hughes, Phil 107, 114
Hulbert, William A. 5
Hunt, Ron 25
Hunter, Catfish 24, 75
Hunter, Torii 107
Huntington Avenue Grounds (home of the Red Sox) 49
Hurdle, Clint 81, 87
Hurley, Michael 110
Hurst, Tim 45–46, 70

infield fly rule 114–117
insect invasions 104–106, 177
Isaminger, Jimmy 47
Isringhausen, Jason 167

Jackowski, Bill (umpire) 74
Jackson, Austin 38
Jackson, Michael (pitcher) 95
Jackson, Reggie 158, 159, 160
Jacob's Field (home of the Indians) 104
Jay, Jon 125, 171, 173
Jeter, Derek 89, 90, 95, 96, 97, 109, 165
Johnson, Ban 47, 59, 61, 133
Johnson, Darrell 156
Johnson, Davey 152
Johnson, Walter 25, 52, 136
Johnston, Charles (umpire) 67, 68, 69
Johnstone, Jimmy 57
Jones, Chipper 84, 92, 94, 115, 122
Jones, Cleon 150
Jones, Garrett 87
Jones, Nippy 151
Jones, Red (umpire) 70–72
Jones, Todd 167
Joyce, Jim (umpire) 2, 38, 39, 174
Judge, Aaron 31
Judge, Joe 136
Judge, Lee 3
Julio, Jorge 82
Jurges, Billy 141
Justice, David 95

Karger, Ed 60
Karstens, Jeff 87
Kauffman Stadium (home of the Royals) 118
Kazmir, Scott 108
Keeler, Willie 48
Kellert, Frank 147, 148
Kelley, Joe 50, 51

Kelley, Shawn 109–110
Kelly, John O. "Honest John" (umpire) 129
Kelly, Mike "King" 128, 129
Keltner, Ken 16, 143
Kendrick, Howie 107
Kerr, Paul 138
Kershaw, Clayton 30
Keunn, Harvey 77
Kimbrel, Craig 115
Kinsler, Ian 170
Kizsla, Mark 83
Klem, Bill (umpire) 6, 27, 55, 57, 60, 64, 131, 134, 135
Knight, Ray 110
Knoblauch, Chuck 96, 98, 99, 100, 165
Konerko, Paul 101, 103
Koosman, Jerry 149, 150, 151
Koufax, Sandy 146
Koy, Ernie 10
Kozma, Pete 115, 116, 174
Kremer, Ray 136
Kubek, Tony 156, 157
Kubel, Jason 108
Kulpa, Ron (umpire) 109, 170, 171, 172

Laabs, Chet 14
Lackey, John 101, 124, 173
Land Shark Stadium (home of the Marlins) 84
Landis, Kenesaw Mountain (MLB commissioner) 137, 138, 139, 141
Langston, Mark 165, 166
Lap, Jack 134
Larson, Don (World Series perfect game) 17–20
LaRussa, Tony 33, 117, 168, 169, 170
Lasorda, Tom 28, 159, 160
LaStella, Tommy 125
Latham, Arlie 45, 53
Lawrie, Brett 177
Layne, Jerry (umpire) 124, 125, 126, 171, 172
Leach, Tommy 49
League Park (home of the Indians) 142
League Park (home of the Reds) 46
Ledee, Ricky 165
Lee, Bill (Cubs) 140
Lee, Bill (Red Sox) 157
Lee, Cliff 111
Lee, Marc 4
Leibrandt, Charlie 162
Lemaster, Denny 22
Lemon, Bob 144, 158
Lester, Jon 107, 124, 173
Lewis, Colby 114
Leyland, Jim 38
Lieb, Fred 45, 64

Little, Will 125
Lloyd, Ashley 46
Lobaton, Michael 125
Lodigiani, Dario 15, 71
Lofton, Kenny 95, 96
Lohse, Kyle 115, 170, 171
Lombardi, Ernie 11
longest game at Turner Field 86–88
Longoria, Evan 84
Lopes, Davey 159
Louis, Joe 140
Lowe, Derek 112
Lowell, Mike 107
Luciano, Ron (umpire) 12, 20
Lugo, Julio 87
Lupica, Mike 176
Lyle, Sparky 76
Lyn, lance 173
Lynch, Thomas 64, 66
Lynn, Fred 155

Mack, Connie 131, 134
MacPhail, Lee 76, 79, 80
Maddon, Joe 1, 111, 125
Maddux, Greg 35, 93, 94
Maglie, Sal 18, 24
Malone, Pat 69
Manfred, Rob 109
Mantilla, Felix 151
Mantle, Mickey 13, 17, 18, 146
Marberry, Firpo 136
Marcus, Jeffrey 83
Maris, Roger 24, 30
Marquard, Rube 132, 133
Marquez, Alfonso (umpire) 168, 169
Marshall, Dave 25
Martin, Billy 17, 74, 75, 76, 77–78, 79, 80, 158
Martin, J.C. 150
Martin, Russell 119
Martinez, Dave 141
Martinez, Sandy 35
Martinez, Tino 96, 165, 166
Martinez, Victor 105, 170
Masi, Phil 144, 145
Matheny, Mike 116
Mathewson, Christy 2, 53, 55, 58, 65, 132, 133, 168
Matsui, Kazuo 82
Matthews, Bobby 44
Matthews, Eddie 151
Mauch, Gene 26
Mauer, Joe 107, 108, 110
May, Lee 153
Mayberry, John 79
Mays, Willie 154
McCaffrey, Harry (umpire) 129

Index

McCann, Brian 84
McCarthy, Joe 68, 69
McCarver, Tim 168
McClelland, Tim (umpire) 78, 79, 80, 81, 83, 108, 110
McCormick, Mike 144
McCormick, Moose 55, 65
McCovey, Willie 25
McCutchen, Andrew 88
McCutchen, Daniel 87
McDougald, Gil 18, 147
McGinnity, Joe 56
McGowan, Bill (umpire) 6
McGraw, John 48, 53, 54, 59, 65, 66, 132, 134
McGriff, Fred 94
McGwire, Mark 31, 32, 117
McHugh, Collin 175–176
McInnis, Stuffy 59, 60, 132
McKean, Jim (umpire) 76, 77, 96, 97, 109
McKechnie, Bill 10, 11, 145
McKenry, Michael 87
McLain, Denny 24
McLaughlin, Jim 152
McLouth, Nate 85
McLean, Larry 67
McNally, Dave 149, 150, 151, 152
McNeely, Earl 136
McRae, Hal 79, 163, 168
McSherry, John (umpire) 94
Meadows, Lee 136
Meals, Jerry (umpire) 35, 36, 37, 86, 87, 109
Medart, William (umpire) 129
Medlen, Kris 115
Merkle, Fred 52, 54, 55, 56, 59, 65, 133, 161
Merkle Game 1, 52–59, 66
Meyer, Dan 84
Meyers, John "Chief" 66, 133
Middlebrooks, Will 173
Midges or "Mayflies" (life cycle) 104
Milan, Clyde 62, 63
Millan, Felix 154
Miller, Bill (umpire) 175, 176, 177
Miller, Bing 71
Miller, Shelby 173
Miller, Stu (windblown balk) 23
"Miracle Mets" 151
Mitchell, Dale 18
Molina, Bengie 114
Molina, Yadier 116, 171, 173
Monahan, Gene 105
Money, Don 74–77
moon landing (U.S.) 149
Moreland, Keith 29
Moreland, Mitch 120

Moret, Roger 157
Morgan, Joe (player) 155
Moriarty, George (umpire) 67, 69, 139, 140, 141, 142
Moses, Wally 71
Moskowitz, Toby (umpire accuracy study) 3
Moustakas, Mike 118
Muchlinski, Mike (umpire) 40, 42
Municipal Stadium (home of Indians) 15
Munson, Thurman 76, 159, 160
Murphy, Cait 52
Murphy, Daniel 125
Murphy, Danny 133
Murphy, Johnny "Fireman" 68
Murray, Dale 78
Murray, Eddie 89
Murray, Jim 26
Murray, Red 66, 133
Musial, Stan 13, 73, 74
Mussina, Mike 31, 42, 89

Nagy, Charles 96, 97
The Naked Gun (Leslie Nielsen film) 108
Napoli, Mike 117, 170
Nash, Bruce 71
Nava, Daniel 173
Navarro, Dioner 119
near-perfect games 37–39, 40–41, 42
Nelson, Jeff (pitcher) 96
Nelson, Jeff (umpire) 119–120
Nettles, Graig 76, 160
Newcombe, Don 147
Niekro, Joe 100
NL Wild Card Game (2012) 114–117
NLCS: (1988) 168; (1997 Game 5) 92–94; (2009 Game 3, Phillies vs. Rockies) 109; (2011) 171
NLDS: (2010 Game 1, Giants vs. Braves) 111–112; (2010 Game 2) 112; (2010 Game 3) 112–113; (2017 Game 5, Cubs vs. Nationals) 123–126
Nolan, Gary 154
Nunamaker, Les 60

Obama, Barrack (U.S. president) 175
obstruction of base runner by fielder rule 174
O'Day, Hank (umpire) 47, 49, 50, 51, 53, 55, 56, 57, 58, 50
Offerman, Jose 99
O'Flaherty, Eric 84
Oldring, Rube 133
O'Leary, Charlie 64
O'Loughlin, Silk (umpire) 59
"$100,000 Infield" (Philadelphia A's) 131, 134

O'Neill, Paul 96, 97, 165
O'Neill, Steve 68, 69
Orie, Kevin 36
"The Oriole Way" 152
Orta, Jorge 163
Ortiz, David 173, 174
Ortiz, Ramon 82
Oswalt 84
Overvall, Orville 53
Owen, Mickey 103
Owens, Brick (umpire) 67
Ozuna, Pablo 103

Padden, Dick 46
Pagan, Dave 76
Paige, Satchel 144
Paisner, Daniel 38
Palermi, Steve (umpire) 168
Palmer, Jim 149
Paul, Josh 102
Paul, Xavier 87
Payne, Fred 62, 63
Peavy, Jake 81, 174
Pedroia, Dustin 173, 174
Peitz, Heinie 46, 50
Pena, Carlos 111
Perez, Pascual 72
Perez, Salvadore 118
Perez, Tony 152, 153, 155
Perry, Gaylord 79, 169
Pettitte, Andy 89, 90, 104
Pfeffer, Fred 128
Pfeister, Jack "The Giant Killer" 54, 55, 58
Phelps, Babe 10
Phillips, Dave (umpire) 79
Phillips, Richie 91
Philly Phanatic 93
Pieper, Pat 73
Pierzysnski, A.J. 101, 102, 103
Pilar, Kevin 119
Pinelli, Babe (umpire) 17, 19, 20
Pine Tar Game (George Brett) 77–80,
Pine Tar Incident (John Mayberry) 79
Pine Tar Rule 79–80
Piniella, Lou 1, 76, 159
Plank, Eddie 131, 133
Polo Grounds (home of the Giants) 55, 58, 132, 133
Pompey, Dalton 119
Porter, Darrell 77, 163
Posada, Jorge 89, 108, 165
Posey, Buster 111, 112
Posnanski, Joe 115
Powell, Boog 149
Price, David 118
Pro Player Stadium (home of the Marlins) 92

Proctor, Scott 87
Puig, Yasiel 175
Pujols, Albert 116–117, 167, 170
Pulli, Frank (umpire) 80, 160, 161
Pulliam, Harry 56
Pytlak, Frankie 68

quick-pitch 119
Quinlin, Robb 102
Quintana, Jose 124
Quisenberry, Dan 162

Radcliff, Rip 69
Raines, Tim 95
Ramirez, Manny 95
Ramirez, Ramon 112
Ramos, Wilson 41
Rasmus, Colby 106
Rawley, Shane 78
Redford, Robert 24
Redmond, Mike 38
Reed, Rick (umpire) 99, 100
Reese, Pee Wee 18, 146
Reichert, Pete 150
Reiker, Rich (umpire supervisor) 102
Reliford, Charlie (umpire) 1,
Rendon, Anthony 123, 125
Reulbach, Ed 53
Reuss, Mark 39
Revere, Ben 119
Reynolds, Allie 19
Reynolds, Harold 118
Reynolds, Jim (umpire) 113, 115
Reynolds, John J. 7
Reynolds, Shane 37
Rice, Jim 155
Rice, Sam 135, 136–138
Richards, Paul 152
Rickey, Branch 3
Rigler, Cy (umpire) 57, 137, 138
Riles, Ernie 28
Ripken, Cal 89
Ripley, Steve (umpire) 72
Rivera, Mariano 89, 98, 99, 107
Rizzo, Anthony 124, 125
Roberts, Dave 176
Robertson, David 114
Robinson, Brooks 12, 149, 150, 152, 154
Robinson, Frank 149, 150, 151
Robinson, Jackie 18, 146, 147, 148
"Robo-Umps" 3–5, 172
Rodney, Fernando 167
Rodriguez, Alex "A-Rod" 1, 107, 114
Rodriguez, Armando (first Hispanic umpire) 7
Rodriguez, Frankie "K-Rod" 101
Rogers, Kenny (pitcher) 167, 168, 169

Index

Rolfe, Red 68
Roosevelt, Franklin Delano 14
Rose, Pete 152, 153, 157
Rosh Hashanah, (Greenberg boycott) 140
Ross, Cody 112
Ross, David 115, 116
Rowand, Aaron 102
Rowe, Schoolboy 139, 141
Rudi, Joe 154
Rue, Joe (umpire) 5, 15
Runge, Brian (umpire) 30
Runge, Ed (umpire) 30
Runge, Paul (umpire) 28, 29, 30
runner misses home plate rule 134
running bases backwards rule 61–64
Russell, Addison 124
Russell, Bill 159, 160
Ruth, Babe 91, 136, 174
Ryan, Nolan 12, 35, 150

Saberhagen, Brett 98, 162
safe-out at home controversies 83, 87, 120, 133–134, 147 152, 154, 173–174
Sain, Johnny 143, 144
Salerno, Al (umpire) 7
Salisbury, Jim 94
Salkeld, Bill 144
Saltalamacchia, Jarrod 173
Santo, Ron 21
Sax, Steve 28
Schaefer, Germany ("steal" of first base) 61–64
Schafer, Jordan 87
Scherzer, Max 36, 40–42, 123–124, 125, 126
Scheurwater, Stu (umpire) 117
Scioscia, Mike 102
Scott, Dale (umpire) 99, 108
Scott, George 77
Seaver, Tom 149, 150
Selig, Bud 1, 107, 31, 33, 39, 112
Selkirk, George 69
Sewell, Luke 69
Seymour, Cy 50, 53, 55
Shafer, Tillie 66
Shaw, Bob (single-game record for balks) 20–23
Shea, Merv 69
Shelton, Derek 105
Sheridan, Jack (umpire) 60
Shibe Park (home of the Philadelphia A's) 132
Showalter, Buck 91
Simmons, Andrelton 115, 116
Simons, Herbert 57
Sizemore, Grady 105
Smith, Earl 136

Smoltz, John 92
"Smudgegate" 166, 168
Snider, Duke 18, 146
Snodgrass, Fred 67, 133
Solters, Moose 69
Sosa, Sammy 31, 32, 80
Spahn, Warren 143, 151
Spalding, A.G. 128, 130
Span, Denard 107
Speaker, Tris 60
spectator interference 33, 65–67, 90–91, 115
spitballers 169–170
Sportsman's Park (home of the Browns) 128
Springstead, Marty (umpire) 77, 109, 160
Stainback, Tuck 142
Stanky, Eddie 144
Stanton, Giancarlo 34
Stark, Dolly (umpire) 140
Stark, Jayson 174
Stassi, Max 110
Steinbrenner, George 75, 80, 95, 106, 158
Stengel, Casey 10, 17, 149, 151
Stern, Bill 148
"Steve Blass Disease" 98
"Steve Sax Syndrome" 98
Stewart, Bill (umpire) 10, 11, 12, 142, 143, 144, 145
Stewart, Dave 23, 31
Stone, Steve 36
Strasburg, Stephen 124
Strawberry, Darryl 29, 95, 165
strike zone controversies 3, 4, 11, 12, 15, 17, 19, 22, 35, 36, 69, 84, 85, 92–94, 108, 110, 112, 117, 119, 166, 171–172, 175–176
Sucre, Jesus 120
Sullivan, David (umpire) 127, 128, 129, 130
Sullivan, Jeff 176
Summers, Bill (umpire) 69, 146, 147, 148
Sutton, Don 169
Swisher, Nick 108, 114
Swoboda, Ron 151

Tabata, Jose 40, 41
Tannehill, Lee
Tarasco, Tony 90
Taylor, Michael 125
Taylor, Sammy 73
Taylor, Tony 26
Teixeira, Mark 108
Telegraph Cup 130
Temple Cup 130
Templeton, Garry 29
Tenney, Fred 54
Thome, Jim 95, 96, 111

Thompson, William G. 6
Thomson, Bobby 73
Thorn, John 1, 6
Tiant, Luis 155, 156
time-in/time-out controversies 61, 63, 76–77
Tinker, Joe 53, 55
Torre, Joe 87, 96, 100, 105, 106, 110, 116, 125
Trachsel, Steve 32
TrackMan (Doppler pitch tracking system) 4
Trosky, Hal 67
Trout, Mike 116
Trump, Donald (U.S. president) 123
Tschida, Tim (umpire) 99, 100
Tulowitzki, Troy 81
Turley, Bob 146
Turner, Trea 124, 125
Turner Field (home of the Braves) 86, 112, 115

Ueberroth, Peter 163
Uehara, Koji 173
Uggla, Dan 87, 115
uncaught third strike rule 102, 103
Uribe, Jose 28
Uribe, Juan 112
Utley, Chase 109

Valentin, John 99
Valentine, Bill (umpire) 7
Vander Meer, Johnny (consecutive no-hitters) 9–12
Van Slyke, Andy 168
Vaughn, Greg 165
Verducci, Tom 31, 118
Verlander, Justin 167
Vickers, Rube 50
Vizquel, Omar 95, 97

Waddell, Rube 62
Wagner, Honus 48, 49, 57
Wainwright, Adam 173
Walker, Neil 87
Wall, Donne 165
Washburn, Jarrod 102
Washington, U.L. 78
Washington, Ron 113, 114, 170
Weaver, Earl 97, 152
Webb, Brandon 30
Weis, Al 150, 151
Welke, Tim (umpire) 79, 111, 115
Wells, David 95, 165
Wendelstedt, Harry (umpire) 4, 25, 27, 41, 124, 135
West, Joe (umpire) 169

West Side Grounds (home of the Cubs) 57
Wheaton, William Rufus (first umpire) 5
White, Doc 26, 47, 62, 63
White, Roy 159
"Whitey Ball" (1985 Cardinals) 162
Wieters, Matt 109, 125
Wiggins, Alan 72
Williams, Art (first black NL umpire) 7, 93
Williams, Bernie 90, 95, 96, 97, 99, 165
Williams, Billy 21
Williams, Jimy 99, 100
Williams, John T. 172
Williams, Matt 30
Williams, Ted 14, 16, 70
Williamson, Ned 128
Willis, Vic 57
Willoughby, Jim 157
Wilson, Brian (pitcher) 112
Wilson, Enrique 96
Wilson, Woodrow 142
Wood, Kerry (20-strikeout game) 34–37, 41
Wood, "Smokey Joe" 60
Woodson, Tracy 28
Woodward, Woody 153
Workman, Brandon 173
World Series: (1903) 49; (1908) 59; (1911) 130–135; (1918) 174; (1919) 101; (1925) 135–138; (1934) 139; (1935) 138–142; (1941) 103; (1948) 142–145; (1955) 145–148; (1956) 18–20, 148; (1957) 151; (1969) 149–151; (1970) 152–154; (1973) 154; (1975) 155–158; (1978) 158–161; (1985) 161–164; (1986) 161; (1998) 164–166; (2013) 172–175; (2017) 175–177
World Series ejections 139, 141, 163–164
World's Championship Series (WCS) 127, 130; (1885) 127–130
Worrell, Todd 163
Wright, Glenn 136
Wrigley Field (home of the Cubs) 35
Wynne, Marvell 29

Yankees–Dodgers rivalry 147, 148, 158, 160
Yastrzemski, Carl 155
"Year of the Balk" (1988) 22–23
"Year of the Pitcher": (1968) 24; (2010) 39
"The Yips" 98, 99
Yom Kippur (Greenberg boycott) 140
Youkilis, Kevin 107
Young, Delmon 111
Yount, Robin 76

Zimmer, Don 147
Zimmerman, Ryan 123
Zobrist, Ben 118, 124
Zullo, Alan 71

www.ingramcontent.com/pod-product-compliance
Ingram Content Group UK Ltd.
Pitfield, Milton Keynes, MK11 3LW, UK
UKHW042003140426
5217IPUK00015B/957